CW01025105

FAITH AND LIFE

FAITH AND LIFE

BENJAMIN B. WARFIELD

THE BANNER OF TRUTH TRUST

THE BANNER OF TRUTH TRUST
3 Murrayfield Road, Edinburgh EH12 6EL
P.O. Box 621, Carlisle, Pennsylvania 17013, U.S.A.

*

First published 1916
First reprint by the Banner of Truth Trust 1974
Reprinted 1990
ISBN 0 85151 585 1

*

Printed in Great Britain by Offset Lithography by
the Alden Press, Oxford.

TO

Ethelbert Dudley Warfield, D.D., LL.D., Litt.D.

A BROTHER BELOVED

IN THE FLESH AND IN THE LORD

CONTENTS

FAITH AND LIFE

THE CAUSE OF GOD

1 Kings 19:9: " What doest thou here, Elijah? "

THE history of Elijah supplies us with one of the most striking, and, we may add, one of the most instructive, sections of the Old Testament. With him begins the wonderful history of Prophetism. Through him we obtain a glimpse which we would not willingly lose of God's dealings with His people: His faithfulness to them when they were unfaithful to Him; His unremitting efforts to withdraw them from sin and keep them in that intimate and obedient relation to Him in which alone was safety to be found.

At first sight the narrative may appear objective to a fault. We are told nothing of who Elijah was, how he had been trained, whence he came as he passes across the page of history. In the midst of Ahab's wicked rule suddenly he stands before the idolatrous King and pronounces the curse of God, which for his sake should fall on the land which he had polluted with his apostasy. And as suddenly as he appears, so suddenly he withdraws again. Hidden at Cherith or at Zarephath for a period measured by years, he appears on the scene of public history once again as unexpectedly and as much a messenger from on high as at first. Everywhere he goes the powers of heaven accompany him, and his appearances and disappearances are almost as sudden as the bolts of heaven themselves.

But, however rapid the action, and however much, at first view, the narrative may seem to wear the appearance of objectivity; however much it may seem to be concerned only with the history of Israel and God's endeavour through the words and works of His prophet to awaken His people to righteousness and rescue them from the slough of their idolatry; the story of Elijah yet manages to be primarily and above all else the story of Elijah. Somehow, as in music sometimes a secondary strain is carried on, shot through the dominant theme of the composition, in harmony with it and yet separable from it, and needing but a little emphasizing to make it the chief burden of the whole; so within the bosom of this narrative of how God sent His prophet to Israel with His thunder-message calling it back to the service of Him, of how He dealt thus faithfully with His people and sought to save them from themselves and for Him, there lies, not hidden, but embraced and preserved for us, the touching account of how God dealt with and trained the prophet himself. As Jesus, when He sat in the judgment hall of Annas offering Himself a victim for the saving of the world, yet had time to turn a significant glance upon Peter as he stood denying Him before the courtyard fire, and thus saved His poor repentant follower in the saving of the world; so God in His use of Elijah for the teaching of Israel also found time to train the heart of the prophet himself.

These chapters are crowded with teaching for us. We must select, from the wealth they bring to us, some one thing on which our minds may especially dwell to-day. Let it be this instructive element in them: God's way of training His prophet. Let us observe in the case of Elijah how God dealt with him in His grace so as to bring him to a better knowledge of himself, of God and of the nature of the work to which he was called. When once we approach the narrative with this purpose in view, it becomes difficult to see anything else in it. We forget Israel in Elijah. Israel seems only the instrument upon which and by means of which Elijah's heart and soul were taught. We have in a word emphasized the subordinate strain until it becomes dominant; and the very possibility of this is a clear proof that the subordinate strain was planted in the music by the Great Composer, and that it was meant that our ears should hear it.

We are told, we say, nothing of the early life, the early training, or directly, of the character of

Elijah. He appears suddenly before us as the messenger of God's wrath. Like his great antitype—who was greater, our Lord being witness, than even he—he is a voice from the wilderness crying the one word, Repent! He is the human embodiment of the wrath of God. Wherever he goes destruction accompanies him. Drought, fire from heaven, floods of rain, death for the enemies of God, follow hard on his footsteps. He is embodied law. And as such he is a swift witness against his people. Obedience, repentance, strict account, these form the essence of his message.

God chooses appropriate instruments for His work. And we have reason to believe that the sternness of Elijah's mission was matched by the sternness of his aspect and the sternness of his character. We are therefore justified in having said that he was, not merely the messenger of God's law and wrath, but their embodiment. He was by natural disposition, as framed under providential circumstances, and by virtue of the side of God which he had as yet apprehended, nothing loath but rather naturally inclined to act as the witness of God against his people, well-fitted to call down the vengeance of God upon them and to delight in the overthrow of His enemies. He was in danger of thinking of God only as a lawgiver and the just avenger of His wounded honour. Hence arose the necessity of the training of the prophet. Every incident of his career, as it is recorded for us, entered into this training. As we cast our eye over it, we observe that what Elijah needed to be taught was (1) dependence on God; (2) fellowship with man in his sufferings; (3) confidence in God's plans; and (4) a sense of their essential and broad mercifulness.

These lessons are brought home to him by means of two stupendous miracles over nature, wrought for the purpose of teaching the people that Jehovah and He alone is God,—so closely intertwined were the two lines of Divine work, the training of the people and the training of Elijah. No sooner had the prophet declared to the apostate King the word of God sent to him, "As the Lord, the God of Israel liveth, before whom I stand, there shall not be dew nor rain these years but according to my word," than a special personal message came from the Lord to him saying, "Get thee hence, and turn thee eastward, and hide thyself by the brook Cherith, that is before Jordan. And it shall be that thou shalt drink of the brook, and I have commanded the ravens to feed thee there." Thus it was brought about that both Israel and Elijah were simultaneously learning the lesson of the littleness of man before God. But diversely. Israel was learning that it could not with impunity break God's law; Elijah that even God's servants depend on Him for their every want. The self-willed nation was learning to submit to its Lord;

the perhaps too self-confident prophet was learning the weakness of flesh and man's utter dependence on his Maker.

In the silence of the wilderness, hidden in one of those torrent-clefts which fall into the Jordan valley, Elijah was dependent on God's hand for his daily food; on the water which flowed at first in quantities full enough for his needs over the rocks of the brook's bed, but gradually grew less and less until it trickled in drops scarcely numerous enough to moisten his parched lips; on food brought to him by the unclean ravens. Thus gradually he learned to sympathize with his suffering fellows and to rest on God. It was meet that he who seemed to have the dominion of the heavens in his hands, who prayed that it should not rain and it rained not, should share in the want which resulted; and should learn to sympathize with poor suffering, even if sinful, humanity, like that greater one who was yet to come and learn also how to sympathize with us through His participation in our griefs. How fully he learned his lesson the subsequent narrative tells us in the beautiful story of his dealings with the widow of Zarephath with her cruse and barrel, and her sick and dying child—one of the most Christlike narratives among all the Old Testament miracles. Thus then as Israel was prepared for repentance, the prophet was prepared inwardly to be a fit messenger to his suffering brethren, bringing them relief from their sore affliction. We repeat it, God sends His messages by fit instruments.

And so, in due time, Elijah comes to bring the famished land relief. We all remember the story of the tremendous scene wherein Elijah—the "prodigious" Tishbite, as an old author calls him—challenges the prophets of Baal to meet him in a contest of worship on Carmel, and defeats them by simply calling on his God; and then draws down rain on the parched ground by the almighty virtue of his prayer. No scene of higher dramatic power is to be found in all the world's literature. As we read, we see the prophet ruling on the mount; we see him bent in prayer on the deserted summit; we see him when, the hand of God upon him, he girded up his victorious loins and ran before the chariot of Ahab, the sixteen miles through the driving storm, from Carmel to Jezreel. No scene we may say could have been more nicely fitted to his mind or to his nature. Here the king of men was king indeed and his victory seemed complete. But God's children must suffer for their triumphs. Were there no thorns in the flesh, messengers of Satan, sent of God to buffet them, there would be no one of men who could serve the Lord in the scenes of His triumph without grave danger to his own soul. And Elijah needed to learn other lessons yet. He needed to learn that God's victories are not of the external sort and are not to be won by the weapons of men.

How quickly after the triumph comes the moment of dismay. "And Ahab told Jezebel," says the simple narrative, "all that Elijah had done, and withal, how he had slain the prophets with the sword. Then Jezebel sent a messenger unto Elijah, saying, 'So let the gods do to me and more also, if I make not thy life as the life of one of them by to-morrow about this time.' And when he saw that, he arose and went for his life and came to Beersheba." Thus, Elijah has his lesson to learn again after his miracle. We need not wonder at his sudden flight. It is the price that strong, fervent spirits pay for their very strength, that they suffer a correspondingly strong reaction. So it was with the prophet's antitype, John the Baptist, when in the prison he lost his faith and sent to ask Him whom God had Himself pointed out to him on the banks of Jordan, whether, indeed, He was the Coming One. So it was with Peter also, who could venture on the waves, but only to cry, "Lord save me, I perish"; who could draw his sword and smite the High Priest's servant, but only at once to deny his Lord at the challenge of a servant maid. So now it was with Elijah. God's hand had been outstretched at his call. He had shut up the heavens at his bidding and had nourished him at Cherith and given him miraculous sustenance at Zarephath, and the widow's son back from the grave. He had sent down His fire from heaven and delivered the priests of Baal into his hand and opened the heavens at his prayer. But Elijah could not trust God, now, to deliver him from a woman's hate; and that, although her very message bore in it the betrayal of her weakness.

Was there not a deeper spring for this distrust still? With all his training, Elijah did not as yet know his God. His life had fallen on evil days, times of violence that demanded violent remedies for their diseases. And he could not believe in the efficacy of any but violent remedies. Fresh from Carmel and the slaughter of the priests he was impatient of the continuance of evil, and expected the miracles of Carmel to be but the harbinger of the greater miracle of the conversion of the people to God in a day. When Elijah awoke on the morrow and found Israel altogether as it had been yesterday, he was dismayed. Had then the triumph of yesterday been as nothing? Was Jezebel still to lord it over God's heritage? What then availed it that the fire had fallen from heaven? That the false priests' blood had flowed like water? That the rain had come at his bidding? Was the hand of God outstretched only to be withdrawn again? Elijah loses heart because God's ways were not as his ways. He cannot understand God's secular modes of working; and, conceiving of His ways as sudden and miraculous only, he feels that the Most High has deserted His cause and His servants. He almost feels bitter towards the Lord who had let him begin a work which He leaves him without power to complete. Hence Elijah must go to the wilderness to learn somewhat of the God he serves. After his first miracle of closing the heavens, he learned what man was in his sufferings and in his needs. Now he has opened the heavens and is to learn what God is and what are the modes of His working and the nature of His plans.

There is no mistaking the purpose of God in leading the prophet into the wilderness; nor the import of the teaching He gives him there. The disheartened prophet, despairing of the cause of God because all things had not turned out as he had anticipated, throws himself on the desert sands to die. But there God visits him; and leads him on to Horeb, where the Law had been given, where it had been granted to Moses to see God's glory, the glory of the Lord, the Lord God, merciful and gracious, slow to anger and plenteous in mercy and truth. Reaching the Mount the stricken prophet seeks a cave and lodges in it. And then the word of the Lord came to him with the searching question, " What doest thou here, Elijah? " We do not need to doubt that there was reproof in the question; but surely it is not reproof but searching inquiry that forms its main contents. The Lord had Himself led Elijah here, for his lesson. And now the Lord probes him with the deepest of questions.

After all, why was Elijah there? The question calls for reflection; and reflection which will bring light with self-condemnation; and with the self-condemnation, also self-instruction. "What doest thou here, Elijah?" The honest soul of the prophet gives back the transparent truth: "I have been very jealous" . . . and so on. Here we see distrust in God and despair of His cause; almost complaint of God, for not guarding His cause better; nay, more, almost complaint of God that He had left His servant in the lurch. The Lord deals very graciously with His servant. There is no need now of reproof; only the simple command to go forth and stand upon the mount before the Lord. And then the Lord passed by; first a great, strong wind rent the mountains and brake in pieces the rocks before the Lord; but it was not in the wind that the Lord was. And after the wind, an earthquake; but the Lord was not in the earthquake. And after the earthquake, fire; but the Lord was not in the fire. And after the fire, a sound of gentle stillness. Elijah does not now need to be told where the Lord is. The terror of the storm, of the earthquake, and of the flame, is as nothing to the awesomeness of the gentle stillness. "And it was so, when Elijah heard it, that he wrapped his face in his mantle, and went out and stood in the entering in of the cave." Did he already begin to suspect that he had mistaken the storm that goes before Jehovah for Jehovah's self? The terror of the law for the very hand of Him whose essence is love? The terrible preparation for the Gospel for the Gospel itself? But there is still no word of direct instruction. Only the old question still sounds in his ears. "And behold there came a voice to him and said 'What doest thou here, Elijah?'" To it he returns the same answer as before; but surely in deep humility of spirit. Be that as it may, however, the Lord proceeds to tell him that He has yet work for him to do and sends him back with instructions which imply that there is a long future for the fruition of His plans. And whether at once or more slowly we cannot doubt that the lesson had its effect and Elijah learned not to lose hope in God's cause because God's ways in accomplishing it are not our ways.

How full all this is of lessons to us! Let us at least not fail to learn from it: (1) That the cause of God does not depend on our single arm to save it. "I, I only, am left," said Elijah, as if on him alone could God depend to secure His ends. We depend on God, not God on us. (2) That the cause of God is not dependent for its success on our chosen methods. Elijah could not understand that the ends of God could be gained unless they were gained in the path of miracles of manifest judgment. External methods are not God's methods. (3) That the cause of God cannot fail. Elijah feared that God's hand was not outstretched to save and fancied that he knew the dangers and needs better than God did. God never deserts His cause. (4) That it is not the Law but the Gospel, not the revelation of wrath but that of love, which saves the world. Wrath may prepare for love; but wrath never did and never will save a soul.

We close then, with a word of warning and one of encouragement. The word of warning: We must not identify our cause with God's cause; our methods with God's methods; or our hopes with God's purposes. The word of encouragement: God's cause is never in danger; what He has begun in the soul or in the world, He will complete unto the end.

OLD TESTAMENT RELIGION

Psa. 51:12: "Restore unto me the joy of thy salvation."

"AND David said unto Nathan, I have sinned against the Lord. And Nathan said unto David, The Lord also hath put away thy sin." It may almost seem that David escaped from his crime too easily. We may read the narrative and fail to observe the signs of that deep contrition which such hideous wickedness when once recognized surely must engender. There is the story of the sin drawn in all its shocking details. Then Nathan comes in with his beautiful apologue of the ewe-lamb, and its pungent application. And then we read simply: "And David said unto Nathan, I have sinned against The Lord. And Nathan said unto David, The Lord also hath put away thy sin." After that comes only the story of how the child of sin was smitten, and how David besought the Lord for its life and finally acquiesced in the Divine judgment. One is apt to feel that David was more concerned to escape the consequences of his sin than to yield to the Lord the sacrifices of a broken and a contrite heart. Does it not seem cold to us and external, David's simple acknowledgment of his sin, and the Lord's immediate remission of it? We feel the lack of the manifestations of a deeply repentant spirit, and are almost ready, we say, to wonder if David did not escape too easily from the evil he had wrought.

It is merely the simplicity of the narrative which is deceiving us in this. The single-hearted writer expects us to read into the bare words of David's confession, "I have sinned against the Lord," all the spiritual exercises which those words are fitted to suggest and out of which they should have grown. And if we find it a little difficult to do so, we have only to turn to David's penitential Psalms, to learn the depths of repentance which wrung this great and sensitive soul. One of them —perhaps the most penetrating portrayal of a truly penitent soul ever cast into human speech—is assigned by its title to just this crisis in his life; and I see no good reason why this assignment need be questioned. The whole body of them sound the depths of the sinful soul's self-torment and longing for recovery as can be found nowhere else in literature; and taken in sequence present a complete portrayal of the course of repentance in the heart, from its inception in the rueful review of the past and the remorseful biting back of the awakened heart, through its culmination in a true return to God in humble love and trusting confidence, to its issue in the establishment of a new relation of obedience to God and a new richness of grateful service to Him.

Let us take just these four, Psalms 6, 38, 51, 32.

In Psa. 6 sounds the note of remorse—it is the torment of a soul's perception of its sin that is here prominently brought to our most poignant observation. In Psa. 38, the note of hope—not indeed absent even from Psa. 6—becomes dominant and the sorrow and hatred of sin is coloured by a pervasive tone of relief. In Psa. 51, while there is no lessening of the accent of repentance there is along with the deep sense of the guilt and pollution of sin which is expressed also a note of triumph over the sin, which aspires to a clean heart and a steadfast spirit and a happy service of God in purity of life. While in Psa. 32, the sense of forgiveness, the experience of joy in the Lord, and the exercises of holy and joyful service overlie all else. Here we trace David's penitent soul through all its experiences; his remorseful contemplation of his own sin, his passionate reaching out to the salvation of God, the gradual return of his experience of the joy of that salvation, his final issuing into the full glory of its complete realization.

In some respects the most remarkable of this remarkable body of pictures of the inner experiences of a penitent soul, is that of Psa. 51. It draws away the veil for us and permits us to look in upon the spirit in the most characteristic act of repentance, just at the turning point, as it deserts its sin and turns to God. Here is revealed to us a sense of sin so poignant, a perception of the grace of God so soaring, an apprehension of the completeness of the revolution required in sinful man that he may become in any worthy sense a servant of God so profound, that one wonders in reading it what is left for a specifically Christian experience to add to this experience of a saint of God under the Old Testament dispensation in turning from sin to God. The wonderful depth of the religious experience and the remarkable richness of religious conception embodied in this Psalm have indeed proved a snare to the critics. "David could not have had these ideas," says Prof. T. C. Cheyne, brusquely; and, indeed, the David that Prof. Cheyne has constructed out of his imaginary reconstruction of the course of religious development in Israel, could not well have had these ideas. These are distinctively Christian ideas that the Psalm sets forth, and they could not have grown up of themselves in a purely natural heart. And therein lies one of the values of the Psalm to us; it reveals to us the essentially Christian type of the religion of Israel; it opens to our observation the contents of the mind and heart of a Spirit-led child of God in the ages agone, and makes us to know the truly Christian character of his experiences in his struggle with sin and his aspirations towards God, and thus also to know the supernatural leading of God's people through all ages.

For consider for a moment the conception of

God which throbs through all the passionate language of this Psalm. A God of righteousness who will not look upon sin with allowance; nay, who directs all things, even the emergence of acts of sin in His world, so that He may not only be just, but also "may be justified when He speaks and clear when He judges." A God of holiness whose Spirit cannot abide in our impure hearts. A God of unbounded power, who governs the whole course of events in accordance with His own counsels. But above all, a gracious God, full of lovingkindness, abundant in compassion, whose delight is in salvation. There is nothing here which goes beyond the great revelation of Ex. 34:6, "a God full of compassion and gracious, abundant in lovingkindness and truth; keeping lovingkindness for thousands, forgiving iniquity and transgression and sin." Indeed the language of the Psalm is obviously modelled on this of Exodus. But here it is not given from the lips of Jehovah, proclaiming His character, but returned to us from the heart of the repentant sinner, recounting the nature of the God with whom he has to do.

And what a just and profound sense of sin is revealed to us here. The synonymy of the subject is almost exhausted in the effort to complete the self-accusation. "My transgression, my iniquity, my sin;" I have been in rebellion against God, I have distorted my life, I have missed the mark; I have, to express it all, done what is evil in Thy sight—in the sight of Thee, the Standard of Holiness, the hypostatized Law of Conduct. And these acts are but the expression of an inner nature of corruption, inherited from those who have gone before me; it was in iniquity that I was born, in sin that my mother conceived me. Shall a pure thing come from an impure? Nay, my overt acts of sin are thought of not in themselves but as manifestations of what is behind and within; thrown up into these manifestations in act, in Thine own ordinance, for no other cause than that Thy righteous condemnation on me may be justified and thy judgment be made clear. For it is not cleanness of act merely that Thou dost desire, but truth in the inward parts and wisdom in the hidden parts. Obviously the Psalmist is conceiving sin here as not confined to acts but consisting essentially of a great ocean of sin within us, whose waves merely break in sinful acts. No wonder the commentators remark that here we have original sin "more distinctly expressed than in any other passage in the Old Testament." Nothing is left to be added by the later revelation in the way of poignancy of conception—though much is, of course, left to be added in developed statement.

Accordingly, the conception of the radicalness of the operation required for the Psalmist's deliverance from sin, is equally developed. No surface remedy will suffice to eradicate a sin which is thus inborn, ingrained in nature itself. Hence the passionate cry: Create—it requires nothing less than a creative act—create me a clean heart—the heart is the totality of the inner life—and make new within me a constant spirit—a spirit which will no more decline from Thee. Nothing less than this will suffice—a total rebegetting as the New Testament would put it; an entire making over again can alone suffice to make such an one as the Psalmist knows himself to be—not by virtue of his sins of act which are only the manifestation of what he is by nature, but by virtue of his fundamental character—acceptable to Him who desires truth in the inward part; nay, nothing less than this can secure to him that steadfastness of spirit which will save his overt acts from shame.

Nor does the Psalmist expect to be able, unaided, to live in the power of his new life. One of the remarkable features of the doctrinal system of the Psalm is the clear recognition it gives of the necessity, for the cleansing of the life, of the constant presence and activity of the Holy Spirit. "Take not thy holy Spirit from me and uphold me with a spirit of willingness." Thine to lead, mine to follow. Not autonomy but obedience, the ideal of the religious life. The operations of the Holy Spirit in the sphere of the moral life, the ethical activities of the Spirit, His sanctifying work, are but little adverted to in the Old Testament, and when alluded to, it is chiefly in promises for the Messianic period. Here, David not merely prays for them in his own case, but announces them as part of the experience of the past and present. His chance of standing, he says in effect, hangs on the continued presence of the Holy Spirit of God in him; in the upholding within him thereby of a spirit of willingness.

Thus we perceive that in its conception of God, of sin, of salvation alike, this Psalm stands out as attaining the high-water mark of Old Testament revelation. It was by a hard pathway that David came to know God and himself so intimately. But he came thus to know both his own heart and the God of grace with a fullness and profundity of apprehension that it will be hard to parallel elsewhere. And it was no merely external knowledge that he acquired thus. It was the knowledge of experience. David knew sin because he had touched the unclean thing and sounded the depths of iniquity. He knew himself because he had gone his own way and had learned through what thickets and morasses that pathway led, and what was its end. And he knew God, because he had tasted and seen that the Lord is gracious. Yes, David had tasted and seen God's preciousness. David had experience of salvation. He knew what salvation was, and He knew its joy. But never had he known the joy of salvation as he knew it after he had lost it. And it is just here that the special poignancy of David's repentance comes in: it was not the repentance of a sinner merely, it was the repentance of a sinning saint.

It is only the saint who knows what sin is; for only the saint knows it in contrast with salvation, experienced and understood. And it is only the sinning saint who knows what salvation is: for it is only the joy that is lost and then found again that is fully understood. The depths of David's knowledge, the poignancy of his conceptions—of God, and sin, and salvation—carrying him far beyond the natural plane of his time and the development of the religious consciousness of Israel, may be accounted for, it would seem, by these facts. He who had known the salvation of God and basked in its joy, came to know through his dreadful sin what sin is, and its terrible entail; and through this horrible experience, to know what the joy of salvation is—the joy which he had lost and only through the goodness of God could hope to have restored. In the biting pain of his remorse, it all becomes clear to him. His sinful nature is revealed to him; and the goodness of God; his need of the Spirit; the joy of acceptance with God; the delight of abiding with Him in His house. Hence his profound disgust at himself; his passionate longing for that purity without which he could not see God. And hence his culminating prayer: "Restore unto me the joy of Thy salvation."

THE WRATH OF MAN

Psa. 76:10:—"Surely the wrath of man shall praise thee."

THE Seventy-sixth Psalm is represented by a very old tradition—it is already embodied in the Septuagint version—as a hymn of praise to God for the destruction of Sennacherib. There is no reason why this tradition may not be supposed to preserve the truth. But its truth or falsehood does not particularly concern us. The Psalm was in any case written upon some such occasion as the destruction of Sennacherib. It celebrates a great deliverance wrought by the power of God; a deliverance beyond all expectation, wrought by God alone. The essence of its representation is that Jehovah is a man of war, above all comparison great. When He enters the field, all the machinery of conflict stops. The lightning-like arrows which fly from the bow cease in their courses; the shield and the sword fall helpless to the ground; the stoutest-hearted with their chariots and horses drop into the inactivity of death. For Jehovah is terrible. None can stand before Him when His wrath begins to burn but a little.

As the Psalmist contemplates the certain destruction that befalls all the foes of Israel, when Jehovah speaks, he rises from the particular to the general. He proclaims the praises of the eternal and universal providence of God, as it is illustrated in the great fact that even the most violent passions of men are under His control, and conduce only to the fulfilment of His ends. "Surely," he cries, "the wrath of man shall praise Thee, and the residue of wrath Thou wilt restrain," or "the residue of wrath wilt Thou gird upon Thee." The fundamental sense is that the ebullitions of the wrath of man, however violent and outbreaking they may be, are, nevertheless, like all else that occurs, under the complete control of God and are employed by Him as instruments for working out His ends. Like all else that comes to pass, then, they illustrate God's glory. For the rest, the passage teaches, according as we construe the last half of the verse, either that all the wrath of man which would not conduce to the divine glory God restrains and does not permit to manifest itself in action, so that the completeness of His control over man's wrath is what is emphasized; or else, that after all the wrath of man raging in its utmost fury has exhausted itself in vain struggles against the rising wrath of Jehovah, there remains to Jehovah, in opposition to it, the fullness of wrath, with which He girds Himself for action, so that the resistless might of Jehovah as over against the puny weakness of man is what is emphasized. We need not now attempt to decide between the two interpretations; it is enough to fix our minds on the main declaration—this to wit: that the wrath of man also is under divine control, and it too, like all else that occurs in the world, conduces only to the divine glory.

It is well for us to remind ourselves of this great fact in a time like this. It may seem to us as if the fountains of the great deep were broken up and the world were on the point of being overwhelmed by the violence of human passion. Men seem to have broken away from the government of conscience, and even from the guidance of the common instincts of humanity. The whole earth appears to have become a churning mass of rage. We see millions of our fellow-creatures flying at one another's throats in a ruthless struggle, and whole countries harried and reduced to ruin. Up from the battle-fields, and up from the wasted lands behind the battle-fields, rise only cries of rage and despair. It is good for us to remember that the Lord God Omnipotent reigns over all. That all this welter of blood and iron He holds well in hand. That none of it would have occurred without His direction; that nothing can occur in it apart from His appointment; and I do not say merely that He will overrule it all for His glory, but that all of it will conduce to His praise. For, "surely the wrath of man is to Him for praise, and the remainder of wraths will He restrain."

It may be hard for us to understand or even to believe it—for our sight is dim and the range of our vision is narrow—but all things work together under God's governing hand for good. Even the things which in themselves are evil, in all their workings work together for good in this world of ours; for it is God's world after all, and He is the Governor of it, and He governs it for good, and that continually. John Calvin reminds us that though Satan may rage about like a roaring lion seeking whom he may devour, yet he has a bit in his mouth and it is God who holds the reins. "Oh, Assyrian, the rod of My anger," cries Jehovah. It was for his own ends—lust of conquest, delight in power— that the Assyrian on his part was doing it. He knew not that he was but the instrument in God's hands for working higher ends, and that when they were secured, the sword would drop from his inert fingers and he would himself fall on sleep. "Glorious art Thou and excellent," sings the Psalmist, "more than the mountains of prey: the stout-hearted are made a spoil, they have slept their sleep; and none of the men of might have found their hands. At thy rebuke, O God of Jacob, both chariot and horse are cast into a dead sleep." In the midst of the turmoil of war, let us remember that war too is of God, and that it, too, will in His hands work for good: that even the wrath of man shall be to Him for praise.

But there is more than even this in the Psalm for our learning, at least by implication. We read in it not only of the wrath of man, but also of the wrath of Jehovah; and the wrath of Jehovah is set over against the wrath of man as greater than the wrath of man—greater, more lasting, more prevailing. None can stand when the wrath of Jehovah only begins: when all other wrath is quenched the wrath of Jehovah abides—He girds Himself with it and is terrible to the kings of the earth. We must not then fall into the fancy that all wrath is evil, and that we must always and everywhere suppress it. There is a righteous anger, as well as an unrighteous. Else we would not read, "Be ye angry, and sin not." If to be angry were already sin, we could not be exhorted not to sin in our anger. God is angry. He is angry with the wicked every day. His wrath is revealed from heaven against all that work iniquity. If it were not so, He would not be a moral being: for every moral being must burn with hot indignation against all wrong perceived as such. That is precisely what we mean by a moral being: a being which knows right and wrong, and which approves the right and reprobates the wrong. If we do not react against the wrong when we see it, in indignation and avenging wrath, we are either unmoral or immoral.

Therefore also, Christ was angry. The Gospels are filled with instances of the manifestation by Him of the emotion of anger in all the varieties of this emotion: from mere annoyance, as when He rebuked His disciples for forbidding the children to be brought unto Him, to burning indignation, as when the unfeeling Scribes would not permit Him to heal the suffering on the Sabbath day—yes, even to what the Evangelists do not scruple to call outbreaking rage which shook with its paroxysm His whole physical frame, as when He advanced to do battle with death and sin—the destroyers of men—at the grave of Lazarus. Even the Lamb feels and shows wrath. Christ is our perfect example. And if we are to be His perfect imitators, we not only may, but must, be angry; we not only may, but must, exhibit wrath—whenever, that is, good is assaulted and evil is exalted. We too, must be found, on proper occasion, with the whip of small cords in our hands; we too, must not draw back when righteousness is to be vindicated or when the oppressed are to be rescued. In this sense too, the wrath of man is to God for praise. We please Him when we are righteously angry. He who never feels stirring within him the emotion of just indignation is not like God in that high element of the image of God in which he was made—His moral nature. Indignation is an inevitable reaction of a moral being in the presence of wrongdoing, and it is not merely his right, but his duty to give it play when righteousness demands it.

No doubt we are to seek peace and ensue it. But this is the peace not of the condonation of evil, but of the conquest of it. We are to conquer evil in ourselves. We are to know no inordinate anger. We are to be slow to anger and quick to put it aside: we are not to let the sun go down upon our wrath. We are to remember that anger is a short madness, and not trust ourselves too readily in wreaking it on others—even when we think it righteous: not avenging ourselves, but giving place to the wrath of God, knowing that in His own good time and way He will avenge us. We are to conquer it in others: by the soft word which takes away anger, by the patient endurance which disarms it, by the unwearying kindness which dissolves it into repentance and love. Love is the great solvent; and love is the bond of peace. Where love is, there wrath will with difficulty live, and only that wrath which is after all outraged love can easily assert itself. But so long as there is wrongdoing in the world, so long will there be a place in the world for righteous indignation.

It is only when the world shall have been remade and there is no longer anything in it that can hurt or destroy that the lion and the lamb shall lie down together—because now the lion has ceased to be a lion. These things are to us an allegory. They mean that peace is the crowning blessing of earthly life and comes in the train of righteousness. Peace is, in the strictest sense, a by-product and is not to be had through direct effort. He works best for the world's peace who works for the world's righteousness. It is only when the world shall come to know the Lord and obey Him, that the peace of God can settle down upon it. We may cry, "Peace, peace," and there be no peace. But he who cries, "Righteousness, righteousness," will find that he has brought peace to the earth in precisely the measure in which he has brought righteousness. Jesus Christ is the Prince of Peace, because He takes away sin; and you and I are workers for peace when we preach His Gospel, which is the Gospel of peace just because it is the Gospel of deliverance from sin. Sin means war, and where sin is, there will war be. Righteousness means peace, and there can never be peace where righteousness has not first been realized.

FOR CHRIST'S SAKE

Matt. 5:11:—"For My Sake."

"He came to his own and his own received him not." Though they had been for generations under the tutelage of the law, the schoolmaster to lead them to Christ; though the forerunner had come to prepare the way before Him, proclaiming repentance to be the gate to His spiritual kingdom; yet He found the majority of the people inflamed by earthly hopes and passions and wedded to their expectation of a kingdom of flesh, in which they as kings and priests should revel in the discomfiture of all their enemies. Consequently we find our Lord taking an early opportunity in His ministry, when He saw the multitudes before Him, to teach them the real nature of the kingdom which He came to found. In this aspect, the Sermon on the Mount is closely analogous to the marvellous discourse on the Bread of Life, recorded for us in the sixth chapter of John. In both alike our Lord found Himself in the presence of a carnal-minded crowd whose hopes were set upon an earthly kingdom of might and worldly glory, and who sought Him only in the hope that through Him they might gratify their ambitious aspirations. In both alike the purpose of the

Divine teacher is instruction and sifting, or sifting through instruction. They knew not of what spirit they were; He would open to them the nature of the work He came to do, the nature of the spiritual kingdom He came to found.

By historical necessity, the Sermon on the Mount is, then, the proclamation of the law of the kingdom. How beautifully it opens! Not, as the listening crowd, hanging eagerly upon the lips of the wondrous teacher, expected, with a clarion call to arms, or a ringing promise of reward to him who fought valiantly for Israel. Not as we might expect, with a stinging rebuke to their carnal hopes and a stern correction and repression of their ungentle spirit. But gently and winningly, wooing the hearers to the higher ideal, by depicting in the most attractively simple language the blessedness of those in whom should be found the marks of the true children of the kingdom. When the Lord speaks to His children it is not in the voice of the great and strong wind that rends the mountain and breaks in pieces the rocks, nor in that of the earthquake, or of the fire, but in that still small voice or "sound of a gentle stillness" in which He spoke to Elijah in the mountain. The Lion of the Tribe of Judah had come and He opens His mouth and blesses the people in the voice of a Lamb.

Look at this ninefold twisted cord of the beatitudes and learn what the followers of the Lamb must be. As we look does it seem a mirror giving us back the lines and features of our own faces? Or rather, some strange picture of an unknown race brought home by some traveller to a far country—a race of almost unhuman lineaments, so different are they from our own? Indeed, here is the portrait of the dwellers in a far land, even a heavenly; here we trace in living characters the outlines of those who live with God; the citizens of His kingdom whose home and abiding city is above, where Jesus is on the right hand of God. They are not of lofty carriage—but "poor in spirit"; nor are they of gay countenance—they "mourn" rather, and "hunger and thirst" eagerly "after the righteousness" which they lack within themselves; they are "merciful, poor in heart, peacemakers." Surely then, they are well-esteemed among men! Nay, this is another of their characteristics. They are supremely lovable; but men hate them. They are persecuted for their very righteousness' sake. But they have their reward. Blessed are they—nay, "blessed are ye—when men shall reproach you and persecute you and say all manner of evil against you falsely for Christ's sake. Rejoice and be exceeding glad, for great is your reward in heaven."

The promises of Christ are not earthly but heavenly. He promises His servants evils here below; so true is it that "prosperity is the blessing of the Old Testament, adversity of the New."

Yet in the midst of all this lowliness and evil, they are blessed. As heaven is higher than earth so high is their blessedness above any earthly success or glory or delight. Though they see their earthly house of this tabernacle being literally worn away, then, by afflictions oft and endurances many they need not faint; for even this affliction is light in comparison with the weight of yonder glory. More, they may rejoice and be exceeding glad, for great is their reward in heaven. The more suffering for Christ here, the more glory with Christ there. As an old writer has it, the more the vessels of mercy are scoured here, the more may they be assured that God wants them to shine there; the more clear it is that we are being preserved not in sugar but in brine, the more clear that God is preserving us not for a season but for eternity. The last of the beatitudes thus pronounces blessed those who suffer affliction for Christ's sake and bids them rejoice and be exceeding glad, because their reward shall be great.

Let us punctually observe, however, that it is not affliction in itself that is pronounced blessed. It is affliction for Christ's sake. This is the key-phrase which locks up the whole list of beatitudes. For Christ's sake. It is this that transmutes poverty of spirit into heavenly humility, that brings comfort to the mourning, and glorious riches to the meek, and plenty to those that hunger and thirst after righteousness. It is this that has been the spring of mercy in the merciful, of purity in the pure of heart, of peace in the peacemakers. And it is this and this only that makes it a glory to endure the scoffs and revilings and persecutions of men. As truly as we may say that the blessedness of affliction and persecution is due to its relation to the reward, is due to the fact that it is the gateway to the kingdom, so also may we say that it depends on its cause. For Christ's sake is the little phrase that points us to its source and law.

When we selected these three words, "For my sake" as the centre of our meditation this afternoon, therefore, we elected to ask you to give your attention this hour to the great determining motive of the Christian life, above which the Scriptures know no higher, above which no higher can be conceived. Christ adverts to it as the great moving spring of Christian activity and endurance in the ninth beatitude. When reproach and persecution and reviling are endured on Christ's account, then and then only are we blessed. But this is not the only place or the most moving way that this motive is adduced. The Scriptures are full of it. Let us sum up what we have to say of it in two propositions. (1) For Christ's sake is the *highest* motive which could be adduced to govern our conduct. (2) For Christ's sake ought and must be our motive in *all* our conduct. In other words it is the grandest and most compelling, and we should make it our universal and continual motive, in all our conduct of life.

Let us consider then, the greatness of this motive as a spring of action, and here let us observe, first, that its greatness as a motive is revealed to us by the greatness of the requirements that are made of us on its account. This ninth beatitude is an example in point. Men are expected to endure reproaches and persecutions and all manner of evil for Christ's sake. That is, "for Christ's sake" is expected to sweeten the bitterest cup, and to make every affliction joyful to us. Disgraceful scourgings, unjust imprisonments (Matt. 10:18), burning hates (10:22), malignant slanders (Luke 6:22), death itself (Matt. 10:39), and that with the utmost refinement of cruelty and the deepest depths of disgrace; all these are enumerated for us as things before which no Christian should hesitate when it is for Christ's sake. All these are things which Christians have joyfully met with praises on their lips for Christ's sake. The enumeration in the eleventh chapter of Hebrews is but a bare catalogue of what since then has been endured with delight by those who bore this strengthening talisman in their bosom, For Christ's sake. These too have had trial of mockings and scourgings, of bonds and imprisonments, of stonings and sawings asunder, and of long lives of privation in deserts and caves and have for Christ's sake witnessed a good confession. These all, in one word, have testified to us the supreme strength of the motive "for Christ's sake," by joyfully suffering everything for Christ, that they might be glorified with Him, becoming sharers in His sufferings that they might be participants in His glory.

And this leads us to observe, secondly, that the greatness of this motive is revealed to us by the greatness of the promises that are attached to living by it. So in this ninth beatitude, those who are afflicted for Christ's sake are pronounced blessed, and are called upon to rejoice and be exceeding glad, because—because, so it is added, "great is your reward in heaven." And so is it everywhere. "Every one" it is said, without exception (Matt. 19:39), "every one that hath left houses or brethren or sisters or fathers or mothers or children or lands for my name's sake, shall receive a hundredfold and shall inherit eternal life." Thus it is that those whose eyes are opened may see the recompense of the reward and may be enabled to account the reproach of Christ greater riches than the treasures of Egypt. He that denieth Christ before men may, indeed, receive the applause of men; but men pass away and their applause is empty air. But, he that denieth men for Christ's sake is received into the eternal habitations. "He that findeth his life shall lose it; but he that loseth his life for my sake shall find it." If we suffer with Him so also shall we be glorified together with Him (Rom. 8:17). There is, indeed, no limit to the reward promised; truly "great is our reward in heaven." And the greatness of the motive may be justly measured by the greatness of the reward. As high as heaven is above earth, as long as eternity is beyond time, as great as perfection is above lack, as strong as stability is above that which endureth but a moment; so high is the heavenly reward above the earthly suffering and so strong is the motive to act for Christ's sake.

But, thirdly, let us observe that the greatness of this motive is revealed to us by the fact that God honours it as the motive of His own most mysterious acts of redemption. He not only asks us to do for Christ's sake what is hard for us, but He Himself for Christ's sake does what is hard for Him. What could be more difficult for a just and holy God than to pardon sin and take the sinner into His most intimate love and communion? Yet for Christ's sake God does even this. "I write unto you, little children," says the beloved Apostle, "because your sins are forgiven you for his name's sake" (1 John 2:12). All the instrumentalities of grace are set at work in the world, only for Christ's sake. It is for His sake that we are accepted by God, that we have the gift of the Spirit, that we are regenerated, adopted, justified, sanctified, glorified. Nay, even the little things of life are for His sake. It is not only for His sake that we are received by God, but for His sake that we are treated even here and now while yet sinners as God's children, allowed freedom of access to the Throne of Grace, and have all our petitions (little and great alike) heard and answered. "Verily I say unto you," says the Saviour, "whatever ye shall ask in my name, that will I do" (Jno. 14:13).

And thus we are led finally to observe that the greatness of the motive rests on the greatness of Christ's work for us. As He has stopped at nothing for our sakes, so we must not stop at anything for His sake. All that we are and all that we have are His. And as He has loved us and given Himself for us, so must we love Him and give ourselves to Him. Behind the phrase "for thy sake" lurks thus all the motive power of a great love, the fruit of a great gratitude. As we can never repay Him for our redemption, so there is nothing that we can pause at, if done for His sake. Is not this the core of the whole matter? What difference will it make to us what men may judge or what they will do? Need we hesitate because they consider us beside ourselves? If this is lunacy, it is a blessed lunacy! Nay, shall we not rather say with the Apostle of old, "whether we be beside ourselves it is to God. . . . For the love of Christ constraineth us." And why should the love of Christ constrain us? "Because we thus judge, that if one died for all then all died; and He died for all that those that live should no longer live unto themselves, but unto Him who for their sakes died and rose again." Yes, here it is: for our sakes He died and rose again. And because He died for our sakes, we shall live for Him, yea, and if need be, for His sake also die. Is there, can there be asked, a stronger motive than this?

Or need we ask at this point how universal is this obligation—how far, into what details of life, we should carry it as our motive? It is clear that there can be no call so great that this motive should not dominate it; we must be glad and willing to go to death itself "for His sake." But perhaps, the other side needs emphasis too. Can there be a call so small that this motive need not govern us? Nay, we are bought with a price and are asked not only to be ready to die, but also (sometimes a harder task) to be ready to live for Christ. Whatever we do, however small, however seemingly insignificant—must needs be for Him. We are now new creatures—no more worldlings but Christ's children; let us see to it that we live like Christ's own children; doing all we do for Him and for His sake. So the Scriptures teach us to do: "Whatsoever ye do in word or in deed, do all in the name of the Lord Jesus, giving thanks to God the Father through Him."

"Whatsoever ye do, do from the soul, as unto the Lord, and not unto men; knowing that from the Lord ye shall receive the recompense of the inheritance." (Col. 3:17, 23.) As Christians, let us be Christians, recognizably followers of Christ, doing His will in all we do and trying our duty at every stage simply by these questions: Is it according to His will? Does it subserve His glory? Is it for His sake? So doing, we cannot but approve ourselves before man and God as followers of Him.

THIS- AND OTHER-WORLDLINESS

Matt. 6:33:—"But seek ye first his kingdom and his righteousness; and all these things shall be added unto you."

THIS verse is in a sense the summing up of the whole lesson of the Sermon on the Mount up to this point. This great discourse had opened with an enumeration of the classes to whom the advent of the kingdom would bring joy and blessing, in whom the leading characteristic is seen to be other-worldliness. It then proceeded to enunciate the law of the kingdom, which demanded holiness before God rather than external righteousness before men. At the nineteenth verse of the sixth chapter the summing up begins with a direct appeal to lay aside care for earthly things and to set the mind on heavenly things. This summing up culminates and finds its fullest expression in the verse before us: "But seek ye first the kingdom of God and his righteousness; and all these things shall be added unto you." This is the precipitate of the whole sermon; in a few words it contrasts the two cares which press on man, the two seekings which may engage his attention. It does not commend to us a nerveless life of Buddhist-like retirement from desire and destruction of activity. It presupposes in all men who are men, desire, energy, activity directed to a goal. But it discriminates activities and goals. We are to seek. But not what the heathen seek—worldly ease and goods and advantages. We are to seek heavenly things. Hence, it bans one class of seekings and commends the other. Our chief cnd is not to gain earthly things but heavenly.

Approaching the verse somewhat more closely, we observe of it—that it is a protest against practical atheism. There is a formal atheism of opinions and words and reasonings which declares that there is no God and seeks to sophisticate the understanding into believing that there is none. This the Bible describes as an open folly: the fool has said in his heart, There is no God. But even when the lip and the mind behind the lip are true to right reason and confess that there is a God who rules the world and to whom we are responsible in our every thought and word and deed, there is often a practical atheism that lives as if there were no God. Formal atheism denies God; practical atheism is guilty of the possibly even more astounding sin of forgetting the God it confesses. How many men who would not think of saying even in their hearts, There is no God, deny Him practically by ordering their lives as if He were not? And even among those who yield, in their lives, a practical as well as a formal acknowledgment of God, many yet manage, practically, to deny in their lives that this God, acknowledged and served, is the Lord of all the earth. How prone we are to limit and circumscribe the sphere in which we practically allow for God! We feel His presence and activity in some things but not in others; we seek His blessing in some matters but not in others; we look for His guidance in some affairs but not in others; we can trust Him in some crises and with some of our hopes but not in or with others. This too is a practical atheism. And it is against all such practical atheism that our passage enters its protest. It protests against men living as if they were the builders of their own houses, the architects of their own fortunes. It protests against men reckoning in anything without God.

How are we to order our lives? How are we to provide for our households—or, for our own bodily wants? Is it true that we can trust the eternal welfare of our souls to God and cannot trust to Him the temporal welfare of our bodies? Is it true that He has provided salvation for us at the tremendous cost of the death of His Son, and will not provide food for us to eat and clothes for us to wear at the cost of the directive word that speaks and it is done? Is it true that we can stand by the bedside of our dying friend and send him forth into eternity in good confidence in God, and cannot send that same friend forth into the world with any confidence that God will keep him there? O, the practical atheism of many of our earthly cares and earthly anxieties! Can we not read the lessons of the birds of heaven and the lilies of the field which our Father feeds and clothes? What a rebuke these lessons are to our practical atheism, which says, in effect, that we cannot trust God for our earthly prosperity but must bid Him wait until we make good our earthly fortunes before we can afford to turn to Him. How many men do actually think that it is unreasonable to serve God at the expense of their business activity? To give Him their first and most energetic service? How many think it would be unreasonable in God to put His service before their provision for themselves and family? How many of us who have been able to "risk" ourselves, do not think that we can "risk" our families in God's keeping? How subtle the temptations! But, here our Lord brushes them all away in the calm words, "Seek ye first the kingdom of God and his righteousness; and all these things shall be added unto you." Is this not a rebuke to our practical atheism?

But the verse does not take the form of a rebuke; it takes the form of an appeal; and we observe next of it, therefore, that it is an appeal to make God's kingdom and righteousness the prime objects of our life. And looking closely at it we see that it is not an empty appeal but includes a promise. We are, primarily, to make God's kingdom and righteousness our chief concern; but, doing so, we shall more surely secure the earthly things we need. The passage does not proceed on the presumption that we do not need these earthly things; it asserts our need of them. It does not proceed on the assumption that they are not to be in their appropriate place and order and way the objects of seeking. It merely corrects our mode of seeking them. We may seek them without and apart from God or we may seek them in and of God. It tells us that the former way—the atheistic way, in which we seek to provide for ourselves—is the way not to get them; the latter way in which we seek them in and from God is the way to get them. Who can doubt it?

In the first place we have God's promise. He tells us that if we will seek first His Kingdom and His righteousness He will add all these things. He tells us in effect that to godliness there is the promise both of this world and of the world to come. Men find it hard to believe this. It is a standing problem of the wise of the earth and has been from Job's day down. But we have the promise.

In the next place we may add, despite the difficulties of life and the clouding of judgment, it, after all, does stand to reason. Isn't, after all, it the best way to secure the reward, to enter into the service of the King? And God is the King of all the earth. How shall we obtain the goods of the earth better than by hearty service of the

King of the earth? True we shall obtain them as gifts and not as acquired by us. But is not the best path for man, to seek them at His hands? The King suffers not His faithful servants to want.

But more fundamentally still, we may add that it belongs to the very nature of things. If we want to enjoy those earthly goods which God has placed in this world for the benefit and use of His children, the best way to secure their enjoyment is obviously not to seek to do it individually but socially. It is a social axiom that everything that betters the condition of society as a whole increases our enjoyment of our material goods. A savage acquires a pot of gold. How shall he enjoy it? His fellow savages covet it; and who shall secure it to him? He is liable to be waylaid at night for it. Every bush hides an enemy; the poisoned arrow may fly upon him from any tree; his sleep is driven from him as he seeks to protect his life. Hidden by friendly darkness he may bury his treasure under some great tree in the tangled forest; and anxiously guard its neighbourhood lest he may have been watched and still be bereft of it. In such conditions there is no enjoyment of the treasure for him; he can enjoy only the protection of it. But, now, he is a wise savage and instead of giving his energies to protecting his treasure, he gives it to civilizing his people. Out of the savage tribe rise the rudiments of a state;

the majesty of law emerges—protecting under its powerful ægis the person and property of its citizens. What a change! No need of hiding the treasure now. He can wear it displayed upon his person. He now can enjoy at least its possession. But a higher stage is still possible; the community may be not only civilized but Christianized; Christian principles take the place of external laws; love the place of force. And he, touched with the same spirit, goes about with his treasure, transmuting it into aid for the suffering and needy. Now he is truly enjoying it, enjoying, not only protecting it, not only possessing it but using it. When such a time fully comes to this world of ours—that is what we mean by the Millennium—the kingdom of God has come for which we daily pray in the prayer our Lord has taught us, when men no longer prey on one another but help and support one another.

Meanwhile how shall we approach it? By our Lord's prescription—by seeking the kingdom of God and His righteousness. In proportion as we seek and find this kingdom, in the measure in which we bring it into practical life in the narrow circle around us, is it not necessarily true that we shall have and enjoy the best goods of this earth? Is there not a deep foundation in the nature of things for our Lord's promise: "Seek ye first the kingdom of God and his righteousness; and all these things shall be added to you?" Is not this the most hopeful way to obtain and hold and enjoy these other things?

But it is time for us to take note of another and the most characteristic element in this appeal. When we observe it narrowly we will see that it is not an appeal to seek the kingdom of God and His righteousness on the ground that this is the best way to obtain the other goods. It does not say: "Seek ye first the kingdom of God and His righteousness" "because"—but simply "and"—"and all these things shall be added unto you." It is a fact that Godliness has also the promise of this life, but that is not the reason why Godliness should be sought. It is a better reason that it has the promise of the life to come. It is a better reason still that it is Godliness. Nor does our passage itself fail to bring this out. It does not say "and all these things shall be your reward." It does not propose to pay us for seeking God's Kingdom and righteousness by giving us earthly things. It says: "and all these things shall be added unto you." The Greek word is not the word for pay, reward, but for the small gratuitous addition to the promised wages, given as we should say "in the bargain." The worldly goods that come to us are in a word here represented not as our reward, but as something "in the bargain." The appeal of the passage is made to rest elsewhere; that is, in the contrast between goods earthly and goods heavenly. We are to seek the heavenly, not for the sake of the earthly, but for their own sake. For, as Paul says, after all the Kingdom of God is not meat and drink but righteousness. And our passage sets, as Bengel points out, this celestial food and drink over against the earthly.

Herein resides the "lift" of the passage. It places the highest good before us—God and His righteousness—fellowship with God; and pries at our hearts with this great lever of, Who will seek earthly food and drink when they can seek the kingdom of God and His righteousness? In the restitution of the harmony between man and God thus involved, every blessing is included. Here is something worth losing all earthly joys for. Here is something worth the labour of men, the very end of whose being is to glorify God and enjoy Him forever. Would we not purchase it with loss of all earthly—if we can speak of loss in the exchange of the less for the greater? Will we not take this for our seeking when in addition to this great reward, we shall have also "all these things added to us"? See the tenderness of our Lord in this constant regard for our human weakness.

And there is another tender word in the passage when restored to its right reading, which reaches down into our hearts to summon another motive from their depths, whereby we may be led to seek God's kingdom and righteousness. The fact that this is the best way to obtain these very earthly blessings which we need may be a sufficient motive. The glory of the things sought may be a higher and more prevailing motive. But there is a more powerful one still; it is love—love not to a principle but to a person. And our Lord does not fail to touch on this. In its right reading the passage does not run: "Seek ye first the kingdom of God and His righteousness," but "Seek ye first His kingdom and His righteousness." And the antecedent to "His" is "your heavenly Father." Here our Lord is tugging at our hearts. "For your heavenly Father knoweth that ye have need of all these things. But seek ye first His kingdom and His—your heavenly Father's—righteousness; and all these things shall be added unto you." Did we say the passage is a protest? Did we say it is a command? Do we not now see that it is rather a pleading? O, the subtlety of love! Love speaks here to us; will not love respond in us? Under such pleading what can we do but seek first our heavenly Father's kingdom, our heavenly Father's righteousness? And because He is our Father, we are sure both that we shall find it, and with it—how comparitively little it seems now!—whatever else we need, added to us.

LIGHT AND SHINING

Mark 4:21–25:—"And he said unto them, Is the lamp brought to be put under the bushel, or under the bed, and not to be put on the stand? For there is nothing hid, save that it should be manifested; neither was anything made secret, but that it should come to light. If any man hath ears to hear, let him hear. And he said unto them, Take heed what ye hear: with what measure ye mete it shall be measured unto you; and more shall be given unto you. For he that hath, to him shall be given: and he that hath not, from him shall be taken away even that which he hath."

ONE of the peculiarities of our Lord's method of teaching is His repeated use of a number of favourite sayings—or maxims, we may call them—in varied connexions and in differing applications. This gives a remarkable piquancy to His speech and must at the time have served the double purpose of fixing the several teachings which He embodied in these gnomic sayings firmly in the minds of His hearers, and of attracting them to the matter of them as something peculiarly weighty. In the passage before us we have a cluster of these "proverbs," all of which meet us elsewhere and sometimes with other applications, but which are combined here to give pregnancy and force to the specific message of this passage. Here is the beautiful parable of the lamp. Here is the amazing paradox of secrecy in order to openness. Here is the crisp proverb that ears are given for hearing. Here is the simile of equitable measures. Here is the gnome of the relation of possession to receptivity. No one of these is a stranger to readers of the Gospels. They are found elsewhere also in much the same connexion as here; but they are found elsewhere also in other connexions. They are marshalled together here to give wings to a specific teaching.

What is that specific teaching?

Well, there is too much in it—too much depth of suggestion, too many implications of meaning, for us to attempt to draw it all out at once. But we may direct our attention to at least four things that lie on the surface. Obviously this cluster of sayings lays before us an important declaration, presses on our attention an urgent exhortation, reveals to us a profound philosophy of life, and founds on this a serious warning. Let us attend for a moment to these four things.

The important declaration that is made in these sayings amounts to this: that there is no esoteric element in Christian teaching. This is the primary suggestion of the parable of the lamp and the explicit assertion of the startling paradox which immediately follows it, to the effect that "there is nothing hid save that it may be manifested, neither has anything been made secret save that it might come abroad." For a lamp exists, the parable tells us, for no other purpose but to illuminate; it comes not to be put under the bushel or under the couch, but on the stand—that its light may shine. And, the paradox adds, there is to be nothing cryptic or apocryphal in the whole sphere of Christian teaching. It is, in effect, the very contradiction of Christianity as truth, to imagine that it can exist for any other end but to serve the purpose of truth—to enlighten.

The strength of our Lord's emphasis on this important declaration just on this occasion finds its explanation of course in the need that had arisen to guard from misapprehension His own methods of teaching. For a change had just been introduced into His modes of instruction, from which His disciples might be tempted to infer that Christianity was a double system, with an esoteric and an exoteric aspect. Our Lord, who had hitherto spoken plainly, had suddenly begun to speak in parables; and He had not concealed from His disciples that His object was to veil His meaning. Was there not introduced thus the full-blown system of esoterism? It is to correct this not unnatural inference that our Lord declares so emphatically that the truth He is teaching—even in parabolic form—is a lamp, and has for its one end to shine; that what is now hid and made secret under this parabolic veil, is hid and made secret not that it may not be made known, but just that it may be made known. The impulse to use parables thus arises from wisdom and prudence in teaching, not from a desire to conceal. He teaches in parables in order that He may teach; not in order that He may not teach. This method of veiled teaching, in a word, is forced on Him by the conditions under which He is teaching and arises from the state of mind of His hearers; it is not chosen by Him in order to conceal His meaning, but in order to convey it to those for whom it is intended. It is with Him either to teach thus or not to teach at all; and He consequently teaches thus. This is the fundamental doctrine of parabolic teaching. I do not say it is the whole account to be given of it; we may see in the sequel that there is more to say, and that the adoption of parabolic teaching has a punitive side—as, indeed, it could not fail to have—with reference to those who could and would not endure sound doctrine; whom it puzzled, therefore, rather than instructed. But this is the fundamental account of it.

We may see this from an illustration. Take as such the teaching which was the immediate occasion of these remarks of our Lord's. He had just been delivering the first cycle of the parables of the Kingdom. Why had He taught the fundamental facts as to the Kingdom in parables? Briefly, because He could not have taught them in any other way. For His conception of the Kingdom was at just the antipodes of that of the people He was addressing. Should he have plainly and didactically proclaimed just what their error was, just what the truth was? He certainly would have been understood in that case. But there would have been an end to His teaching and so of His mission as Teacher. And so, instead, He told them some beautiful stories. In these stories He embodied the whole fundamental doctrine of the Kingdom. What was the effect? To those open to His instruction the whole doctrine of the Kingdom was conveyed. Those not receptive to it were simply puzzled; instead of being outraged and driven to violence, they were simply puzzled and thrown back into dull inertia. When He said, the Kingdom of Heaven is like the sower, and the like, they could only look perplexed and shake their heads. The Kingdom of Heaven as they understood it was like nothing less than these things. What could He mean? And thus He obtained opportunity—the Great Sower that He was—to sow His seed and to exemplify His own parable. Meanwhile receptive souls pondered and understood, understood, that is, more or less. For even His own disciples, nay, the Apostles themselves, were not yet capable of receiving the truth in its purity and entirety. And, accordingly to them too, He taught as occasion offered, in parables, by which He lodged the truth in their minds that it might germinate and grow.

Nothing is more obvious than that this wise

prudence in the mode of disseminating the truth has nothing in common with esoteric teaching; and our Lord's broad denial of esoterism was as justified as it was needed. A lamp that is shaded is shaded, not for the benefit of the lamp, as if it were too good for common use, or existed for some other end than enlightening, but for some extrinsic end. There may be a violence of wind from which it needs temporary protection; there may be weakness of eyes which require guarding. So with the truth which Jesus came to teach. It is not too sacred for the knowledge of men; it exists to be known. But it may require temporary protection from violent opposition; it may require veiling because of the weakness of men's understanding. Hence it is spoken under the veil of parables. But this is that it may be spoken, that it may be made known, and not that it may be concealed. No crypticism, no apocryphalism is in place here!

Accordingly, then, within this declaration there is embodied also an urgent exhortation. It is interlaced with the declaration in this passage of Mark so as to be scarcely distinguishable from it. Elsewhere it is brought out most explicitly and with tremendous emphasis. It is an exhortation to the recipients of the truth to see to it that it is not quenched in the darkness of their own hearts, but permitted to act in accordance with its nature as light—to shine. In Matthew, for example, we read: "Even so let your light shine before men, that they may see your good works and glorify your Father which is in heaven." Here it appears only in the way of implication. Jesus says in effect: The truth I am delivering in this veiled form is, like all truth, of the nature of light; it comes to enlighten; temporarily it is veiled, but, emphatically, it is hid only that it may be manifested; it is made secret only that it may come to light. Ye are my chosen witnesses; to you I say with significant emphasis, "If any man have ears to hear, let him hear." There is a subtle implication that not the truth only which He spoke is the lamp, brought to be put on the stand; but these disciples of His, to whom the truth has been brought, have been lighted by the truth, and having been lighted, are lighted that they too may shine. In effect, there is a solemn commission given here to His disciples—not to His Apostles only, but (as verse 10 shows), to the whole body of His disciples, to see to it that what He is now preaching in parables shall be in its due season brought out on the housetop. There is careful provision made, in a word, for the cultivation of the seed He was now sowing. He was speaking in parables—the times required it—but they are to see to it that what is thus taught veiledly shall in due time be announced openly.

No doubt, in this whole procedure, there is divine sanction given to the principle of wise adaptation of our preaching to times and circumstance. But, O, how easy it is to misapply this principle and pervert it to cowardly ends of personal profit. Preach to our times? Yes, of course. But preach what to our times? Our Lord's example does not give warrant to the suppression of unpalatable truth. It only sets an example of how still to preach the unpalatable truth while staving off for the fitting time the inevitable rupture, and providing for its full proclamation in the end. He spoke in parables? Why in parables? First, because by speaking in parables, He could still teach the unpalatable truth. If He had been willing to suppress the unpalatable truth He would have had no need of preaching in parables. There will be no need of a veil if we remove the thing to be veiled. And secondly, because He would so teach the unpalatable truth, that men must needs hear it before they know what they are hearing, and thus He would catch them with holy guile. You see there is nothing here so little as an example of suppression of the truth. There is only an example of finding a way to preach to men, despite their opposition, what they do not choose to hear.

Christ does not yield to men; He triumphs over men. And this is the commission He gives to us: Let your light shine! Do not think you are imitating Him when you quench your light; when you permit the clamours of men to drown your voice of teaching. You imitate Him only when, despite men's opposition, you find a way to make your voice heard and the truth with which you are charged a power among them. Silent, Christ was not; compromising, He was not; He was only persistently inventive in modes of proclamation. You imitate Him least of all when you put your light under a bushel or under a couch; to be like Him you must let your light shine.

It is already clear to us, no doubt, that there is implicit in this passage a fully developed philosophy both of teaching and of life. Why did Christ preach in parables? To conceal the truth or to teach the truth? The proper answer is, of course, both. The two are not mutually exclusive. Fundamentally we say, it was in order to teach the truth. Proximately it was, of course, so far to conceal the truth as to be able to teach it in the circumstances in which He stood. People who would not listen when He told them plainly what the Kingdom He came to found was like, would listen to His story and so have the unpalatable truth told them before they were aware. But this is not the whole story. There is more to be said and Christ says it. Truth so taught becomes a touchstone and discriminates among men. When Jesus said "the Kingdom of God is like to . . ." that was an opening familiar enough to the whole body of His audience. The most rigid Pharisee, the most fanatical zealot would prick up his ears at that. But when He went on and told them what—in His view—the Kingdom of God was like, what would the Pharisee, what would the zealot, make of that? Nothing. The disciples themselves could not make much of it. The others naturally could make nothing. Thus, the method of teaching by parables, certainly did not succeed in illuminating all. The plainest teaching under heaven could not have illuminated those minds. They were too filled with preconceptions, prejudices, personal desires, to be accessible to the truth. How could veiled teaching dispel their darkness? It could only avail to make the darkness of their minds deeper; they could only say in puzzlement, "We do not understand!" How can the glorious Kingdom of Heaven—God come to triumph over Israel's foes, how can this be like the sower sowing His seed, and the like? So our Saviour explains that the teaching is given to them in parables, that seeing they may see and not understand. In effect, parabolic teaching becomes the test of men. Whether men understand or do not understand the teaching veiled in the parable, is the revelation of their state of mind and heart, or, as it is fashionable nowadays to call it, of their receptivity. Parabolic teaching then comes into the world as a rock of decision; those who are open to the truth understand, those not open to the truth do not understand.

Observe how pointedly our Lord develops this idea in the later verses of our passage; with what piercing directness He asserts the effect in the last verse of all: For he that hath to him shall be given, and he that hath not from him shall be taken away even that which he hath. Here is the underlying philosophy of parabolic teaching; and along with it of all teaching. And is it not so, our own hearts being the judge? Let the parables fall on the ears of one instructed in the Kingdom of Heaven and how beautifully rich in their teaching they are. Points of attachment are discovered at every step and the conceptions that rest half-formed in us are developed in the richest manner. Let them fall on the minds in which no thought of the Kingdom of Heaven was ever lodged; and they are but as rocks in the sky. All teaching as to divine and heavenly things is, in a measure, parabolic; we can reach above the world and ourselves only by symbols. All such teaching comes to us, then, as a test, and the proximate account of its varied reception may be found in the condition of the ears that hear it. Have we ears to hear this music? Or does it beat a vain jangling discord only in our ears? The philosophy of the progress of the Kingdom in the world rests on the one fact—the condition of the hearer. He that has ears to hear, hears; he that has no ears to hear this music, remains unmoved.

Accordingly, then, the passage culminates in a great warning. "Take heed how ye hear." And this warning is supported by the verses already incidentally adduced: "With what measure ye mete . . ."; "He that hath . . .; He that hath not . . ." The warning is, of course, of universal application. It is spoken here to Christ's immediate disciples, and it is most immediately a warning to them to look with care and loving scrutiny on the teaching He was giving about the Kingdom. Do you not fail, it says, to hear and ponder; to understand and profit by this teaching. But it stretches further. As we, too, are His disciples it comes in these times also to us. Let us not fail to-day to hear and ponder and understand and profit by the teaching brought to us by these pungent words!

CHILDLIKENESS

Mark 10:15:—"Verily I say unto you, Whosoever shall not receive the Kingdom of God as a little child, he shall in no wise enter therein."

THE declaration embodied in this verse, apparently very simple, and certainly perfectly clear in its general sense, is not without its perplexities when examined in its detailed implications. The occasion of its enunciation was an incident in the life of our Lord which manifests His beautiful tenderness as few others of those narrated in the Gospels. In the prosecution of His mission He went up and down the land, as we are told, "doing good." It was characteristic of His teaching that the common people heard Him gladly. It was of the essence of the beneficent impression that He made that He drew to Him all who were afflicted and were suffering with diverse diseases.

The Evangelists stud their narratives thickly with accounts of how the people flocked to him, bringing all their sick and receiving from Him healing of body and mind. This appeared to His closest followers well worth while. It was all part of his office as One sent from God to heal the hurt of Israel. But the people did not stop there. Mothers brought their babies also to Him, and asked Him to lay His hands on them and bless them, too. Here His disciples drew the line. These babies were not sick and did not need the healing touch of the Great Physician. By the very fact that they were babies they were incapable of profiting by His wonderful words. To intrude them upon His attention was to interfere unwarrantably with His prosecution of His pressing labors, and to supplant those who had superior claims on His time and strength. So the disciples rebuked the parents and would fain have sent the babies away.

But the Lord, perceiving what was toward, was moved with indignation and intervened with His great, "Let the little children come to me, prevent them not." And taking them in His own arms, He laid His hands on them and blessed them; the word employed being a very emphatic one, meaning a calling down fervently of blessings upon the objects of the prayer. The mothers went away comforted, bearing their blessed babies in their arms.

What a picture we have here of the Master's loving-kindness! It is not strange if, when we read the narrative, we stop, first of all, to adore and love Him. It is a revelation of the character of Jesus; and what can we contemplate with more profit than the character of Jesus? But we soon begin to realize that the incident is freighted with instruction for us relatively to our Lord's mission as well, and to question what messages it brings us from this point of view. We ask why was our Lord "moved with indignation" at His disciples for intercepting the approach of the mothers with their babies to Him. They meant well; surely He needed protection from unnecessary and useless draughts upon His energies. Indignation was certainly out of place unless there was some very harmful misunderstanding somewhere.

And so it begins to dawn upon us that the disciples ought to have known better. And that means ultimately that they ought to have known better than to suppose that Jesus' mission was summed up in instruction and healing. Were this all that it was, it had been right enough to exclude the babies from His presence. Only if He had something for these babies too; only if His blessing on them—not needing healing and incapable of instruction—nevertheless, brought to them the supreme benefit; would it be a crime to shut them out from His offices. Whence we may learn that the blessing which Jesus brought was something above His instruction and superior to His healing ministry. A great physician, yes; a prophet come from God, yes; but above and beyond these, the bearer of blessings which could penetrate even to the helpless babes on their mothers' breasts.

Perhaps if the disciples stopped short of this,

it is not inexplicable that men of to-day, having proceeded so far, should show a tendency to stop right here and utilize this much gain with such devotion that they do not stay to search further. We have obviously here a warrant for infant baptism, they say. For does not Jesus declare that infants are to be permitted to come to Him and are not to be hindered—affirming further that the Kingdom of Heaven is of such, and taking them in His arms and blessing them? And can His Church, representing Him on earth, do less? Must not His Church suffer the infants to be brought to Him and take them in her arms and mark them with His name and bless them? Nay, say others, this and more: A warrant here for confidence in the salvation of infants. For how can we believe that He who on earth so tenderly and solemnly took them in His arms and blessed them, forbidding their access to Him to be hindered, will now in heaven refuse to receive them when they come flocking to His arms? And does He not distinctly declare that the Kingdom of God belongs to such; and does that not mean first of all—whatever else it may mean—just this simple thing, that infants as such are citizens of His heavenly kingdom and must be accredited with all the rights of that heavenly citizenship?

It is no part of my purpose to stop and examine the validity of these inferences. Let it be enough for us to-day to note clearly, merely that they are inferences. And having noted that they are inferences, let us for the moment at least pass them by, and engross ourselves in the teaching which is explicit and for the sake of which, therefore, we must suppose that the incident is recorded. For our Lord did not leave His disciples to draw inferences from the incident, unaided. He draws one for them; and that one is what we have chosen as the subject of our meditation to-day. In this inference He withdraws our minds from the literal children He had taken and blessed, and focuses them upon the spiritual children who should constitute the Kingdom of Heaven.

You will observe that He passes at once from the one to the other. When He says "For of *such* is the Kingdom of God," He does not mean that the Kingdom of God consists of literal infants, but rather of those who are like infants. You may assure yourselves of this by turning to the first beatitude: "Blessed are the poor in spirit; for theirs"—or "of them"—"is the Kingdom of heaven." That is to say, the Kingdom of heaven belongs to—or is constituted of—the "poor in spirit." So, here, if what were intended were that the Kingdom of God belongs to —is constituted of—infants, we should have: "For of *them*"—or "theirs"—"is the Kingdom of God." What we do have, however, is not that, but, on the contrary, "For of *such as they*—of *their like*—is the Kingdom of heaven." The

Kingdom of heaven is declared, therefore, to be constituted not of children but of the childlike. And the declaration is at once clinched by the words of our text, introduced by the solemn formula "Verily," "Verily I say unto you, Whosoever shall not receive the kingdom of God as a little child, he shall in no wise enter therein."

The message which the incident is made by our Lord to bring us, therefore,—and which, accordingly, the passage directly teaches us with no inferences of ours—does not concern either infant baptism or infant salvation, but distinctly the constitution of the Kingdom of God. The Kingdom of God, it asserts, is made up, not of children, but of the childlike. And that concerns directly you and me. The Kingdom of God, our text asserts, is made up of people like these children whom our Lord took in His arms and blessed. And that being so, we are warned that no one can enter that Kingdom who does not receive it "like a little child." This is as much as to say, not only that childlikeness characterizes the recipients of that Kingdom, but that childlikeness is the indispensable prerequisite to entrance into it. It certainly behoves you and me who wish to be members of the Kingdom of God to know what this childlikeness means.

Well, many think at once of the innocence of childhood. The statement is, in effect they say, that the Kingdom of God consists solely of those who are in their moral innocence like children. Only such can enter it. A grave difficulty at once faces us, however, when we enunciate this view. That is that Jesus does not seem elsewhere to announce innocence as a—as the—condition of entrance into the Kingdom which He came to establish. On the contrary, He declared that He came not to call the righteous, but sinners, and announced that His mission was to seek and save what is lost. The publicans and harlots, He tells us, go into the Kingdom before the righteous Pharisees. To give point to this we note that in Luke's narrative the parable of the publican and pharisee praying in the temple immediately precedes the account of our present incident, and is placed there evidently because of the affinity of the two narratives. It would read exceedingly oddly if the publican was justified and the pharisee, with all his righteousness, rejected, and immediately afterwards it were asserted that the Kingdom was solely for the innocent. No, there is nothing clearer than that Jesus' mission was specifically to those who were not innocent—that it is characteristic of those who enter His Kingdom that they do not feel innocent—that, in a word, the Kingdom is built up from and by the "chief of sinners" like Paul, and those who say of themselves that "if any man say he hath no sin he is a liar, and the truth is not in him," like John. Not the "righteous" but "sinners" Jesus came to save.

Remembering the pharisee and publican, shall we not say, then, that the trait of childhood here celebrated is, if not exactly innocence, at least humility? It was precisely humility that characterized the prayer of the publican and our Lord elsewhere commends humility as in some sense the primary Christian grace. "Blessed," He says in that first beatitude, which we have already cited, "blessed are the poor in spirit, for theirs—of them—is the Kingdom of heaven." Is not this an express parallel to our present passage, saying in plain words what is here said in figure? When we read, then, that the Kingdom of heaven belongs to those who are childlike, and only he can enter it who receives it as a child—is not the very thing meant, that none but the humble-minded, the poor in spirit, can possess the Kingdom? Indeed, is not this very thing spoken out in so many words in a closely related previous incident when Jesus took a child and set it among His disciples, as they were disputing as to who should be greatest, and bade them to humble themselves and become as that little child if they would be great in the Kingdom of heaven—enforcing the lesson moreover with a declaration almost the same as that of the text: "Verily I say unto you, Except ye turn and become as little children, ye shall in no wise enter into the Kingdom of heaven"? It certainly seems as if in that passage at least the humility of little children is just the thing signalized, and entrance into the Kingdom is hung on the possession of that specific virtue.

Even in that passage, however, it may be well to move warily. Is humility the special characteristic of childhood? To become like a child may certainly be an act of humility in one not a child, and it is very intelligible that our Lord should, therefore, tell those whom He was exhorting to become like a child that they can only do it by humbling themselves. But is that quite the same as saying that humility is the characteristic virtue of childhood, or that a humble spirit is the precedent condition of entering the Kingdom of heaven? We seem to be in danger of reading the passage too superficially. Our Lord tells His disciples that they cannot enter the Kingdom which He came to found except they turn and become like little children; and He tells them that they cannot become like little children except by humbling themselves, and, therefore, that when they were quarrelling about greatness they were not "turning and becoming like little children." But He does not seem to tell them that humility of heart is the characterizing quality of childlikeness; in this statement it is rather the pathway over which we must tread to attain something else which is the characterizing quality of childlikeness. Childlikeness is one thing; that by which that state is attained is another.

Much less is humility suggested to us in our present passage as the constitutive fact of child-likeness. These babies that Jesus took into His arms, in what sense were they lowly minded, and the types of humility of soul? If they were like other children of their age, they were probably, so far as they showed moral characteristics at all, little egotists. There is no period of life so purely, sharply, unrelievedly egotistic as infancy; and there is, consequently, no period of life less adapted to stand as the typical form of that lowliness of mind which seeks another's, not one's own, good.

Others have gone further and I think done better, therefore, when they have suggested that it is the simplicity of childhood, its artlessness and ingenuousness, which is the trait which our Lord intends when He declares that the Kingdom of Heaven is made up "of such" as they, and that no one who does not receive that Kingdom like a child—that is, in childlike simplicity and ingenuousness—shall enter into it. Above everything else the mental life of a child is characterized, perhaps, by directness. It lacks the sinuosities, double motives, complications, of the adult intelligence. The child does not think of "serving two masters," but gives itself altogether to one thing or the other, and possesses at least the single purpose if not always that precise singleness of eye which our Lord commends. We know what an encomium our Saviour passed on that singleness of eye because of which the whole body should be full of light; and what an echo of this teaching His apostles sound in the praise of that singleness of heart or simplicity of soul in which they make the Christian disposition to consist. May it not, then, be this lack of duplicity in thought and feeling, this clear simplicity of heart which results in singleness of devotion, that our Lord declares here to be characteristic of childhood and of those spiritual children who alone may be true disciples?

This is a very attractive idea; but attractive as the idea is, it seems a little artificial and not easily deducible from the passage itself. It might fit very well in the eighteenth chapter of Matthew—and, indeed, would give a far better sense there than the conception of humility; but it seems to be outside the scope of our present passage. These children were mere babies—and in what clear and outstanding sense are babies characterized by simplicity of heart and singleness of soul?

We feel, then, that a great step is taken when others step in and suggest that the particular trait which our Saviour has in mind when He declares that only the childlike can enter His Kingdom is the trustfulness of the child. Here we touch, indeed, what seems really the fundamental trait of the truly childish mind, that colors all its moral life, and constitutes, not merely its dominant but we might almost say, its entire disposition—implicit trustfulness. The age of childhood is, above everything else, the age of trust. Dependent upon its elders for everything, the whole nature of the child is keyed to trust; on trust it lives, and by means of trust it finds all its means of existence. Its virtues and its faults alike grow out of trust as its fundamental characteristic. There is no picture of perfect and simple and implicit trust discoverable in all the world comparable to the picture of the infant lying peacefully and serenely on its mother's bosom. And we must remember that this is the spectacle that our Lord had before Him. The mothers were bringing their babies to Him to be blessed; He looked at them as they approached; and, observing the utter trustfulness of the attitude of the child reclining in the nest of its mother's arms, He announced that here is the type of the Kingdom of God and of its children. In these trusting babies He saw the symbol of the citizens of His Kingdom. "Of such as these," He declared, "is the Kingdom of God"; and then He added that no man who did not receive the Kingdom like one of these little trustful babies, could even enter it. Trust, simple, utter trust, that is the pathway to the Kingdom.

We cannot doubt that in thus directing its attention to the trustfulness of little children as their characteristic trait, the mind has been turned in the right direction for the proper understanding of our Lord's declaration. But even yet, I think, we have scarcely reached the bottom fact. You will observe that all the suppositions hitherto made move in the subjective sphere. Dispositions of mind alone have been suggested; men have been seeking to discover the disposition of mind which is most characteristic of childhood; to which we may suppose, therefore, that our Saviour, referred, when He declared that His disciples must be like children if they would enter His Kingdom. But our passage says nothing of dispositions of mind; and why should we?

Why not seek an objective characteristic here? These babies, which Christ took in His arms—what dispositions of mind had they? We must now revert to the narrative, and observe with care that these children were, in point of fact, mere babies. Perhaps we have been thinking of them rather as well-grown children, and picturing them as standing around our Lord's knees, giving Him eager, if wondering attention, as He spoke to them. Nothing of the kind. They were babies in arms, perhaps of only a few weeks or months old, perhaps of only a few days. They had no disposition of mind. Luke calls them distinctly infants, and speaks, therefore, of their being brought as remarkable: "They were bringing to Him *even* their babies." And that is the reason why the disciples rebuked their parents for bringing them—mere babies who could get nothing from the Master. The same thing is less clearly but equally really suggested in the other narratives; we read that they were *brought*; that Jesus took them *in His arms*, and the like. We must think of them, then, as distinctively babies. What dispositions of soul were characteristic of them? Just none at all. They lay happy and thoughtless in their mother's arms and in Jesus' own arms. Their characteristic was just helpless dependence; complete dependence upon the care of those whose care for them was necessary. And it would seem that it is just this objective helpless dependence which is the point of comparison between them and the children of the Kingdom.

What our Lord would seem to say, then, when He says: "Of such is the Kingdom of heaven," is that the Kingdom of heaven is made up of those who are helplessly dependent on the King of the Heavens. And when He adds that only those who "receive" the Kingdom like a child can enter into it He seems to mean that the children of the Kingdom come into it like children of the world into the world—naked and stripped of everything, infants who are to be done for, who can not do for themselves. There is every indication of this as our Lord's meaning. Among others we note that the record of the incident is followed immediately in all three Gospels by the record of the incident of the rich young man—which goes on, you see, to illustrate the same idea. For what was the trouble with the rich young man? Just this: that he could not divest himself of everything and come into the Kingdom naked. "He had great possessions." "How hard, children,"—this "children" is possibly a reminiscence of His demand that they should be "like children"—"children, how hard it is for a rich man—or for anyone—to enter the Kingdom of heaven." Into this Kingdom we can enter only as poor and naked and helpless as children enter the world. That we have nothing is the condition that we may have all things. Perhaps it may not be too much even to say that what the passage teaches is that we enter the Kingdom of heaven as we enter the world only by a birth—a birth which comes to us—which we do not secure. In that case we have a parallel passage in the third chapter of John which is one of the very few passages in John where the term "Kingdom of God" occurs.

The upshot of it all is, then, this: that the Kingdom of God is not taken—acquired—laid hold of; it is just "received." It comes to men, men do not come to it. And when it comes to men, they merely "receive" it, "as"—"like"—"a little child." That is to say, they bring nothing to it and have nothing to recommend them to it except their helplessness. They depend wholly on the King. Only they who so receive it can enter it; no disposition or act of their own commends them to it. Accordingly the Kingdom of God is "of such as little children." The helpless babe on the mother's breast, then, now we can say it with new meaning, is the true type of the Christian in his relation to God. It is of the very essence of salvation that it is supernatural. It is purely a gift, a gift of God's; and they who receive it must receive it purely as a gift. He who will not humble himself and enter it as a little child enters the world, in utter nakedness and complete dependence, shall never see it.

THE GLORY OF THE WORD

John 1:1:—"In the beginning was the Word, and the Word was with God, and the Word was God."

THE first verse of the Gospel of John contains one of the most weighty statements of the deity of our Lord in the New Testament. It is not the only weighty statement, much less the only distinct statement, of the deity of our Lord in the New Testament. Rather, the whole New Testament is a testimony to our Lord's deity; and we can read no part of it sympathetically without catching this note sounding through it.

Particularly we need to disabuse our minds of the banality by which the Synoptic Gospels used to be distinguished as the Gospels of the human Jesus, from the Gospel of John as the Gospel of the Divine Jesus. The Synoptic Gospels teach the deity of Jesus as truly and, indeed, as emphatically as the Gospel of John, though not in precisely the same manner. Whatever else William Wrede did or did not do with his book on the Gospel of Mark, he made it impossible forever afterwards to look upon Mark as a naïve collection of all that His followers could recall of the human Jesus; and Johannes Weiss will not be gainsaid when he points out that the Jesus of "the oldest Gospel" has already advanced far toward the Jesus of the latest Gospel. He is to be criticized only for speaking of an "advance" in this connexion, and of that "advance" as not quite complete. Recent critics are fairly falling over one another in their rush to recognize that the conception of a Divine Messiah was not only Primitive-Christian, but Pre-Christian, and that belief in the deity of Jesus, was, therefore, already included in acceptance of Him as Messiah.

We meet no new thing, then, when we read in the first verse of John's Gospel a crisp declaration that Jesus is God. But we do meet something new in the manner in which this declaration is made. It would not be quite exact to say that it is new that John begins his Gospel with a declaration of the deity of Jesus. Mark also begins his Gospel with a declaration of the deity of Jesus; if, at least, the reading is right which makes him use the term, "the Son of God," in his opening sentence—"The beginning of the Gospel of Jesus Christ, the Son of God." It can hardly be maintained that the "Son of God" is not to be understood here in its ontological sense. The difference between the Synoptics and John here is only a difference in what we may call their mode of approach to the common theme. It would not be misleadingly expressed if we said that in the Synoptics the divine nature of the man Jesus is exhibited, while in John the human life of the divine Word is portrayed. In this sense, John does take his start from the deity of our Lord as the Synoptics do not. The deity of our Lord is made by John his point of departure in his delineation of this divine life in the world, while the Synoptics take their start from the birth of Jesus, or the opening of his public ministry.

It is due to this difference that John's Gospel alone opens with a prologue, which takes us back at once into the depths of Eternal Reality, and tells us who and what that being actually was, whose life-history in the world is about to be depicted. There is probably no more pregnant piece of writing in the world than this prologue to John's Gospel. And there is no part of this pregnant prologue more pregnant than its first verse. There are just seventeen words in it; we can count only eight different words in it: but these few words are simply bursting with significance. In the first place, our Lord is designated here by a unique name, and that a name big with meaning. And then, under this unique name, three declarations are calmly made of Him—so calmly as almost to betray us into taking them as mere matters of course—each of which, separately considered, is of tremendous import, and the three together, in combination, of more tremendous import still. When we have read these three limpid sentences—"In the beginning was the Word, and the Word was with God, and the

Word was God"—we have read things which even the angels, desiring to look into them, might well despair of plumbing.

When we say that the name given here to our Lord—the "Word"—is unique, we have, of course, the New Testament only in mind. And even so, to be absolutely exact, we must note that John repeats it a little lower down in this prologue, when he tells us of this Word, here declared to have been in the beginning, with God, and Himself God, that he became flesh; and indeed echoes it in the opening words of his first Epistle and in a splendid description of the conquering Christ in the Apocalypse. These instances, however, do not abate the fact that this designation belongs in a very special sense to these opening clauses of John's prologue. There is nothing to prepare us for it here: it just suddenly appears before us in these three great declarations in unrelieved startlingness. And perhaps the most striking thing about it is that John does not present it to us as a mysterious designation of Jesus, as a remarkable designation of Him, or, we must add, even as a new designation of Him. He employs it quite simply and without apparent consciousness that he is doing anything either startling or new.

That it is not a new designation of our Lord to either John or to his readers, is already apparent from the fact that no emphasis falls on it whatever. It occurs three times, it is true, in these three short clauses. But the words are so arranged that the emphasis is always thrown elsewhere—on what is asserted of the Word, not on the designation itself—while the designation appears as a matter of course. And the employment of the same designation in the opening words of the contemporaneous First Epistle of John is a clear proof that it was not first applied to our Lord in this prologue. We must dismiss from our minds, therefore, the fancy that John invented the designation, "The Word," for our Lord. We must suppose it to have been a current designation of our Lord in the circles for which John was writing, and that it needed no explanation from him of its meaning.

Whence the term came, and precisely what it means when applied to Jesus, are, of course, another matter. We cannot talk of its being borrowed from Philo, or from the philosophy which Philo represents. There is nothing more certain than that John does not use it in the sense which it bears in Philo, or in the philosophy which lies behind Philo. It is not much more likely that it was borrowed directly from the native Jewish speculations, which, like the speculations of Philo and those whom he most closely followed, are governed by the need for something to mediate between the transcendent God and the world of space and time. But this general type of thinking was very widely diffused, and the modes of speech which it developed naturally penetrated, in more or less modified meanings, much more deeply into the life and language of the people than the conceptions these modes of speech were invented to express. All terms of this sort have their roots in some system of thought, but come to those who ultimately employ them with a varied history behind them, in the course of which they have lost much of the shades of suggestion with which they started, and have picked up others on the way. We have no safe guidance to their meaning on the lips of any given speaker, except his actual usage of them. And to judge by John's actual usage of the term, "the Word," applied as a designation to our Lord, it has travelled far indeed from its Neo-Stoic or Philonian beginnings—if those were its beginnings—before it reached his hands. What he means by it is obviously so different from what Philo or the Neo-Stoics meant by it, that, in most important respects, it is its precise contradiction. What is clearest about it is that he uses it as a designation of Jesus of the highest import, as attributing to Him properly divine functions, if not directly a properly divine nature. As a man's word is the expression of his being, so, when Jesus is spoken of as the Word by way of eminence, that is, as the Word of God, He is designated as the manifested God.

Speaking thus of Jesus by this great designation, John makes three assertions concerning Him. In the first of these he declares His eternal subsistence. In the second, His eternal intercommunion with God. In the third, His eternal identity with God. Let us look briefly at these three great assertions in turn.

The first of them runs in our English version thus: "In the beginning was the Word." This rendering, however, scarcely brings out its full sense. The words are so ordered in the original as to throw all the emphasis—and it is a strong emphasis—on the words, "in the beginning," and "was." The verb "was," in other words, is not a mere copula, but a strong assertion of existence. We might perhaps bring part of its meaning out by changing the order of the words and reading: "In the beginning the Word *was*." What is declared is that "in the beginning"—not "from the beginning" but "in the beginning,"—when first things began to be, the Word, not came into being, so that He might be the first of those things which came into being, but already *was*. Absolute eternity of being is asserted for the Word in as precise and as strong language as absolute eternity of being can be asserted. The Word antedates the beginning of things; He already *was*—the imperfect of continuous existence—when things began to be. Go back now to the first verse of Genesis, of which there is an obvious echo here, and read that in the beginning God created the heavens and the earth—the Hebrew periphrasis for the universe. The Word already *was* before God thus began to speak things into existence. We cannot be surprised, then, to read in the next verse, with the emphasis of accumulated assertion, that "all things" without exception "were made by Him, and apart from Him there was not one thing made which has been made." The Word was not made; He always *was*. All that has been made was made by Him.

To this great assertion of express eternity of being, there is now added in the second clause another equally great assertion; or rather a greater assertion, for these three clauses are arranged in a climactic series. "In the beginning the Word already was—and the Word was with God." This new assertion is still under the government of the words, "in the beginning": it declares the eternal mode of existence of this eternally existent Word. And the mode of existence declared for Him places Him in an ineffable immediacy of relation to God. The phrase, "with God," is not the common expression for "with God," but a more pregnant one. It intimates not merely co-existence, or some sort of local relation, but an active relation of intercourse. The Word, existing from all eternity, exists from all eternity in intercommunion with God. His eternal existence was not a solitary one. A relation is asserted; and a relation implies a duality. The relation which is asserted is a very intimate one; and it is a distinctly personal one. There can be intercourse only between persons. When it is said, then, that the Word "was"—it is still the eternal "was" of continuous existence—"in the beginning" in communion with God, the eternally distinct personality of the Word is not obscurely suggested. From all eternity the Word subsisted alongside of God in personal intercommunion with Him. He has been from all eternity God's Fellow.

The intimacy of the relation intimated is startlingly brought home to us by a later phrase of this prologue. Here we are told in language of almost unexampled pregnancy that the Word—called on this occasion by the tremendous name of "God Only-begotten"—is (the timeless present of eternal existence) ceaselessly, not merely in, but "into the bosom of God." This is the expression for the closest and most intimate relation conceivable for persons; and the language in which it is cast conveys the idea at once of a continuation of its unbroken continuity and of its ceaseless renewal. It is in this intimacy of communion that the Word is declared to have been eternally "with God."

But even this great assertion is not enough to declare of the Word. There is a supplement to even it; and a supplement which is so far a correction that it seems purposely added to prevent it from being supposed that enough has already been said. The Word is not merely even thus closely associated with God; He is God Himself. "And the Word was with God—and the Word was God." Eternally subsisting alongside of and in communion with God, the Word is yet not a separate Being over against God. In some deep sense distinct from God, He is at the same time in some high sense identical with God.

It is difficult to reproduce in English the strength of this assertion. The term "God" not only occupies the position of emphasis, but is placed in immediate juxtaposition with the words "with God" of the preceding clause, and, therefore, in sharp contrast with them. The term "God" thus comes out with a tremendous corrective force. "The Word was with God, do I say—nay *God* is what the Word *was!*" The rapidity of the movement of thought and the stress thrown thus on this new assertion are extreme. The meaning is that John was not willing to have the one statement made without its complement being at once added to it. He wishes us to understand that it is too little to say of the Word even that He is God's co-eternal Fellow. We must say of Him that He is the eternal God's very self.

The term God in this great assertion is without the article. This does not weaken the affirmation. It is primarily merely a grammatical fact. The predicate regularly lacks the article; quasi-proper names, like "God," require it only when an individualizing emphasis is necessary. The bearing of the absence of the article here on the force of the assertion is that thus there is thrown into relief the quality of Godhood in the God with whom the Word is identified. Whatever makes God the Being which we call God, that John affirms the Word to have eternally been. Thus the Word is with the utmost energy and explication asserted to be all that God is; and yet the correction of the assertion that the Word "was with God" as incomplete, is not pushed into a contradiction of it as untrue. The Word, though identical with God, is not in such a manner identical with God, that he may not also be declared to be "with God"—in communion with God. There remains a duality of Persons standing in the express relation of intercommunion, while there is established an identity of Being. What is asserted is that He who has been eternally with God has been at the same time in an ineffable fashion eternally God's self.

Certainly these are three tremendous assertions which John makes here of that Word, who, having become flesh, we know as Jesus Christ—eternal subsistence, eternal intercommunion with God, eternal identity with God. The conception in which they can combine is certainly not an easy or a simple one. It is what we know as the doctrine of the Trinity. In telling us who and what Jesus Christ really is, John thus introduces us to the doctrine of the Trinity. If we were told nothing about the Trinity except what we are told in this single verse, it would yet lie before us in its whole principle. There is no other key which will unlock the mystery of the eternal Being of the Word as here described to us. We are but expressing John's meaning, then—in other words, but nevertheless nothing but his meaning—when we declare that Jesus Christ is the Second Person of the Adorable Trinity. This is, in brief, what John teaches us in the first verse of his Gospel.

LOOKING TO MEN

Jno. 5:44:—"How can ye believe, which receive glory one of another, and the glory that cometh from the only God ye seek not?"

THE fifth chapter of John marks one of the great turning points of his narrative. Up to this point, he has given us great typical representations of how Jesus wrought faith in the hearts of His hearers—at Jerusalem (in the case of Nicodemus), in Samaria (in the case of the Samaritan woman), in Galilee (in the case of the nobleman of Capernaum). Now he begins to show us the development of the opposition. With the fifth chapter the conflict begins; and in three great typical instances, each gathering around a miracle, we see how Jesus' work gathered opposition to itself, until opposition culminated in the black tragedy of His death. Here we have laid bare the springs, nature and deeds of unbelief.

Not that we have no longer an exhibition of Jesus begetting, by word and work, faith in His life-giving Person. In each instance in which the process of the hardening of unbelief is pictured to us, there is a picture of faith too, in contrast with it. The impotent man, the man born blind, the family of Lazarus, are heroes of faith, and nothing can be more beautiful than the manner in which it is shown how simple, unsophisticated faith fixed itself on Jesus. But on each occasion of faith-begetting work, blind unbelief hardened itself to deeper and deeper blackness, and it is this progress which forms the salient feature of the narrative.

In the fifth chapter the grounds of unbelief are laid bare to us, as rooted in an essentially self-seeking and worldly spirit. No part of the chapter is unimportant for understanding the lesson which is most pointedly expressed in the verse more especially before us. The miracle out of which grew the discourse, of which this verse is the culmination, is, of course, appropriate to its lesson; and the conversation and discourse are carried inevitably up to this end.

The miracle was wrought on an impotent man, and out of it was to grow the discourse which was to uncover the impotence of sinners, on their own part, to believe in the Saviour of the world. Long had the man lain helplessly by the very pool of healing, where the ordinary means of cure were; but he had no power to make a healing use of them, nor was there any to help him—until Jesus passed by and spoke the wonderful word of healing to his weary soul. But it was on the Sabbath day, and the Jews, the types of that Pharisaic religiosity which loved to make long prayers on the corners of the streets and to make broad their phylacteries to be seen of men, whose religion in a word was a religion for men to mark and praise, at once judged that the due observance of the Sabbath law was of more importance than the healing of a diseased sinner. At once are brought into contrast the religion that seeks God's approval and that which seeks the applause of men. Jesus meets the healed man and bids him sin no more; they meet Jesus and in their rage at the disregarding of their laws seek to slay him.

Our Lord does not permit the contrast to pass unnoticed. And this is the burden of His discourse. All He did was of the Father and to the Father and for the Father; and sought only His approval. All they did was of man and to man and for the approval of man. His eye was turned upwards, theirs downwards. And, therefore, they were impotent to believe in Him; though He, the water of life, was in their reach, they could not reach out and take and live. How could they believe, though in word and work the Father was bearing witness to Him, when they cared nothing for the Father, but only for men; when they were receiving glory from one another and not seeking glory from God, the Only One.

Now note:—

(1) Our Lord asserts that the Jews were unable to believe. He asserts a true inability to faith in them; but by no means allows that they have thereby become irresponsible. How can ye—how are ye able to—believe?

(2) He traces this inability to its source in a

wrong disposition. He asserts that the reason that they could not believe was because of their condition of mind and heart. How are ye able to believe, seeing that ye are receiving glory one of another and seek not the glory that cometh from the Only One?

(3) The special sin that darkened their eyes to Christ's truth and worthiness as one sent from God was the sin of living for the world's eye, not God's; of seeking the world's applause, not God's approval. They wished a Messiah for worldly glory, not for salvation.

The passage will teach us then:

(1) That a true inability may well consist with responsibility; an inability that rises out of the moral condition and is constituted by the immanent choice.

(2) That the habit of living for the applause of our fellow men in religious things is deadly to the religious affections and life, which in their very nature are Godward and must look upwards only to Him.

(3) That from God alone can true glory come; and He is the sole source of the Christian's glory.

There can be no doubt that our Lord asserts of these Jews that they could not, were not able, had not the ability to believe. And He assigns the reason for this; a reason not derived from any outward compulsion, and not due to any lack of evidence. They had sent to John and John had testified to Jesus, and if they would look to the Scriptures they witnessed to Him; nay, would they look to heaven, heaven itself bore witness to Him in His wonderful works. They were caught in a network of evidence. Whence it all the more fully follows that if they believed not, it was due to some inability. Yes, a true inability, an induration of believing tissue which rendered it unable to react to any testimony, however great. But this inability did not render them irresponsible for their lack of faith. Our Lord closes His discourse with a solemn asseveration that they did not need Him to accuse them to the Father: "There was one that accused them, even Moses, on whom they had set their hopes. For if they believed Moses, they would have believed Him, for he wrote of Him." In a word, our Lord arraigns them for their inability to believe, not as though it was an excuse for their lack of faith, but as though it was the blackest item in the indictment against them. They could not believe, but it was because of their wicked hearts, because they had set their hearts on earthly things and cared not for the heavenly.

And now we understand why the healing of the impotent man is the miracle out of which this discourse grows. All Christ's miracles are parables. For thirty-eight years this man had lain there just alongside the healing floods, and he was impotent to use them for the healing of his disease—neither had he anyone who could apply them to him. And here before these Jews stood One offering the water of life, and they were impotent to reach out their hand to take it, because they were receiving their glory one from another and sought not the glory that comes from the Only One. It is the impotence of man by his natural powers to believe—be the evidence never so convincing—that Jesus would teach us by His parable and by His discourse. The impotent man might have ocular evidence every time the water moved of its healing virtues. What good did the demonstration do him, when he could not reach out and take the healing floods? These impotent Jews might have, did have, demonstrative evidence that the Lord of Life stood before them. John had spoken, God in His word had spoken, God by sign and miracle had spoken. And yet what good did evidence do them so long as they could not believe, because their hearts were set on the earth and not on the heavens?

Is it not plain to you that it is not evidence alone that produces faith? Did the abundant evidence of the Divine mission of Christ convince the Jews; who sought His life the more vindictively for every item of evidence they could not resist; who answered His demonstration of deity by hanging Him on the tree? Nay, be the evidence never so perfect, we cannot believe who have evil hearts of unbelief. Never until that Divine voice, freighted with supernatural power, which said to the impotent man, Arise, take up thy bed and walk, has sounded with a personal message to our souls, do we gain the power to believe, though Moses himself and the law written in our hearts pronounce us inexcusable.

Now as we have learned a doctrinal lesson from our text, let us learn also a practical one. Surely the text teaches us that the habit of living in religious things for the observation and applause of our fellows is deadly to all religious affections, and, indeed, to all religious life itself. Nor could it indeed be otherwise. Are not the religious affections in their very nature Godward? And is not the religious life dependent on our preserving in ourselves an attitude of dependence and receptivity with reference to God? Turn our eyes from Him, and religion in any true sense of the word is gone. Rites may remain; forms may remain; genuflections and prayers may remain; a strict mode of life may remain, but not religion. The husk of religion—like the shell of nuts—may endure when the kernel is gone; it is often harder to destroy the hull and husk than that subtle kernel, for which alone the husk exists. But of what worth is the husk after what it was formed to protect is gone? Of course this is not to condemn the outward forms of religion. This is involved in the very figure used. Like the shell of a nut, it is needed; needed for the protection and preservation of the kernel. But without the kernel? That is a different matter.

As ministers, we have, and we ought to recognize it, special temptations to religiosity, as distinguished from religion. We are professionally religious men. Let the lesson come home especially to us then, that the habit of being religious for the eye of men is deadly to true religion. It does not follow that we ought to be careless of our influence over men. It only follows that we ought to be careful with respect to what we influence them. We should set an example to them to be truly religious, lovers of God and seekers only of His approval; and not only to seem to be religious. How subtle the temptation is! How grand a thing to have the reputation of being the most religious man in the community, the most careful in our religious services, the most punctual in our religious duties! Well, the Pharisees were all this. No men in the land were more religious; they were models for all men in the strictness of their lives. And they could not believe! There is a better thing than having the reputation of being religious; and that is being religious. And the difference is just this: That the one has praise of men and the other of God.

And thus we are led to lay emphasis, in closing, on the third point of teaching which I would have you receive from our text: that all true glory comes from God only. This is the pointed antithesis of the text; and Christ uses it as the sufficient uncovering of the failure and folly of the Jews. They received glory from their fellow men, and did not remember that true glory comes from God only. It is hard for men to feel this. We do so long after the approval of our fellows. Men go in crowds. Truth has a poor show, when the tide sets against it. How hard it is to face the gibes of our companions. "Old Fogy," "Narrow-minded"—these are not very bad words in themselves, but they have a baleful power. How natural to desire to be "in the swim"! How delightful to feel the approval and to enjoy the aid of our fellows pressing us on. It is human to love human applause and to seek it.

But it is Divine to stem the tide for God. Jesus preached unpopular truth. Men could so little endure it that they crucified Him for it. Paul preached unpopular truth, and suffered a thousand deaths for doing so. Will we say that they were wrong? After all, it is only when the "vox populi" is really the "vox dei" as well, that we can afford to follow it. When the "vox populi" stands in opposition to the "vox dei," let us breast it at all hazards! In other words, let it be the "vox dei" that we unhesitatingly and unwaveringly follow; and if the "vox populi" agree with it, so much the better for the "vox populi." As ministers of

God's grace let us make up our minds firmly and once for all to seek His glory and not men's. After all, is it not to his own Master that every man stands or falls?

A HALF-LEARNED CHRIST

Jno. 6:68, 69:—"Simon Peter answered him, Lord to whom shall we go? Thou hast the words of eternal life. And we have believed and know that Thou art the Holy One of God."

THE first impression made on us by this response of Peter's to our Lord's pathetic appeal, "Surely ye too will not wish to go?" is the nobility of the confession which it contains. We are not surprised to find one of the commentators, therefore, speaking of it as "this immortal reply"; nor are we surprised that it is commonly treated by commentators and expounders alike from this point of view. Thus, for instance, one expounder develops it as a "serious answer" to our Lord's "searching inquiry"; and finds in it, (1) a "reverential address"— "Lord"; (2) a significant inquiry," which is only a "strong way of asserting not alone that our Lord's disciples intended to adhere to Him, but that they reckoned Him the only Teacher, Messiah, Saviour, to whom they could adhere"; (3) a "confidant avowal"—viz., that He had the words of eternal life; and (4) a "simple confession," that they saw in Him none other than "the Holy One of God,"—God's own incarnate Son.

Now, we should certainly be sorry to miss this

side of the matter. Surely, the verse does contain, fundamentally, a confession of Peter's and through him of the apostles' faith; and assuredly this confession is, in contrast with the thought of Jesus entertained by the crowds which had been flocking to Him, a very noble confession, which explains why the twelve cleaved to Him in the midst of the general defection that had now set in. At bottom, this confession does mean that these men were seeking in Jesus satisfaction for spiritual and not carnal wants; and that they, therefore, understood Him incomparably better than the crowds of carnal men which had hitherto surrounded Him; and that, finding satisfaction in Him for their spiritual needs, they could not leave Him as the others left Him, however puzzlingly He spoke, but could not fail to recognize in Him the very consecrated messenger from God whom their hearts craved.

To mean this was, at that time and in those circumstances, to mean almost incredibly much. But it is not to mean everything. There is another side to the declaration, and this other side is obviously the side that was in John's mind when he recorded it. For clearly he does not put it forward as a supreme confession, marking a complete appreciation of Jesus' person and claims, and standing out, therefore, in startling and instructive contrast with the unbelief of others, to the manifestation of which the whole preceding chapter is consecrated—as exhibiting in a word the immense contrast of the fullness of the apostles' faith and appreciation with the slowness or rather grossness of heart of the lesser followers of Christ. On the contrary, he presents it evidently as standing in contrast, indeed, with the unbelief and incapacity to believe of the others, and therefore marking out the apostles as Christ's especially faithful followers; but as, nevertheless, exhibiting more fully the great crisis that had come into our Lord's life by showing how, even among His closest companions, there existed no full appreciation of Him in His work and claims. When Jesus, out of the midst of the scenes that lay about Him, turned to this innermost circle of His followers with the sorrowful inquiry: "Surely ye too will not go away!"—Oh, the pathos of it!—He obtained no doubt a reassurance. No, they would cleave to Him. And this reassurance must have been a balm to His wounded human spirit. But the reassurance He obtained was so little to His mind, that He felt it necessary to meet it with a rebuke: "Was it not I that chose you—the twelve; and of you, one is diabolical!" This very confession was an element, thus, in the crisis through which He was passing, the manifestation of how little even those who were nearest to Him really understood Him or were ready to carry on His work.

Surely it will not be without its lessons to us to

seek, without derogating from the essential nobility of the confession, to trace out also the elements of incompleteness that enter into it, and that make it less than what a confession of Christ ought to be.

First of all, then, we notice that there seems to be an element of boastfulness in this confession. This suggests itself by the obtrusion of the personal pronoun. We might read our English version and think of the emphasis falling on the believing and knowing which is asserted. We cannot so read the Greek. The emphasis falls rather on the "we." "And as for us," says Peter, "we at least" have believed. Peter is contrasting himself and his fellow apostles with others and priding himself on the contrast. We will remember that our Lord had just said, "The words that I have spoken unto you are spirit and are life; but there are of you some who do not believe." Peter seems to swell with pride to think that he is not of these. Repeating his Master's words, he says, "Thou hast words of eternal life, and as for us, we at least have believed!" You see Peter is Peter himself in this confession. How often do we find him pushing forward with his rash and boastful words. "That be far from Thee, Lord," he cries on a similar occasion—to receive the sharp rebuff, "Get thee behind me, Satan!" "Although all shall stumble," he had yet to boast on still another occasion, "yet will not I. If I must die with Thee, I will not deny Thee." We all know with what sorrowful sequence. And so here; "As for us, we, at least, have believed." We perceive the pride in his faith which dictated the words. And now we understand the sharpness of our Lord's rebuke, with its emphasis on the personal pronoun. "You boast yourselves," replies Jesus, "that you at least have believed—was it after all you that believed in Me, or I that chose you—the twelve? And even so, of you, one at least is a devil!" Poor Peter—always boasting and always getting the "Get thee behind me, Satan."

How plain the lesson to us is. A warning, clear, sharp, overwhelming, against all spiritual pride. I am afraid that we too are prone to pride ourselves on what we have only received, as if by our own power we had done these things. There is nothing more unlovely than pride in spiritual things. Do we not feel it moving in us sometimes, however, in the precise form in which it attacked Peter here? Are we not inclined, not merely to felicitate ourselves, but also to boast ourselves that we have believed in Jesus, as if it were the mark of some peculiar excellence in us? But, brethren, if we do indeed believe, who, who is it that has made us thus to differ? Is it that we have believed, or that He, our Lord and Master, has chosen us? Surely it is not we but He who deserves the glory. Let the "Soli Deo Gloria" ring ceaselessly in our breasts. For, we may well believe it, not pride but humility is the root of the Christian life; not boasting of ourselves but glorying in God the Saviour is becoming in us. God give us that small measure of humility which will be willing to acknowledge that it is of Him and not of ourselves that we are partakers of Christ. So shall we learn Peter's lesson: "It is not ye that have believed, but I that have chosen!"

We notice in the second place that Peter's confession in its form looks very much like what we may perhaps call a counsel of despair. "Lord, to whom shall we go," he asks, "Thou hast words of eternal life?" Here, too, our English version may lead us astray as to the tone of the remark. There is no emphasis on the "Thou"; there, indeed, is no "Thou" at all in the Greek. Christ's person, in other words, is not put prominently forward. It is rather conspicuously kept in the background. Neither is there any article to give significance to "words of eternal life." We do not read "*the* words of eternal life" as if Peter recognized in Jesus' words their supreme peculiarity, that they were themselves spirit and life. The phrase is purely general; Peter has found "words of eternal life" in Jesus' talk; that is all. In fact, there is little more here than an echo of our Lord's words a few verses earlier. Our Lord had declared that the words He had spoken were words of spirit and life; Peter echoes that Jesus' words were words of eternal life. It is to his credit that he recognizes them as such; it shows that he is really at bottom spiritually minded. But we cannot help feeling that—like echoes in general—there is some lack of substance in this. There appears to be exhibited acquiescence rather than intense conviction. Peter was, as a spiritually minded man, in search of spiritual nourishment; his heart was keyed to and set upon eternal things—the everlasting welfare of his soul rather than the temporal pleasure of his body. He finds satisfaction in Christ. He finds such satisfaction in Him as he had found in no one else. He cannot look with anything but dismay at losing Him. He recognizes Him as unique among the teachers of Israel and rejoices in Him as such. But there he seems as yet half inclined to stop. And to stop there is to stop fatally short of a true appreciation of Jesus. For there is something negative rather than positive attaching to this position. It would, doubtless, be going too far to say that it all amounts to no more than satisfying oneself with Jesus in the absence of a better. But there is a suggestion of such a state of mind in it. "Will you too leave me?" Jesus asks. "Why, to whom should we go?" is the reply; "Thou hast words of eternal life." There is no adequate entering into the supremeness of Jesus' claims here; there is only a recognition that none better than He could be found. Now, it is not its uniqueness that makes a thing really precious to us. That is a negative attribute. It is the appreciation of the positive content of preciousness in anything which makes the thing unique—because nothing conceivable could surpass it or take its place.

It is well worth our while, brethren, to ask ourselves seriously to-day if we are perhaps ourselves adhering to Christ only because, and so far as, and while, we have no one else to go to? Is our reason for enrolling ourselves His summed up only in this—that we know no better? Well, it is certain that we shall never know a better. For a better does not and cannot exist. Because He is the Supremely Best. Better recognize this at once, however, and feel the uplift of His glory! "Christ and other Masters"—in collocation—is derogatory to Him. His uniqueness is absolute, not relative; and our attitude to it must be a positive and not a negative one. There is enthusiasm demanded here. Let us be bound to Christ by a true appreciation of what He actually is, and we will never question whether perchance we may not some time discover a better; and will never feel an impulse to express our devotion to Him in such words as these, "We must cling to Him because we know not to whom else to go." No, no, we must cleave to Him because He is such that to separate from Him would be to separate from all that makes life worth living, all that gilds this world or blesses the next. This is the attitude that does justice not to what we would fain find in Him but to what He really is.

And this leads us to notice an element of (shall we say?) selfishness in Peter's confession. Peter adheres to Jesus because—so he says—he does not know where else to find the blessings which Peter wants. Now Peter was a spiritually minded man and he was not seeking earthly but heavenly good. This is greatly to his credit. It shows a high and noble nature, with high and noble aspirations, living on a high and noble plane, above all the dross which satisfies so many men. But it is possible to be selfish even on this high plane; and a dash of this selfishness seems to show itself in Peter's confession. He cleaves to Christ, for what reason? Because his longing for words of eternal life is satisfied by Christ. It would be going too far to say that Peter clung to Christ for what, as the coarse saying goes, he could get out of Him. But this coarse language hints at the true state of the case. Surely we will feel that there is something lacking in this attitude, the attitude which cleaves to Jesus because we do not know where else to go to obtain what we want, even though we want the highest good—eternal life itself. Does it not place it on a distinctly lower plane than that fine self-abandonment which cleaves to another, like Ruth to Naomi, out of pure appreciation and love? Think of

Ruth and think of Peter: do not we feel that Ruth was living on a higher plane?

Now, I am not going to preach to you the gospel of "disinterested love" in the sense of the mystics. You all know the fine story of the vision of a woman going forth with fire and water, to burn up heaven and put out hell, that men may hereafter love God neither for fear of hell nor for desire for heaven, but for His Lovely Self alone. We feel the inspiration of it. But we feel doubtless that there is something a little too absolute in its antithesis. There is a proper self-seeking—a proper place for self-love—to which Jesus Himself appeals, and which should be operative to draw us to Him. It is not wrong, but distinctly right, to long for heaven and to fear hell. And that we find all the higher wants of our souls satisfied in Christ is surely no mean commendation of Him to us. The desire for eternal life is no low longing. He who can supply this desire is worthy of our adherence and love.

There is assuredly a place in life for all these things. But after all, they are not quite the highest things. They are the things with which we should begin, not those with which we should end. Let us come to Christ for our own sakes—for our own sakes how can we not come to Him!—but when, having come to Him for our own sakes, we find all that He is, let us learn to love Him and cleave to Him for His own sake. For His own sake, because He is altogether lovely and One to be desired above our chief joy. Why, even in these earthly unions, which we call marriage, we take the loved one "for better, for worse." Shall we take Jesus only for better? And should the worse come to the worst, are we to leave Him and seek some other one who seems to us to have words of eternal life? There is a sense, let us try to understand that, in which it would be better, infinitely better, to perish with Jesus, than to live without Him. Thank God, such an alternative can never occur. With Him is life, and nothing but life; life ever more and more abundantly. But it is well worth our while to distinguish and to see that we love Him and cleave to Him, not merely for the life that is in Him for us, but for all the glorious perfections that are in Him Himself.

To do this we must, of course, know Him as He is and in all that He is. And here we see the final flaw in Peter's confession. He had not yet come to know Christ fully. And that is, doubtless, the ultimate reason of all the other shortcomings we have found in it. Had he known Christ fully, he never would or could have confessed Him only thus—with a boastful spirit as if he had found Christ out instead of having been found by Him; with half-hearted zeal as if He were only the best he had yet found; and with a somewhat selfish outlook as if it were only because he could obtain from Him satisfaction for his felt needs. I am not blaming Peter for not yet knowing Christ better. It rather is wonderful, when all is considered, that he knew Him actually so well, and was ready boldly to declare Him, in the face of all, to be "God's Holy One." It was a great thing for Peter to have seen this clearly; and a great thing for him to have been ready to announce it in the presence of the great defection which was going on at the moment. Herein lies the nobility of this noble confession. But there is a great deal more than this to be known and confessed about Jesus, and Peter afterwards learned it.

The point of importance to us is, Have we learned it? We may be quite sure that our whole attitude to Christ will turn on the fullness and the intimacy with which we know Him. We have no such excuses as Peter had for not knowing Christ in all the fullness of His Being and all the splendour of His Nature. Surely, He must, for instance, be something more to us than "the Holy One of God"—"God's saint"—that is to say, no doubt, by way of eminence, the one whom God has chosen and consecrated and endowed for His service. We have seen how in Peter's case even, such a knowledge of Him did not suffice to make a full confession. And surely He must be something more to us than "the historical Christ"—especially if we begin to doubt or bicker over what history it is that we will accept as a trustworthy account of this "historical Christ." Christ the

Teacher, Christ the Example, Christ the Founder of the Kingdom of God, Christ the King—surely He must be something much more than even all these to us if we are to confess Him aright. The historical Christ, yes, but also the exalted Christ. Christ our Prophet, yes, and Christ our King; but also Christ our Priest and Christ our Sacrifice. Christ that died and also Christ that rose again. The Son of Man and also the Son of God. To Peter as yet He was not all these things, though Peter was feeling His way towards them. To us He is all these things, and more, even Christ, the All in All. Ah, brethren, if we could only see Him in His beauty, how our hearts would go out to Him! No boastful, half-hearted, selfish confession then! Only adoration and joy and unspeakable satisfaction in Him! Let us see and know and confess Him, as He is, and in all that He is!

THE CONVICTION OF THE SPIRIT

Jno. 16:8–11:—"And he, when he is come, will convict the world in respect of sin, and of righteousness and of judgment: of sin, because they believe not on me; of righteousness, because I go to the Father, and ye behold me no more; of judgment, because the prince of this world hath been judged."

THESE chapters which contain the closing discourse of Christ to His disciples are wonderingly dwelt upon by every Christian heart, as the deepest and richest part of the riches of this Gospel. That we may obtain an insight into the marvellous words which we take as the subject of our meditation to-day, it is essential for us to realize the setting which our Lord gave them in the midst of this discourse. He had described to His disciples the conditions of their life, in continuous union and communion with Him, purchased as they were by His death for them and elevated to the lofty position of His special friends from whom He withholds nothing—not even His life itself. Then He had opposed to this picture of their exaltation, a delineation of their condition in the world, opposed and hated and persecuted and slain; while they, on their part, were to bear quietly their witness, endure their martyrdom, and trust in their Redeemer. But was this all? Were they condemned to a hopeless witness-bearing through all the coming years, while the world triumphed over them and in them over their crucified Lord? What an end to the hope they had cherished that this was He who should redeem Israel!

No, says the Lord, not the world but they were to win the victory; the laurel belongs by right not to Satan's but to His own brow. But we will not fail to notice the air of reproof with which He opens the section of His discourse which He has consecrated to an exposition of the victory over the world which He intended that they—as His—should win. "But now," he says, "I am going to Him that sent me, and no one of you asketh me, 'Whither goest thou?', but because I said these things to you, sorrow hath filled your hearts." They had, indeed, expected Him to redeem Israel. It was therefore that they had given Him their trust, their love; that they had left their all to follow Him. But now sad days had come; and they saw their trusted Lord on the eve of giving Himself up to death. Was not this a dashing of their hopes? And had they, then, been so long time with Him and had not learned that the Father had ten myriads of angels who were encamped about Him and who would bear up His every footfall lest by chance He might dash His foot against a stone? Nay, that He had Himself power to lay down His life and to take it again? How could they look upon this coming death as an interference with His plans, the destruction of their hopes, and so sorrow as those without hope, instead of rejoicing as those who see the bright promise of the coming day in the east?

On the lines of these needs of the babes with which He had to deal, our Lord disposes His comforting words. The sorrow of their hearts He deprecates, not merely because He might expect them to rejoice like friends in His approaching departure to the higher and better life, but because He might expect them, after so much that He had done in their sight and spoken in their hearing, to have confidence in His mission and work, and to know that the power of Satan could not prevail against Him. What a spectacle we see here! The Master girding Himself for His last stroke of battle with the joy of victory in His eyes, while His surrounding friends are with streaming tears anointing Him for burial! He plants His foot firmly upon the steps of His Eternal Throne; and they smite their breasts with the sorrowful cry, "We had hoped that thou mightest have been He that should have redeemed Israel!" No wonder that He gives them the loving rebuke, "But now I go my way to Him that sent me,"—to Him that sent me; on the completion of His work, then; not as balked, defeated,—"and no one of you asketh me 'Whither goest thou?', but because I have said these things sorrow hath filled your hearts."

Note how our Lord presses forward His personality here. "But I tell you the truth"—none of you has asked me, but I lovingly volunteer to tell you,—"It is good for you that I go away." This departure is not a forced one, by way of defeat and loss; it was planned from the beginning and is part of the great plan by which I am to redeem not only Israel but the world. Note the emphatic "I": "It is good for you that *I* go away." Why this emphasis? Because there is another to whom this work has been committed and whose offices are necessary for the consummation of the work. "Because *unless I* go, *the Helper* will not come to you; but if I go, I will send Him to you; and it is *He* who, on *His coming*, will convict the world as to sin, and as to righteousness and as to judgment."

Let us observe:—

I. That Christ proclaims the victory.

II. That He announces the agent through whose holy offices the victory will be realized in the world.

III. That He describes the manner in which the victory will be realized—by convicting the world.

IV. That He names the three elements in which this conviction takes effect—sin, righteousness and judgment. And finally,

V. That He points out the means which the Spirit uses to bring home this conviction, in each element, to the hearts of men.

Christ, I say, proclaims here the victory. Why are ye fearful, O ye of little faith? he says in effect to his tearful disciples. I go to the Father, and the world will hate you as it hated me, and the world will persecute you and the world will slay you. But still the world is conquered. It is not because Satan is victor that I go to the Father; it is because I have completed my work, because redemption has been won, and I go to take my place upon the throne, that from that throne I may cause all things to work together for your good,—that from it I may send the Helper forth to you, who will convict the world.

Here He announces the agent through whom the victory is to be realized in the world. He has won the victory; the Spirit is to apply His work that the fruits of the victory may be reaped to the full. A new age has dawned on this sin-stricken world; the Prince of the Power of the Air is dethroned; the Prince of Peace reigns. Henceforth men strive not single-handed against the spiritual hosts of wickedness in high places; they have a Comforter, Advocate, Helper, Paraclete ever at their right hand, and He will give them the victory. It will be observed that Christ is here dealing with His apostles, not merely as individuals striving against the sin that is within them, but as His Lieutenants, leading His hosts against the sin that is in the world. The world may persecute them—and slay them. But they will win the victory; by the power of their Helper they will lead captivity captive.

Hence the nature of the victory that is to be realized in the world is here declared for us. It is a moral victory, a spiritual victory, and its essence is not physical subjection but mental and moral conviction. That Christ dies, that His followers are imprisoned, persecuted, slain, in no wise detracts from the victory; these things are disparate to it; they move on different planes and cannot conflict. What the Helper is to do is to convict the world; and in this conviction rests their victory.

It is easy to see that this was a hard saying. No doubt when it was spoken it fell like a deeper knell on the hearts of the apostles; instead of comforting, it pained, instead of encouraging, it slew. But then, Christ was not yet risen and their eyes were holden that they should know neither Him nor His victory. But turn to Pentecost. Then the Spirit came as He was promised and gave the convicting power to Peter's sermon that here was announced. See the joy in the victory, the exulting courage of the apostles, from that day to the end. Paul declares that he spoke not in the wisdom of the world but in the demonstration of the Spirit and in power. Although he uses a different word, what he means by the demonstration of the Spirit seems to be what Christ here promised under the name of the proof, convincing, conviction of the Spirit. This phrase of Paul's, indeed, is perhaps the best verbal commentary on our passage. The best actual commentary is found, doubtless, in the narrative of the results of the apostolic preaching in the Book of Acts. This, then, is the victory; not an external one over men's bodies, but the conquest of the world to Christ by the demonstration of the Spirit in the proclamation of the Gospel, whereby the world is convicted of sin and righteousness and judgment. The conquest is a spiritual one; the apostles are the agents in it; but the source of the power is the Holy Ghost—our one and true Helper in the world, who convicts the world of sin and righteousness and judgment.

We approach now the center of our subject and perceive what it is that the world is convicted of by the demonstration of the Spirit. The Saviour pointedly discriminates between the three elements: As to sin, as to righteousness, as to judgment. Conviction of the world is the work of the Holy Ghost. Conviction as to what? (1) As to sin. The world which as yet knows not sin is convicted of it as the first and primary work of the Holy Ghost. It is not without significance that this is placed first. There is a sense in which it underlies all else, and conviction of sin becomes the first step in that recovery of the world, which is the victory. Once convicted of sin, another conviction is opened out before it. (2) It may then be convicted of righteousness, that is, of what righteousness is and what is required to form a true righteousness, and (3) it may be convicted of judgment, that is, of what judgment is, what justice requires and its inevitableness. These two together form the correlates of sin. It is only by knowing sin that we can know righteousness; as it is only by knowing darkness that we know light. We must know what sin is and how subtle it is, before we can realize what righteousness is. We must know how base the one is before we can know how noble the other is. We must know the depth that we may appreciate the heights. In like manner we must know sin in order to know judgment. We must know sin in its native hideousness that we may understand its ill-desert, and perceive with what judgment the sinner must be judged. So, too, we must know righteousness to know judgment. Not only the depths of sin, but also the heights of righteousness are involved in the judgment. Sin on the one side, righteousness on the other; these give us our true conviction of judgment. And the work of the Holy Ghost in the world is declared to be conviction; and by convicting men He conquers the world. The Gospel is preached and it everywhere brings a crisis to men. Shall they hear or forbear? Some hear; to some it is hid; but on all the conviction takes effect. Sin is made known; righteousness is revealed; judgment is laid bare. And men convicted of their sin have but a choice of the righteousness or judgment.

For our Saviour does not leave us in ignorance of the import and instruments of this threefold conviction.

(1) "Of sin," he says, "because they believe not on me." This does not seem to mean that there would be no sin save for rejection of Christ, but that the proclamation of Christ is the great revealer of sin, the great distinguisher of men. When Christ is preached the touchstone is applied and men are convicted of being sinners and of the depths and hideousness of their sin by their exhibited attitude towards the Son of God. The Gospel is never hid save to them whose eyes the god of this world has blinded, lest they should see the glory of the Saviour and come to Him and be saved. There is no revelation of character so accurate, so powerful, so unmistakable, so inevitable, as that wrapped up in the simple question, "What think ye of Christ?" Like a loadstone passing over a rubbish heap, His preaching draws to His side all that is not hopelessly bad. And all who come not are demonstrated to be sinners, and the depth of their sin is thus revealed.

(2) "As to righteousness," he adds, "because I go to my Father and ye see me no more." This seems to mean that the fact of Christ's completed work, closed by His ascension to His primal glory, is the demonstration of righteousness. Convicted

of sin, the world is also convicted of righteousness; that is, of the need of a righteousness such as it cannot frame for itself, and such as will match in its height, the depth of its own sin. This is brought to light only in the Gospel, in which a righteousness of God is revealed from faith to faith. The convicting of the Holy Ghost consists no more of a conviction of human sinfulness and need of salvation than it does of the perfect righteousness of Christ wrought out on earth and sealed and warranted by His triumphal departure from this world. Men are convicted of sin, because of their unbelief in Christ: of righteousness because of His finished work.

(3) But there is one more step. "As to judgment, because the Prince of this world has been judged." If there is a sin, and a righteousness, there is also a judgment. And men must know it. The third element in the Spirit's demonstration is the conviction of men of the overhanging judgment. This He performs by means of the obvious condemnation in Christ's person and work of the Prince of this world, involving those who hold of his part in the same destruction. That the world and all that is in it is of the Evil One, that there is no life in it and no help for the children of men, is one element of the Spirit's testimony to the preached Gospel; that this world is under condemnation and reserved for the eternal fire is but another element of it. Everywhere

where the Spirit carries His demonstration men know what judgment is, and they know it by perceiving the judgment of the Evil one.

We should not permit to slip from our minds that we have here the Saviour's own exposition of the method and manner of His spiritual conquest of the world. This conquest is assured. It is the Spirit who performs it. And the method of His work in it is by accompanying the preached word with His demonstration and power. This demonstration of the Spirit consists in convicting the world of sin, of righteousness, and of judgment. Is conviction of sin then, we may ask, necessary to salvation? Is conviction of sin the first step of salvation? Let those smitten souls at Pentecost answer, who cried aloud, Men and Brethren, what shall we do? Is conviction of righteousness necessary to salvation? A convinced and convicted appreciation of the needs of our soul which alone can be found in Christ Jesus? Ask him who has proved to us that the whole world lies alike under the wrath of God, and that by the works of the law no flesh can be justified, and who adds to this word of terror the only word of hope: But now apart from the law a righteousness of God has been revealed, even the righteousness of God through faith in Jesus Christ, unto all them that believe; for there is no difference, for all have sinned and fallen short of the glory of God. And as to conviction of judgment, ask Felix, who trembled as this same Paul reasoned of righteousness and temperance and judgment to come.

Assuredly, my brethren, would we be saved, we must know what sin is, we must know what righteousness is and where it may be found, and we must tremble before the judgment which that righteousness must pass on our sin. Christ has performed His work, and with the shout of "It is finished" upon His lips, has ascended to His throne on high, and there, seated by the right hand of God, He has shed forth this which we even now see and hear. The Spirit is in the world and wherever the Gospel of God's grace is faithfully preached He attends it with His demonstration and power. And what does He demonstrate to our souls? That we are sinners; that we need a God-provided righteousness; that otherwise we must partake in the judgment of the Prince of this world. This is God's way and it is the only way. Let us be fully assured of it!

CHRIST'S PRAYER FOR HIS PEOPLE

Jno. 17:15:—"I pray not that thou shouldst take them from the world, but that thou shouldst keep them from the evil one."

THE text suggests strongly the contrast between the world and heaven, and the relations which the servants of Christ bear to each. The world and heaven are contrasted ideas; contrasted places, and contrasted states. And the peculiarity of the relations which Christians bear to these contrasted places and states is that they may be at the same time in very express relations to both. Our Lord Himself, while walking this earth of ours as a man among men, was yet in the bosom of the Father. And the Christian, His follower, while still in the world, the object of the world's hate and the recipient of its persecution, may yet be in the heavenly places with his Lord. Let us resolve the paradox, by considering in turn:

I. Our Lord's idea of "the world."
II. His idea of heaven.
III. His desire for His followers.

It is often said, and this is the first thought that occurs to us on facing this paradox, that our Lord's idea of "the world," as recorded in John, is an ethical rather than a local one. But this must not be taken too exclusively. Our present verse is the disproof of too exclusive an attribution of the ethical idea to the Lord. Christ prays that his followers should not be taken out of the world, but yet should be kept from the evil. In this single prayer, the word "world" is used in quite a variety of implications. In the fifth verse it means apparently the universe, as a creation. In the eleventh verse, it is equivalent to the earth, with the implication that it is the world of man that is in mind. It is plainly the world of man in the fifteenth verse. But as man is sinful man, it usually in this sense has the connotation of what we call the sinful world, and this sense comes out strongly in the ninth verse, where Christ's followers are contrasted with the world, and more strongly still in verses fourteen and sixteen, where the world is said to hate the good, and so also in the twenty-first and twenty-third verses. In a word, then, the term world means usually the world of mankind, which, because man is universally sinful, comes to bear the implication of the world of sinful man, which then is brought into contrast with Christ's children in whom the power of sin is broken and a radical divergence from the world begun. Accordingly, when they come to Christ, they come "out of the world," even though they remain in the world. The "world" therefore designates a place, but this place as the abode of man, and this man as sinful. And though there is an ethical colouring to the term, yet this ethical colouring does not constitute its essence. Because there is an ethical colouring to it Christ represents His people as gathered out of the world; and because this ethical colouring does not constitute its essence, we can, nevertheless speak of them remaining in the world while kept from its evil.

The idea of heaven, as the contrast to that of the world, must, therefore, partake of this twofold sense. It is primarily a place, to which Christ's children would be removed if they were taken out of the world. But as the world is a bad place, so heaven, its contrast, is a good place; and those who are good are, therefore, already in principle in it. Therefore Paul tells us that our citizenship is in heaven, and that we may even here and now be with Christ in the heavenly places. The word "heaven" does not occur in this prayer. It does occur in the introduction to it, where we are told that "Jesus, lifting up his eyes to heaven, said Father," as if His pure eyes pierced the wall of space and saw the Invisible One. Heaven is, therefore, in this context, the place where God is in His manifested glory, in contrast with the world where the "god of this world" manifests his power for a season. Accordingly our Lord speaks of it as the place where God can be known and enjoyed, or with more personal point and pathos, as the place where He Himself should be, in His destined glory which was also His primal glory; where He, as He is, and not as, in His humiliation, He has seemed, should be and be manifested, and where His children should be partakers of His glory.

And now what is Christ's desire for His people? It is certainly not that they should remain in the world, in its ethical sense. Already they had been given Him out of the world, and therefore they were no more of the world—no more than Christ Himself was. The truth had already been given them, that truth which should free from sin,—God's own name had been manifested to and in them,—and they were in radical opposition to the world, so that the world hated them. Accordingly His prayer distinctly is that they should be kept from that evil which constituted the very characteristic of the world, and that their sanctification should be continued in the truth. He does not desire them to remain in the world in this sense. He has instituted a radical contrariety between them and "the world" ethically considered; and He is providing for this contrariety to widen into an ever broadening gulf.

Just as certainly, it is not that they should remain always in the world, in its more local sense. The tone of joy with which the Lord notes that the time of His sojourn on earth is over and He is ready to re-enter His heavenly glory is unmistakable. Equally unmistakable is the tone of sadness with which He adverts to leaving His followers in the world. They are in danger there; in danger from the world's hate; and in danger from the world's temptation. They are away from their true and proper home there—in the enemy's country—not householders at home, but soldiers on duty, pilgrims on their journey. He longs for them to enter their rest. And though He leaves them joy and the means of more joy in the word of truth, His desire for them is something higher than they can find here below. Nay, His distinct "will" for them is that they also may be with Him where He is to be; that they may behold His glory; that they may share in that glory. He wishes for them what His servant afterwards declared to be "far better," that they too like Him should go out of the world and enter into glory—where Christ is on the right hand of God, where God dwells and His knowledge is, and where love is perfected in all.

But it is that they may temporarily remain in the world, out of which they have in one sense already come, but in which, in the other sense, they are still left, while kept from the evil of it.

Why? Well, for one thing, for their own sakes—that they may be sanctified. God's name has already been manifested to them; God's words have already been given them; and they have received them; and men hate them for it. The good work is already, therefore, begun with them.

Its fruits are already shown in their radical departure from the world and the world's consequent hatred. But the work is not completed. Therefore, the Saviour prays that "they may be sanctified in the truth," that "they themselves also may be sanctified" in truth, just as He had been. They are to remain in the world then for their own sakes that the good work begun in them may be perfected unto the end. This appears as needful. Not, of course, as if they might not conceivably, like the dying thief, be prepared for heaven in a moment. God's almighty grace can work wonders. But that is not God's ordinary way; the muscles of holiness must grow by practice; hence temptation itself and trials are blessings. Hence, too, it emerges that sanctification is to take place in this life, in the ordinary provision of God. God's children are to remain in the world for their sanctification.

For another thing, for others' sake. God's plans need their presence in and work for the world. They are not the whole harvest, but the first fruits only. And that the first fruits may share in the harvest, it is needful to have them stay and labour here. They are to be the seed—"the good seed are they who . . ." And after a while this sowing is to ripen into a goodly ingathering. Accordingly, our Lord prays not only for them but for them also who believe—throughout the whole future—on Him by their word. His glance takes in His whole Church, of all the ages; and these are to abide for it.

For still another thing, for the sake of the world itself. There is a testimony to be borne to the wicked world itself. "The wicked world," apparently, because in contrast here not only with those whom Christ left behind, but also with those who should believe on His name through their word. The world is to be convicted of sin and convinced of Christ's mission and glory. His own are to remain in the world and to propagate and grow into a mighty, unitary Church, in order that the world itself may know that the lowly Jesus whom it has despised and rejected is none other than the Son of God; and that these lowly followers of His, despised and persecuted by it, are loved of the Father even as the Father loves Him. The mighty testimony of the Church of God! How little we are bearing it! How we ought to bestir ourselves to it!

And then, finally, we must say also, for the Son's own sake. For He, too, reaps advantages from their abiding below. So, and humanly speaking, so only, may His mission be vindicated and His glory manifested to the world, in His Church; may His glory be fully manifested to His own, when at last they come to Him; may His love then be perfected in them.

For these reasons, at least, it is well that Christ's people remain for a season in this wicked world.

THE OUTPOURING OF THE SPIRIT

Acts 2:16, 17:—"This is that which hath been spoken through the prophet Joel. . . . I will pour forth of my Spirit."

In any attempt to estimate the significance of the outpouring of the Spirit at Pentecost, considered as the inauguration of the New Dispensation, the following two considerations must be made fundamental.

The Spirit was active under the Old Dispensation in all the modes of His activity under the New Dispensation. This is evinced by the records of the activities of the Spirit of God in the Old Testament, which run through the whole series of the Spirit's works; and by the ascription by the writers of the New Testament of all the working of the Spirit of God in the Old Testament to their own personal Holy Ghost. Thus, for example, the inspiration of the Old Testament prophets and writers is ascribed to the Holy Ghost (2 Pet. 1:21; 1 Pet. 1:11; Heb. 3:7, 10:15; Matt. 22:43; Mark 12:36; Acts 1:16, and 28:25). The authorship of the ritual service of the sanctuary is ascribed to Him (Heb. 9:8). The leading of Israel in the wilderness and throughout its history is ascribed to Him (Acts 7:51). It was in Him that Christ preached to the antediluvians

(1 Pet. 3:18). He was the author of faith then as now (2 Cor. 4:13).

Nevertheless, the change of dispensation consisted primarily just in this: that in the New Dispensation the Spirit was given (so John 7:39; 16:7; 20:22; Acts 2).

The problem, therefore, is to understand how the New Dispensation can be thus by way of discrimination the Dispensation of the Spirit, characterized by the giving of the Spirit, while yet He was active in the Old Dispensation in all the modes of His activity under the New. For the solving of this problem we shall need to exercise a humble courage in embracing the standpoint of Scripture itself.

In order to do this, we must observe that the operations of the Holy Ghost were forfeited by man through sin. Adam enjoyed the influence of the Holy Spirit and it was through the Spirit's inworking that Adam was enabled to withstand temptation, and by it that he might have been led safely through his probation and afterwards confirmed in holiness. When Adam sinned he lost the gift of original righteousness, indeed, but with it also the gift of the Holy Ghost, and the depravation into which he and his posterity sank—according to the fearful history recorded in the first chapter of Romans—has lying at its foundation the deprivation of the Holy Ghost's influences.

The Lord never, indeed, wholly turns away from any work of His hands; did He do so, it would fall at once on the removal of His upholding hand, like the unhooped barrel, back into nothingness. In His providence, and in what we call His common grace, He continues to work among even His sinful creatures who have lost all claim upon His love. But just because they are sinful, they have forfeited all the operations of His grace and deserve at His hands only wrath. After the sin of Adam, the whole world lies in wickedness; and just because it lies in wickedness it is deprived of the inhabitation of the Spirit of holiness.

But though the race has thus by its sin forfeited the right to the inward work of the Holy Ghost, God may in His infinite grace restore the Spirit to man, as soon as, and in so far as, He can make it just and righteous so to do. In the atoning work of Christ, He has laid the foundation for such a restoration in righteousness. But we are dependent on the Scriptures to inform us how far this restoration extends intensively and extensively. We are not authorized to argue that because of the remedy for sin offered in Christ, God must or may treat sin as if it never had existed, so that all that the race has lost in Adam is restored in Christ, and that for all the sinful race alike. It may be consonant with what we could wish to be true, so to argue. But it is obvious that were this, in fact, the state of the case, the race would have been restored in Christ, from the moment of Adam's fall, and would have been continued in holy development unbrokenly. Adam's sin would, in that case, have been a benefit to the race; it would have curtailed its probation and placed the race at once at the goal of attainment which had been promised to obedience. Obedience and disobedience obviously would, in that case, have been all one; the end obtained would have been precisely the same. Whence it would follow that Adam's probation was a mere farce, if not even that the Divine regard for moral distinctions was a pretence.

Nothing can be more obvious according to either Scripture or the experience of the race than that this course was not taken. The Lord did not, at once, treat sin as if it had never occurred. He did, indeed, at once institute a remedial scheme by which the effect of sin might be obliterated to the extent and in the manner which was pleasing to His glorious judgment; but clearly it was not pleasing to Him, on the basis of the atonement, to set aside the fact of sin altogether. How far, on this basis, He was pleased to set aside the fact of sin and restore to men the Spirit of holiness of whom they had been deprived on account of sin, we are wholly dependent upon His Word to tell us.

On the basis of the Scriptural declarations, it is perfectly evident that it was not the plan of God to restore the lost Spirit to man universally. The dreadful fact stares us full in the face that God has thought well to leave some men eternally without the Spirit of holiness. It is obvious that in the execution of His plan of discrimination among men, it was not His plan to distribute the saving operations of His Spirit equally through either space or time. His sovereignty shows itself not only in passing by one individual and granting His grace to another; but also in passing by one nation, or one age, and granting His grace to another. And in His inscrutable wisdom it has obviously been His plan to confine the operations of His grace through many ages to one people of His choice, passing by the nations of the world at large, and leaving them to their sin. This is the meaning of the choice of Israel and the divine guidance of that chosen people.

We cannot fathom all the purpose of God in this disposition of His grace. We may see directly, however, that thus a twofold end was secured. Sin was allowed to work itself out on the stage of a world-wide life, with the result that it exhibited all its horror and all its helplessness. And grace continuously had its trophies on the stage of Israelitish life. Israel thus served as a foil to exhibit the corruption of the nations; and at the same time preserved the continuity of God's people through time and supplied the starting point for the universal extension of His

Kingdom when at length the set time for its inauguration should come. At all events, it is a fact that the Scriptures, on which we are dependent for all knowledge of the work of God's Spirit, confine all their declarations of the work of the Spirit through these gathering years to the theocratic people. Only within and for the benefit of the theocracy does the Spirit of God work from Adam to Christ—from the first man through whom came death to the Second Man through whom came redemption.

And now we are, perhaps, in a position to understand the contrast between the first and second dispensations, when the second is called the Dispensation of the Spirit, inaugurated by the visible outpouring of the Spirit at Pentecost, although the Spirit had been the guide of Israel, and the sanctifier of the people of God from the beginning. The new dispensation is the Dispensation of the Spirit, whether we consider the extent of the Spirit's operations, the object of His operations, the mode of the Divine administration of His Kingdom, or the intensity of the Spirit's action.

The new dispensation is the dispensation of the Spirit because in it the Spirit of God is poured out upon all flesh. This element in the change is made emphatic in the predictions which prepared the way for it—as in the prophecy of Joel which Peter quotes in his Pentecostal sermon; and it is symbolized in the miraculous attestation by which it is inaugurated—in the tongues that distributed themselves on the heads of the agents of the new proclamation—"as if of fire"—and in the "gift of tongues" by which the universality of their mission was intimated. Here is the central idea of the new dispensation. It is world-wide in its scope; the period of preparation being over, the world-wide Kingdom of God was now to be inaugurated, and the Spirit was now to be poured upon all flesh. No longer was one people to be its sole recipients, but the remedy was to be applied to all peoples alike.

The new dispensation is the dispensation of the Spirit, again, because now the object of the Spirit's work is, for the first time, to recover the world from its sin. Of course, this was its ultimate object from the beginning; but during the period of preparation it was only its ultimate, not its proximate object. Its proximate object then was preparation, now it was performance. Then it was to preserve a seed, sound and pure for the planting; now it was the reaping of the harvest. It required the Spirit's power to keep the seed safe during the cold and dark winter; it requires it now to plant the seed and water it and cause it to grow into the great tree, in the branches of which all the fowls of the air may rest. The Spirit is the leaven which leavens the world; in Israel it is that leaven laid away in the closet until the day of leavening comes; when that day comes and it is drawn out of its dark corner and placed in the heap of meal—then, indeed, the day of the leaven has come. Or to use a figure of Isaiah's, during all those dark ages the Kingdom of God, confined to Israel, was like a pent-in stream. The Spirit of God was its life, its principle, during all the ages; it was He that kept it pent in. Now the Kingdom of God is like that pent-in stream with the barriers broken down, and the Spirit of God driving it.

The new dispensation is, once more, the dispensation of the Spirit, because now the mode of the administration of God's Kingdom has become spiritual. This is in accordance with its new extent and its new object, and is intended to secure and to advance its universality and its rapid progress. In the old dispensation, the Kingdom of God was in a sense of this world; it had its relation to and its place among earthly states; it was administered by outward ordinances and enactments and hierarchies. In the new dispensation the Kingdom of God is not of this world; it has no relation to or place among earthly states; it is not administered by external ordinances. The Kingdom of God now is within you; its law is written on the heart; it is administered by an inward force. Where the Jewish ordinances extended, there of old was the Kingdom of God; where men were circumcised on the eighth day, where they turned their faces to the Temple at the hours of sacrifice, and whence they went up to Jerusalem to the annual feasts. A centralized worship we say; for the Temple at Jerusalem was the place where God might be acceptably worshipped and they were of the Kingdom who owned its sway. Now, "where the Spirit of the Lord is, there is the Church"—as Tertullian and Irenæus and Ignatius tell us; wherever the Spirit works—and He works when and where and how He will—there is the Church of God. We are freed from the outward ordinances, Touch not, taste not, handle not; and are under the sway of the indwelling Spirit alone. An inward power takes the place of an outward commandment; love shed abroad in our hearts supplants fear as our motive; a Divine strength replaces our human weakness.

Finally, we may say that the new dispensation is the dispensation of the Spirit, because now the Spirit works in the hearts of God's people with a more prevailing and a more pervading force. We cannot doubt that He regenerated and sanctified the souls of God's saints in the old dispensation; we cannot doubt that He was operating creatively in them in renewing their hearts, and that He was powerfully present in them, leading them in right paths. "Create within me a new heart and renew a right spirit within me" is an Old Testament prayer; and it must represent an Old Testament experience. And yet we seem to be not merely authorized but compelled to look upon the mode of the Spirit's work as more powerful and prevailing in the new dispensation than in the old. For in these new times, God seems to promise not only that He will pour out His Spirit upon all flesh, but that He will pour Him out in an especial manner on His people. In what sense would the fact that He will pour out the Spirit on the seed of Israel be characteristic of the new dispensation, if there were not some advance here on the old? Such a passage as Ezekiel 36:26 or Zech. 12:10 would seem to mean as much as this: that the Holy Spirit will work so powerfully in the hearts of God's people in the new time, that the sanctification which had lagged behind in the old should be completed now. That is to say, there is here the promise of a holy Church. This too, no doubt, is of progressive realization. After a number of Christian centuries we have cause still to weep over the backslidings of the people of God as truly as Israel had. But Christ is perfecting His Church even as He perfects the individual, and after a while He will present it to Himself a holy Church, without spot or wrinkle or any such thing.

Surely it must mean much to us that we live in the dispensation of the Spirit, a dispensation in which the Spirit of God is poured out upon all flesh with the end of extending the bounds of

God's Kingdom until it covers the earth; and that He is poured out in the hearts of His people so that He reigns in their hearts and powerfully determines them to do holiness and righteousness all the days of their lives. Because we live under this dispensation, we are free from the outward pressure of law and have love shed abroad in our hearts, and, being led by the Spirit of God, are His Sons, yielding a willing obedience and by instinct doing what is conformable to His will. Because this is the dispensation of the Spirit we are in the hands of the loving Spirit of God whose work in us cannot fail; and the world is in His powerful guidance and shall roll on in a steady development until it knows the Lord and His will is done on earth as in heaven. It is because this is the dispensation of the Spirit that it is a missionary age; and it is because it is the dispensation of the Spirit that missions shall make their triumphant progress until earth passes at last into heaven. It is because this is the dispensation of the Spirit that it is an age of ever-increasing righteousness and it is because it is the dispensation of the Spirit that this righteousness shall wax and wax until it is perfect. Blessed be God that He has given it to our eyes to see this His glory in the process of its coming.

PRAYER AS A MEANS OF GRACE

Acts 9:11:—"For behold, he prayeth."

WE read these words, "For behold, he prayeth," of Saul of Tarsus, immediately after the account of how, when he was journeying from Jerusalem to Damascus on his persecuting errand, he was smitten to the ground by the Divine hand and raised again by those gracious words—how gracious, how inexplicably gracious they must have seemed to him!—which promised him service for the very One whom he was now persecuting. And when we read them our first thought is likely to turn on the appropriateness of prayer in the circumstances. Thus the theme is obviously suggested of prayer as the appropriate expression of the renewed sinner's heart. On this subject I I shall not, however, speak to you just now. I wish to call your attention, rather, to another subject for meditation which also lies in our passage, though perhaps not so prominently. That is, Prayer as a means of Grace.

If we look closely at this verse we shall see that it suggests prayer as a means of grace. You will notice that it reads, "*For* behold, he prayeth, *and* he hath seen" a vision of Ananaias coming to him to restore him to sight. "*For* behold he prayeth *and*"; that is, this statement is given as a reason, and as a reason why Ananaias should now go to him. And the reason is that Paul is now prepared for the visit. And the preparation consists of the two items that he is praying and that he has seen in a vision Ananaias coming. In other words, that he is in a state of preparedness for the reception of grace in general is evidenced by his being in prayer; while he is prepared for Ananaias' coming in particular through the vision. The passage thus represents prayer as the state of preparedness for the reception of grace; and, therefore, in the strictest sense as a means of grace. We purpose to look at it for a few moments in this light.

Even if we should not rise above the naturalistic plane, I think we might be able to see that the attitude into which the act of prayer brings the soul is one which especially softens the soul and lays it open to gracious influences. Say that we hold with those who believe in prayer, but do not believe in answer to prayer. Well, is not the mental attitude assumed in prayer, at least, an humble attitude, a softening attitude, a beneficial attitude? Do we not see that thus the very act of prayer by its reflex influence alone—could we believe in no more—will tend to quiet the soul, break down its pride and resistance, and fit it for a humble walk in the world? In its very nature, prayer is a confession of weakness, a confession of need, of dependence, a cry for help, a reaching out for something stronger, better, more stable and trustworthy than ourselves, on which to rest and depend and draw. No one can take this attitude once without an effect on his character; no one can take it in a crisis of his life without his whole subsequent life feeling the influence in its sweeter, humbler, more devout and restful course; no one can take it habitually without being made, merely by its natural, reflex influence, a different man, in a very profound sense, from what he otherwise would have been. Prayer, thus, in its very nature, because it is an act of self-abnegation, a throwing of ourselves at the feet of One recognized as higher and greater than we, and as One on whom we depend and in whom we trust, is a most beneficial influence in this hard life of ours. It places the soul in an attitude of less self-assertion and predisposes it to walk simply and humbly in the world.

The significance of all this is, of course, vastly increased, when we rise above the region of naturalism into that of supernaturalism. If when we believe only in prayer but not in its answer, if when we look only for a natural, reflex influence on our life of the attitude into which prayer brings us, we can recognize in it a softening, blessing effect; how much more when we perceive a Divine person above who hears and answers the prayer. If there were no God, we can see that it would be a blessing to men to think there was a God and throw themselves at His feet in prayer. If there is a God who sits aloft and hears and answers, do we not see that the attitude into which prayer brings the soul is the appropriate attitude which the soul should occupy to Him, and is the truest and best preparation of the soul for the reception of His grace? The soul in the attitude of prayer is like the flower turned upwards towards the sky and opening for the reception of the life-giving rain. What is prayer but an adoring appearing before God with a confession of our need and helplessness and a petition for His strength and blessing? What is prayer but a recognition of our dependence and a proclamation that all that we dependent creatures need is found abundantly and to spare in God, who gives to all men liberally and upbraids not? What is prayer but the very adjustment of the heart for the influx of grace? Therefore it is that we look upon the prayerful attitude as above all others the true Christian attitude—just because it is the attitude of devout and hopeful dependence on God. And, therefore, it is that we look upon that type of religious teaching as, above all others, the true Christian type which has as its tendency to keep men in the attitude of prayer, through all their lives.

Every type of religious teaching will inevitably beget its corresponding type of religious life.

And that teaching alone which calls upon man to depend wholly on the Lord God Almighty—our loving Father who has given His Son to die for us—for all the exercises of grace, will make Christians whose whole life is a prayer. Not that other Christians do not pray. But only of these Christians can it be said that their life is an embodied prayer. In so far as any Christian's life is a prayerful life, pervaded by and made up out of prayer, it approaches in its silent witness the ideal of this type of teaching. What other attitude is possible to a Christian on his knees before God but an attitude of entire dependence on God for His gifts, and of humble supplication to Him for His favour? But are we to rise from our knees only to take up a different attitude towards God? Says one of the greatest thinkers of modern times: "On his knees before God, every one that has been saved will recognize the sole efficiency of the Holy Spirit in every good work. . . . In a word, whoever truly prays ascribes nothing to his own will or power except the sin that condemns him before God, and knows of nothing that could endure the judgment of God except it be wrought within him by the Divine love. But whilst all other tendencies in the Church preserve this attitude so long as their prayer lasts, to lose themselves in radically different conceptions as soon as the Amen has been pronounced, the Calvinist adheres to the truth of his prayer, in his confession, in his theology, in his life, and the Amen that has closed his petition re-echoes in the depths of his consciousness and throughout the whole of his existence." That is to say, for us Calvinists the attitude of prayer is the whole attitude of our lives. Certainly this is the true Christian attitude, because it is the attitude of dependence, and trust. But just because this is the attitude of prayer, prayer puts the soul in the attitude for receiving grace and is essentially a means of grace.

But once again, prayer is a means of grace because it is a direct appeal to God for grace. It is in its very innermost core a petition for help and that is—proportionately to its sphere—for grace. The means—the most direct and appropriate, the most prevailing and sure means of obtaining aid from a superior, is to ask for it. If a community desires a boon from the government, it petitions for it. The means above all others by which we are to obtain God's blessing is naturally and properly to petition for it. It is true that all prayer is not petition. The Apostle gives us a list of the aspects of prayer in 1 Tim. ii:1 sq. under the names of "supplications, prayers, intercessions, thanksgivings." All these elements enter into prayer. Prayer in its full conception is then, not merely asking from God, but all intercourse with God. Intercourse, indeed, is the precise connotation of the standing word for prayer in the New Testament—the second in the list of 1 Tim. ii:1, translated in our version simply "prayers." The sacred idea of prayer *per se* is, therefore, to put it sharply, just communion with God, the meeting of the soul with God, and the holding of converse with Him. Perhaps we would best define it as conscious intercourse or communion with God. God may have communion with us without prayer; He may enter our souls beneath consciousness, and deal with us from within; and because He is within us we can be in communion with Him apart from prayer. But conscious communion with Him is just prayer. Now, I think we may say, emphatically, that prayer is a means of grace above everything else because it is in all its forms conscious communion with God. This is the source of all grace. When the soul is in contact with God, in intercourse with God, in association with Him, it is not only in an attitude to receive grace; it is not only actually seeking grace; it is already receiving and possessing grace. And intercourse with God is the very essence of prayer.

It is impossible to conceive of a praying man, therefore, as destitute of grace. If he prays, really prays, he draws near to God with heart open for grace, humbly depending on Him for its gift. And he certainly receives it. To say, Behold he prayeth! is equivalent, then, to saying, Behold a man in Christ! Dr. Charles Hodge used to startle us by declaring that no praying soul ever was lost. It seemed to us a hard saying. Our difficulty was that we did not conceive "praying" purely enough. We can, no doubt, go through the motions of prayer and not be saved souls. Our Saviour tells us of those who love to pray on the street corners and in the synagogues, to be seen of men. And He tells us that they have their reward. Their purpose in praying is to be seen of men, and they are seen of men. What can they ask more? But when we really pray—we are actually in enjoyment of communion with God. And is not communion with God salvation? The thing for us to do is to pray without ceasing; once having come into the presence of God, never to leave it; to abide in His presence and to live, steadily, unbrokenly, continuously, in the midst of whatever distractions or trials, with and in Him. God grant such a life to every one of us!

SURRENDER AND CONSECRATION

Acts 22:10:—"What shall I do, Lord?"

WHEN Paul was stricken to the ground on his way to Damascus by the glory of the risen Christ, bursting on him from heaven, he had but two questions to ask: Who art thou, Lord? and What shall I do, Lord? By the first he certified himself as to the person before whose majesty he lay prone; by the second he entered at once into His willing service.

In this, too, Paul's conversion is typical. No one can call Jesus Lord save by the Holy Ghost; but when the Holy Ghost has moved with power upon the soul, the amazed soul has but two questions to ask: Who art thou, Lord? and What shall I do, Lord? There is no question in its mind as to the legitimacy of the authority claimed, as to its extent and limitations, as to its sphere, as to its sanction. He whose glory has shone into the heart is recognized at once and unquestioningly as Lord, and is so addressed no less in the first question than in the second. Who art thou, Lord? is not a demand for credentials; it is a simple inquiry for information, a cry of wondering adoration and worship. And it is, therefore, followed at once with the cry of, What shall I do, Lord?

In this latter question there unite the two essential elements of all religion, surrender and consecration—the passive and active aspects of that faith which on the human side is the fundamental element of religion, as grace is on God's side, when dealing with sinful men. "What shall I do, Lord?" In that simple question, as it trembled on the lips of Paul lying prostrate in the presence of the heavenly glory, there pulsated all that abnegation of self, that casting of oneself wholly on Christ, that firm entrusting of oneself in all the future to Him and His guidance,—in a word, the whole of the "assensus" and "fiducia," which (the "notitia" being presupposed) constitute saving faith. And saving faith wherever found is sure to take this position, perhaps not purely—for what faith of man is absolutely pure?—but in direct proportion to its purity, its governing power over the life. Surrender and consecration, we may take it then, are the twin key-notes of the Christian life: "What shall I do, Lord?" the one question which echoes through all the corridors of the Christian heart.

And as our life as ministers of the Gospel is nothing else but one side of our Christian life—the flower and fruit of our Christian life—surrender and consecration must be made also its notes. It is in direct proportion as they are made its key-notes that we may hope for success in our ministry; for only in this proportion are we

Christ's ministers and not servitors of our ownselves. Let us, then, approach this holy calling in this spirit, the spirit of Paul before us and of every child of Christ through all the ages. Let us now as we enter these halls to begin or to re-begin our preparation for the great work before us, have no reservations—that we will serve the Lord in this sphere, but not in that; that we will serve Him to this extent, but not to that; that we will serve Him in this mode, but not in that. Let surrender and consecration be our watch-words. "What shall I do, Lord?"—let that question be the spirit of all our lives.

And now let us observe what is involved in such a spirit. I think we may say this much on even a surface survey of the matter—(1) that there is an element of humility that enters into it; (2) that there is an element of true dignity that enters into it, and (3) that there is an element of power that enters into it. Humility, dignity, power—at least these three things.

Humility—what a difference in this regard between Saul the Pharisee and Paul the Christian! Before his conversion Saul seems to have had no doubt of what he should do. His fundamental characteristics seem to have been those of the type of character which we call masterful. He was a man of decision, of energy; somewhat self-sufficient, as indeed a Pharisaic training was apt to make one; little inclined, one would think, to defer to the guidance of others. We must guard against supposing him to have been a man of violent and wicked impulses, as we may be misled into fancying by his career as a persecutor and his own words of subsequent sharp self-rebuke—after his eyes were opened. A man of deep religious heart at all times, set on serving the Lord, his very vices were but the defects of his virtues. But somewhat headstrong, opinionated, undocile, perhaps; bent on serving God with a pure conscience, but constitutionally apt to go his own way in that service—for the God of Israel had never bidden him persecute the saints, and that was an outgrowth, we may be sure, of his habitual self-direction. What can I do to glorify the God of Israel—we may be sure that he had often asked himself that very question—nay, that it was always echoing through his soul and was the lode-star of all his life. There was nothing small or little in Paul's Pharisaic life; no reserves in his devotion to his ideal, and no shrinking from labor, or difficulty, or danger. Paul never was a place-seeker, never was a sycophant, never was self-indulgent, or self-sparing. The elements of a great character wrought in him mightily. What he lacked was not readiness to do and dare; what he lacked was humility. And the change that took place in him on the road to Damascus was in this regard no less immense than immediate. It was a totally new note which vibrated through his being, that found expression in the humble inquiry, "What shall I do, Lord?" It is no longer a question directed to himself: "What shall *I* do?—what shall *I*, in my learning and strength and devotion—what shall *I* do to the glory of God?" It is the final and utter renunciation of self and the subjection of the whole life to the guidance of another. "What shall I do, *Lord?*" Heretofore Paul had been, even in his service to God, self-led; hereafter he was to be, even in the common affairs of life, down to his eating and drinking, God-led. It is the characteristic change that makes the Christian; for the Christian is particularly the Spirit-led man: they that are led by the Spirit of God, they are the sons of God. And as the Christian more and more perfectly assumes the attitude of a constant and unreserved "What shall I do, Lord?", he more and more perfectly enters into his Christian heritage, and lives out his Christian life—the very keynote of which is thus easily seen to be humility.

Dignity—there is an element of dignity which enters into this attitude also. For humility is not to be mistaken for a degrading supineness. Lowliness of mind is far from being the same with lowness of mind. When Paul ceased to be self-led and became Christ-led, he did not by that step become low in mind or morals; it was a step upwards, and not downwards. There is a lurking feeling in most of us, no doubt, that our dignity consists just in our self-government. Self-sufficiency is its note, or, as we perhaps prefer to call it, self-dependence. That man is really a man, we are prone to think, who carves out his own fortune, rests on his own efforts, and seeks favour and certainly direction from no one. Now there is a proper basis for this feeling; we need courageous men who call no man master and swear in the words of none; this self-centred, self-poised, and independent nature is one of the best gifts of God—cultivate it! But it is very easy for a proper self-pride and a high-minded independence to pass into a very improper self-sufficiency. We were not intended to defer with servile incapacity to any fellow-creature's direction; but there is a place for authority in the world after all; and as liberty must not be allowed to lapse into licence, so independence must not be permitted to degenerate into self-assertion. God did not create mankind atomistically but as a race; and it is the part of true dignity to find our true relations and to subject ourselves to them. It is not a mark of manhood to separate ourselves from the bands that unite mankind into an organism, but to take each his place in the organism and thoroughly to fill it.

He who hitches his chariot to a star is not thereby sinking to a lower status. True as this is in worldly matters it is superlatively true in spiritual affairs. The man led by the Spirit of

God—the Christ-led man—is the man of highest, and not of lowest, dignity. As it is the mark of a Christian man that he is "under orders," so it is the source of all his dignity that he is "under orders." With that odd penetration into the essence of things, which so often characterizes the words of Rudyard Kipling, he seems to have grasped and set forth this fundamental fact of the Christian life in the refrain of one of his "Barrack Room Ballads." He says:

> "The 'eathen in 'is blindness bows down to wood and stone—
> 'E don't obey no orders, unless they is 'is own."

The point is, of course, the fine soldierly conception of the value of order and discipline; the soldier recognizes the fact that he is "under orders" as the source of all that gives value and worth to his life; his coming "under orders" was his transmutation from a "hoodlum" into a "soldier"; the discipline of the army has made, as we say, a man of him. But Rudyard Kipling has so phrased his refrain as to make it hint a far wider and higher truth. The characteristic of heathenism, as he sees it, from this soldier-like point of view, is precisely that the heathen man—like the hoodlum,—that the heathen world—like a mob—obeys no orders; each man goes his own way; is left, as the Scriptures say, to his own devices. On the other hand, the characteristic of the Christian man is that he has orders to obey—he is "under orders." And the soldier, conscious of all that being under orders is to him—of what it has wrought in him—of how it has given him self-respect, a sense of his value, a consciousness of dignity and worth,—sees in this parallel fact the essence of Christianity. The Christian man is the man who is under orders; the heathen, he—who like the man in the slums—obeys nothing but his own caprices.

Rudyard Kipling was, perhaps, speaking more wisely than he knew; for what is the primary characteristic of Christendom but just this,—that God has taken charge of it, given it His orders, a revelation we call it; while heathendom is without this book of general orders. And what is the characteristic of the Christian man but just this: that he has found his Captain and receives his orders from Him? "What shall I do, Lord?"—that is the note of his life. And is it not clear that it is the source of an added dignity and worth to his life? Just as the soldier is nothing but the hoodlum licked into shape by coming under orders—under the establishing and forming influence of legitimate and wise authority—so the Christian is nothing but the sinner, come under the formative influence of the Captain of us all.

Power—it lies in the very nature of the case that such a coming under orders is the source of a vast increase also of power. For it is at once to find our place in a great and powerful organism.

So the soldier finds it, though this is not the primary fact of his betterment which he perceives as a result of his coming under orders. That, as Kipling rightly sees, is the subjective effect on himself, the increase of self-respect and of general dignity and conscious worth which comes to him. But the increase of power also is a factor of high moment. A cog wheel is a useless piece of iron by itself; but in its legitimate place in the machine it works wonders. An individual is as nothing in this seething mass of humanity which we call the world; be he never so energetic he can work no effect, but all his activity is like the aimless dashing of a moth about the destroying flame. But let him find his true place in the organism of humanity, and the weakest of us becomes a factor in the inevitable rush of the whole towards its destined end. See, then, the element of power in the question, "What shall I do, Lord?" For we must keep fully in mind that this human race of which we are members is not simply a chance aggregation of individuals, like a mass of worms crawling restlessly this way and that as the native impulse of each directs. It cannot be atomistically conceived. It is an organism, in which each individual has his appointed place and function. It is not merely the dictate of wisdom but the condition of efficiency and power that we should each find this, our place, and fulfil our own function.

If sin had never entered the world, this would doubtless be an easy task; we should each fit well into the place in which we find ourselves and should fulfil our required functions smoothly and easily, and each in his appointed measure advance the race to its destined goal. But sin has spoiled all; and the disjointed mechanism lies broken and dismantled and unable to work at its task. It is, therefore, that Christ Jesus has come into the world, the head of a new humanity, for the restoration of the race to its harmony with itself, the universe, and its appointed work. It is only through Him and through His direction as the Captain of our salvation that we may discover or occupy our place in His Church, which is only another name for reorganized humanity. Therefore the noble figure of Paul, which compares the Church to a body and us to members in particular. How shall the members of a body act? Each going his own way, independently of and inconsiderately of the others? Where then would be the body? But how find our true place and task in this organism of the body of Christ? There can be but one way and that way is pointed to by Paul's question, "What shall I do, Lord?" He and He only can appoint to their functions the members of His body, and thus the way of continued humility and dignity is easily seen to be also the way of power.

Take another example from military affairs.

What shall the soldier in battle do, if he would wish to be effective as a factor in the result? Go his own way, or obey orders? Let each seek to go his own way, and that army is doomed. But let each only strictly obey orders, and if the leading is wise and sure—as our leading under our Divine Captain is—the end is certain victory. Each soldier may seem to himself isolated as he makes his way through the underbrush; he can see no companion; he can hear no neighbour. It may seem to him that on his sole arm is laid the whole burden and heat of the day. Let him but obey orders and he is, on the contrary, a link in the one great design, and after a while, as the brushwood is threaded and the open plain is reached, the bugle sounds the charge, and out he charges—all by himself—to find suddenly that he is not by himself. Out of the ground as it seems, to the right and to the left of him, others start up—who have obeyed orders like himself—and they sweep a united band to the victory. Brethren, that is the way we are to conquer the world; and our part in it is just to obey orders. "What shall I do, Lord?" is to be our one question, and simple obedience to the response our one duty. Ah, in all our ministerial life, if we value success—the success of Christ—let us make Paul's question the one single, simple matter of our lives. Let "Lord, what shall I do?" be our sole chart for all the journey of life.

THE SUMMATION OF THE GOSPEL

Acts 26:18:—"To open their eyes, that they may turn from darkness to light, and from the power of Satan unto God, that they may receive remission of sins and an inheritance among them that are sanctified by faith in me."

We are given in the Book of Acts three accounts of Paul's conversion—one by Luke in the course of his history of the advance of the church, and two from the lips of the Apostle himself in addresses reported by the historian in the course of his narrative. The account in the apology which the Apostle in chains made before King Agrippa is the fullest account of the three, and especially in the report it makes of the words spoken by Jesus to Paul. We may be especially grateful for this. For these words are simply marvellous in the compressed fullness of their content and the richness of their teaching to us, even after the passage of so many ages.

The superior completeness here of the narrative of what passed between the Lord in heaven and him whom He would make a chosen vessel for the conveyance of His precious Gospel to the world, is already apparent in certain preliminaries to the main declaration—comparatively unimportant no doubt, but not without their significance. Here only we are told that the ascended Christ addressed the future Apostle in the Hebrew dialect,—the sacred tongue in which all the prophets had spoken and Moses, when they foretold His sufferings and how first out of the resurrection of the dead He should proclaim light to the people and to the Gentiles. Here only also are we told that to the sad inquiry, "Saul, Saul, why persecutest thou me?" was added that proverbial saying, "It is hard for thee to kick against the pricks" —intimating that like the harnessed ox he was in the hands of a master who would direct his path whither He would, and it was useless for him to strive against the performance of the duties which were appointed him. Better accept the commission given you and perform the work of the Lord assigned to you, with joy that you are chosen to serve the Lord, than to seek hopelessly to go your own way.

But it is not until we reach the words by which Saul was commissioned to be the Lord's Apostle that the full richness of this report breaks upon us. "Arise and stand upon thy feet"—so the record of the words runs—"for it is for this that I have appeared to thee; to ordain thee as a servant and a witness both of those things because of which thou hast seen me and of those things because of which I shall appear to thee, delivering thee from the people and from the nations, unto whom I send thee." Here is Paul's appointment to the apostleship. Was ever man appointed to an office in a manner so authoritative or with words so decisive? Christ comes from heaven itself to make the appointment. The appointment is to the work of a servant, a servant of Himself. The nature of the service required is that of witness-bearing; "a servant and a witness," that is, a servant whose service is witnessing. The matter to be witnessed to is provided by the appointer: "a witness of that with respect to which I shall appear unto thee." The witness is to add nothing of himself but to testify only what he has heard, what he has seen with his eyes, what he beheld and his hands have handled. And as the scope of the testimony is thus set him so also is its sphere; it is to be borne to the "people and the peoples"—to Jew and Gentile,—unto whom, says the voice, "I send you"—with majestic emphasis on the "I."

Truly it is to the office of a servant that Paul is called, a servant with a specific work to do and with specific instructions how to perform it. Thus he was made an "apostle," an apostle by the same call to the same work which all the apostles had received. It is even odd how perfectly Paul's commission accords with the very terms given to his fellows: "Go, and make disciples of all the nations . . . and lo, I am with you always, even to the end of the world." "The people and the Gentiles unto whom I send thee"—here is the universal commission; he is to go to Jew and

Gentile alike, to all the world. "Delivering thee from the people and from the Gentiles, unto whom I send thee"—here is the accompanying promise of "Lo, I am with thee." And note the nature of the apostolic promise. It is not that Paul shall suffer no harm from Jew and Gentile, that he shall not be hard-bested, baffled and persecuted. How could Paul the prisoner have repeated such a promise as that? It was that he should not be balked in his witness-bearing to them; that through divine intervention he should be successful in performing his duty as a servant and witness. Here, says Calvin, we see the Divine hand instilling courage into His servant for his task by assuring him of Divinely given success and at the same time forewarning him of the cross he was to bear. He shall need deliverance; but he shall have it.

What then is the task laid upon this servant? We have it already adumbrated in the call. He is called to serve as a witness. Witness-bearing is his one function. But in the wonderful words which are more particularly before us to-day, we have it opened out to us in all its richness. I send thee to all peoples, says the heavenly King, in imposing upon him His mission: I send thee to all peoples, "to open their eyes." There we have in the briefest compass possible, the whole apostolic mission. The apostles are sent into a world, blinded by sin, sunk in the darkness of soul that comes from sin, "to open men's eyes." Witness-bearers as they are, their duty corresponds with their equipment: they have received of the Lord, let them impart of what they have received to others. They have only to "open men's eyes," to open them to a clear vision of their state, of their danger and destiny, and of the love of God in Christ which has provided a reprieve from the danger.

To what end are they to open men's eyes? "To the end," says the heavenly King, "that they may turn from darkness to light, and from the power of Satan to God." As the whole apostolic duty consists in opening men's eyes, so the end for which they perform this duty consists wholly in the "conversion" of men; they are to open men's eyes to the end that men may "turn"—turn "from darkness to light and the power of Satan to God."

Why should they thus turn? The heavenly King condescends to explain even this to us. It is that "they may receive forgiveness of sins and inheritance among the saints." Those who are in darkness and under the tyranny of Satan, having had their eyes opened to their true state and the provision for their relief made by a loving God, may turn from the darkness to light and from the power of Satan to God. The condition of so doing is to have their eyes opened. This the Apostle was to perform. The effect of so doing was to receive forgiveness of sin and a lot among the saints. This God was to do; and He alone could do it. Turning to God, they receive from God these blessings.

How then do they receive them? The heavenly King does not omit to tell us plainly, though, no doubt, it is involved in the nature of the case. If, by turning to God, they receive from God these blessings, it must needs be by faith that they receive them, for what is faith but a looking to God for blessings? Nevertheless the ascended Christ fails not to state the matter for us and to state it in a manner and in a position in the sentence which throws upon it a tremendous emphasis. "By faith" He says; and He says more, —"by faith in Me." And there is where the Christianity of the declaration comes in.

One might be sent to open men's eyes without being a Christian. Socrates was so sent; and he opened men's eyes to much that was true, and right, and good; and Sakya Muni was so sent; and Zoroaster and Confucius; and since them a host have been so sent, who, by their investigations into nature or their profound philosophy, have made men to know things, and, let us hope, have made men's darkness less intense—though we must never forget that the world by all its wisdom does not know God. Men might be even sent to open men's eyes as to their religious state—so that their religious darkness might be ameliorated and they be led to see some rays of religious light, and to long to be delivered from the power of Satan and to turn to God—without being Christians. Even should we say that we are sent to open men's eyes that they may turn from darkness to light and the power of Satan to God and so might obtain forgiveness of sins and a lot with the sanctified—the proclamation might remain not yet Christian. Nor would the mere addition of the words "by faith" Christianize it. But when we say that all this is obtained by faith in Jesus, and say this as the ascended Jesus has said it here—then, indeed, we have a Christian proclamation, or let us rather say, the Christian proclamation. For in these words we have the very essence of Christianity.

And now, perhaps, we shall be able to understand why, ever since the Book of Acts has been written, men have been accustomed to look upon this little verse as one of the most pregnant in the whole scope of revelation, and why they have learned to call it the "Breviarium Apostolicum," the "Summarium Evangelicum." It is the compendium of apostolic duty. It is the summation of the Gospel. It tells the Apostle briefly that his one duty is to "open men's eyes"; it tells the world briefly that the Gospel consists in forgiveness of sins and a title to eternal life through faith in Jesus. Out of one and out of the other it extracts the core and holds that up to us for our undistracted contemplation. As such it surely is worthy of our most serious consideration.

There is another circumstance about it which gives it an especial claim on our attention. These are the words of the ascended Christ. Men to-day seem to find it very difficult to discern an authority in religion. Surely we cannot trust the mere "ipse dixit" of men in the affair of the salvation of the soul! Let us find firm footing for our feet! And so the cry has risen, Back to Christ! Back even from the apostles whom He commissioned to make Him known to men; back to Christ Himself! But when we go back to Christ, a new doubt seizes the wavering soul. Was not Christ, too, in the time of His sojourn on earth, a man? Mayhap—so it is suggested—mayhap He not only walked as a man and spake as a man, but thought as a man and taught as a man. Can we trust even His deliberate declarations in the days of His flesh? Well, if we are earnest in all this, we may find relief for our souls in a passage like the one before us. In it we have gone back to Christ. It is He who speaks these words to us. And we have gone back, not to the earthly Christ but to the heavenly Christ. It is not the Christ in His humiliation but the Christ in His glorification who here speaks to us. He has put off the Servant-form, and been exalted to the right hand of the Majesty on High; and He rends the heaven to give to men from the very Throne, this

"Breviarium Apostolicum," this "Summarium Evangelicum." It may, indeed, be that like an Old Testament hero we are ourselves unstable as water—"like the surge of the sea driven of the wind and tossed"—and cannot feel our footing firm though the Eternal Rock be beneath our feet. But surely if we are earnestly in search of a secure basis for our faith, the word spoken from heaven by the exalted Christ supplies it to us; making known to us what the duty of the Apostle, and of us, too, the successors of the Apostles in witnessing to the Word, is, and what the Gospel is to which as Christ's messengers we are to bear witness.

Approaching the passage in this spirit, let us mark well the supreme lessons it brings to us, as messengers of the grace of God in the Gospel—as seekers of the salvation that is in Jesus.

Mark, then, first of all, the function which the Ascended Jesus assigns to His witnessing servants. It is summed up in a single term—it is "to open men's eyes." Now, of course, the eye of the heart can be opened only by the Spirit of God; and it is not this unperformable duty which Christ lays on His servants. But the eyes of the mind are opened, in a lower sense, by the presentation of the truth and it is this that the Lord requires of His servants. They are "witnesses"; their duty is not to tickle men's ears or to allay their fears; their duty is to make known the truth, though it is precisely the truth that is not agreeable to their ears and that arouses and gives leash to their most terrifying fears. What men need is to have their eyes opened, and the duty laid on Paul and on all who would be followers of Paul is to open men's eyes. That it was in this sense that Paul understood his commission is obvious from the succeeding context. He was not disobedient to the heavenly vision, he tells the king, but having been sent to open men's eyes, that they might turn to God, he preached the Gospel of repentance and turning to God, bearing his witness to small and great alike. So will we, too, fulfil our commission as messengers of God's grace. We owe, as ministers, a teaching duty and our prime duty—our one duty—is to teach: we must open men's eyes.

We must not fail to mark the honour which is thus put by the Ascended Jesus on what we have learned to call by way of eminence, the Truth,—or, the Gospel message. Everything is made to turn on that. It lies at the root of all. The Apostle's duty is to open men's eyes. Whatever of salvation may come to men comes subsequently to that and as an outgrowth of this root. "Truth is in order to godliness"—that is a true formula. But it must not be read—should we wish to remain in harmony with the Ascended Christ—as a depreciation of the value of "truth" and "knowledge" (its subjective form), but as an enhancement of their importance. Truth exists only to produce godliness; that is true and needs to be kept constantly in mind. But no truth, no godliness,—that, too, is true and that, too, needs to be kept fully in mind. The only instrument in your hands or my hands for producing godliness is the truth; we are not primarily anything else but witnesses to truth; and the truth of God is the one lever by which we can pry at the hearts of men. Preach the Word; that is our one commission. And it is no more true that the Word cannot be preached without a preacher, than that the preacher cannot preach without a Word. Men are in darkness, they need light, and we are sent to give it to them.

It is equally important to observe that the implication of our Ascended Saviour's words of commission as to the condition of men, is that they are in darkness. That is the reason why they require to have their eyes opened. In what darkness let the Apostle who received the commission elsewhere tell us. As to the Gentiles, he tells us sufficiently in the first chapter of Romans; they have held back the knowledge of God in ungodliness until their foolish mind is darkened and they cannot know God; and under what bondage to Satan this has brought them, let the catalogue of evils with which that chapter closes inform us. Nor are the Jews in better case: for a veil lies on their hearts also which will not be taken away except on turning unto the Lord. The dense darkness in which men live, the terrible bondage into which they have been brought; this is part of the revelation of the Ascended Saviour, connected with which is the necessary implication of their hopelessness apart from the preaching of the Gospel. The appointed means of breaking this darkness is the proclamation of the Gospel by which alone can men's eyes be opened.

As it is the single duty laid by the Ascended Christ on His messengers that they shall open men's eyes, the single duty He lays on their hearers is correspondingly that they should turn from the darkness to the light, and (what is the same thing) from the power of Satan to God. It is, of course, as evident that men cannot turn from darkness to light, from the tyranny of Satan to God, in their own strength, as it is that men cannot open other people's eyes by their own power. As in the one case, so in the other, the immanent work of the Holy Spirit is not excluded because it is not mentioned. But as in the one case, so in the other, the action of man is required. Christ requires His apostle to "open men's eyes" —that is, to proclaim the truth which opens their eyes. Christ requires their hearers to turn from the darkness to the light, to shake off their bondage to Satan and turn to God. In both cases, He requires the "sowing" and "watering," while it is He alone who gives the increase. What we need to mark is that in this we have the one requirement of the Gospel. All that the ascended Christ demands is that when the light is brought to the eye the eye shall follow the light; that when the darkness is made visible to it as darkness, it shall not cling to the darkness by preference; that when Satan and God are set before it, it shall not choose Satan's bondage rather than the liberty which is in God.

Let us mark now the declaration made by the Ascended Christ of the benefits received from the Gospel. Those who under the message turn from Satan to God receive "remission of sins and a share with the sanctified," and that is to say, they receive a complete salvation. For what does man want in this world of darkness and subjection to Satan? What but, on the one hand, remission of the sins by virtue of which alone he can be held under Satan's tyranny, and, on the other, a title to the bliss prepared for the saints? Here are the two sides of what is technically termed Justification, proclaimed as the essence of salvation from heaven itself. Freedom from sin—that is the negative side; an inheritance among the saints—that is the positive side. Saints may have an inheritance—a lot or share—in bliss on their own account. But surely a sinner has no right to share it with them. Not even if his sins be forgiven him has he a right to share it. Enough for him that his sins are forgiven. On what ground shall he receive so great an additional reward? But the Gospel offers him not only relief from the penalty of sin but a place among those who are sanctified. "Who have been sanctified"—that he cannot yet say of himself. But by God's grace he has a title to a place among those who can say it. Holy angels and sanctified men—they stand before God's face forever.

Nor must we fail to mark the emphatic adjunction of the means by which they receive these gifts—the instrumental cause of their reception of them. The Ascended Jesus says it is by faith, and adjoins the emphasized definition—"that faith which is in Him." Thus the whole proclamation is bound together. Paul is to be Christ's witness. What he is to preach is what he has seen of Him and is to see of Him. It is Christ that is preached. It is the preaching of Christ which is to open blind eyes and lead men to turn to God. It is, therefore, through faith in this preachment of Christ that men are to receive forgiveness and adoption; through faith in the Christ preached that all the reward comes. Surely here is the centre of the Gospel. Ministers are sent forth to open men's eyes; men's eyes are opened that they may turn to God; men turn to God to receive forgiveness and acceptance; men receive this forgiveness and acceptance by faith—the faith that is in Christ.

THE SPIRIT'S TESTIMONY TO OUR SONSHIP

Rom. 8:16:—"The Spirit himself beareth witness with our spirit that we are children of God."

"THE Spirit himself beareth witness with our spirit that we are children of God." This is one of the texts of the Bible to which the Christian heart turns with especial longing and to which it clings with especial delight. On it has been erected the great Protestant doctrine of Assurance—the great doctrine that every Christian man may and should be assured that He is a child of God—that it is possible for him to attain this assurance and that to seek and find it is accordingly his duty. So much as that it certainly, along with kindred texts, does establish. The Holy Spirit Himself, it affirms, bears witness with our spirit that we are children of God; and then it goes on to develop the idea of childship to God from the point of view of the benefits it contains—"and if children then heirs, heirs of God and joint heirs with Christ."

It is quite obvious that the object of the whole is to encourage and enhearten; to speak, in a word, to the Christian's soul a great word of confidence. We are not to be left in doubt and gloom as to our Christian hope and standing. A witness is adduced and this no less a witness than the Holy Spirit, the author of all truth. We are not committed to our own tentative conjectures; or to our own imaginations and fancies. The Holy Spirit bears co-witness with our spirit that we are God's children. Surely, here there is firm standing ground for the most timid feet.

No wonder that men have seized hold of such an assurance with avidity, and sought and found in it peace from troubled consciences and hesitating fears. No wonder either if they have sometimes, in their eagerness for a sure foundation for their hope, pressed a shade beyond the mark and sought on the basis of this text an assurance from the Holy Ghost for a fact of which they had no other evidence, if, indeed, they did not feel that they had evidence enough against it; an assurance conveyed, moreover, in a mode that would be independent of all other evidence, if, indeed, it did not bear down and set aside abundant evidence to the contrary. This occasional use of the text to ground an assurance which seems to the observer unjustified if not positively negatived by all appearances, has naturally created a certain amount of hesitation in appealing to it at all or in seeking to attain the gracious state of assurance which it promises. This is a most unprofitable state of affairs. And in its presence among us, no less than in the presence of a somewhat exaggerated appeal to the testimony of the Spirit, we may find the best of warrants for seeking to understand just what the text affirms and just what privileges it holds out to us.

And here, first, the text leaves no room for doubt that the testimony of the Holy Spirit that we are God's children is a great reality. This is not a matter of inference from the text; it is expressed by it in *totidem verbis*. Exactly what is affirmed is that "the Spirit himself beareth witness with our spirit that we are children of God." The actuality of the Spirit's testimony to our childship to God is established, then, beyond all cavil; it is entrenched in the same indeclinable authority by which we are assured that there is a Spirit at all, that there is any such thing as an adoption into sonship to God, or that it is possible for sinful mortals to receive that adoption,—the authority of the inspired word of God. That the Spirit witnesses with or to our spirits that we are children of God is just as certain, then, as that there is such a state as sonship to which we may be introduced or that there is such a being as the Spirit of God to bear witness of it. These great facts all stand or fall together. And that is as much as to say that no Christian man can doubt the fact of the testimony of the Spirit that we are children of God. It is accredited to him by the same authority which accredits all that enters into the very essence of Christianity. It is in fact one of the elements of a full system of Christian truth that must be acknowledged by all who accept the system of Christian truth.

It would seem to be equally clear from the text that the testimony of the Spirit is not to be confounded with the testimony of our own consciousness. However the text be read, the "Spirit of God" and "our spirit" are brought into pointed contrast in it, and are emphatically distinguished from one another. Accordingly, not only does H. A. W. Meyer, who understands the text of the joint testimony of the Divine and human spirits, say: "Paul distinguishes from the subjective self-consciousness, I am the child of God, the therewith accordant testimony of the objective Holy Spirit, Thou art the child of God"; but Henry Alford also, who understands the text to speak solely of the testimony of the Spirit, borne not with but to our spirit, remarks: "All are agreed, and indeed the verse is decisive for it, that it is something separate from and higher than all subjective conclusions"—language which seems, indeed, scarcely exact, but which is certainly to the present point. It is of no importance for this whether Paul says that the Spirit bears witness with or to our spirit; in either case he distinctly distinguishes the Spirit of God from our spirit along with which or to which it bears its witness. And not only so but this distinction is the very nerve of the whole statement; the scope of which is nothing other than to give the Christian, along with his human conclusions, also a Divine witness.

Not only, then, is the distinction, here emphatically instituted, available, as Meyer reminds us, as a clear *dictum probans* against all pantheistic confusion of the Divine and human spirits in general, and all mystical confusion and intersmelting of the Divine and human spirits in the Christian man, as if the regenerated spirit was something more than a human spirit, or was in some way interpenetrated and divinitized by the Divine Spirit; but it is equally decisive against identifying out of hand the testimony of the Spirit of God here spoken of with the testimony of our own consciousness. These are different things not only distinguishable but to be distinguished. The witness of the Holy Ghost is something other than, additional to, and more than the witness of our own spirit; and it is adduced here, just because it is something other than, additional to, and more than the witness of our own spirit. The whole sense of Paul's declaration is that we have over and beyond our own authority a Divine witness to our childship to God, on which we may rest without fear that we shall be put to shame.

It is to be borne in mind, however, that distinctness in the source of this testimony from that of our own consciousness is not the same as separateness from it in its delivery. Paul would seem, indeed, while thus strongly emphasizing its distinct source—namely, the Divine Spirit—nevertheless to suggest its conjunction with the testimony of our own spirit in its actual delivery. This, indeed, he would seem frankly to assert, if, as seems most natural, we are to understand the preposition in the phrase "beareth testimony with," to refer to our spirit, and are to translate with our English version, "The Spirit itself beareth witness with our spirit." So taken, the conjunction is as emphatic as the distinction. It must not be overlooked, however, that some commentators prefer to take "our spirit" as the object to which the testimony is borne: "the Spirit beareth witness to our spirit"—in which case the emphasis on the conjunction of the testimony of the Spirit of God with that of our spirit may be lost. I say, may be lost: for even then the preposition in the verb will need to be accounted for; and it would seem to be still best to account for it by referring it to our spirit—"the Spirit itself beareth its consentient witness to our spirit," its witness consenting to our spirit's witness. And I say merely that the emphasis on the conjunction may be lost; for even if this interpretation be rejected and the force of the preposition be found merely in the accordance of the witness with the fact, by which it is the truth and trustworthiness of the testimony alone which is emphasized; nevertheless the connection of the verse with the preceding one is still implicative of the conjoined witness of the two spirits. For it is in our crying "Abba, Father," that the witness of the Spirit of God is here primarily found—the relation of this verse to the preceding being practically the same as if it were expressed in the genitive absolute—thus: "the Spirit which we received was the Spirit of adoption whereby we cry Abba, Father,—the Spirit Himself testifying thus to our spirit that we are children of God."

The fact that the conjunction of the two witnesses thus dominates the passage, however its special terms are explained, adds a powerful reason for following the natural interpretation of the terms themselves and referring the preposition "with" directly to the "our spirit." It is with considerable confidence, therefore, that we may understand Paul to say that "the Spirit himself beareth witness together with our spirit that we are children of God," and thus not merely to imply or assert—as in any case is the fact—but pointedly to emphasize the conjunction, or, if you will, the confluence of the Divine testimony with that of the human consciousness itself. Distinct in its source, it is yet delivered confluently with the testimony of our human consciousness. To be distinguished from it as something other than, additional to, and more than the testimony of our human consciousness, it is yet not to be separated from it as delivered apart from it, out of connection with it, much less, in opposition or contradiction to it. "The Spirit of God," says that brilliant young thinker whose powers were the wonder, as well as the dependence, of the Westminster Divines, "is not simply a martyr—a witness—but co-martyr—*qui simul testimonium dicit*—he bears witness not only to but with our spirit; that is, with our conscience. So that if the witness of our conscience be blank, and can testify nothing of sincerity, hatred of sin, love to the brethren, or the like, then the Spirit of God witnesses no peace nor comfort to that soul; and the voice that speaketh peace to a person who hath no gracious mark or qualification in him, doth not speak according to the Word, but contrary to the Word, and is, therefore, a spirit of delusion."—"So that in the business of assurance and full persuasion, the evidence of graces and the testimony of the Spirit are two concurrent causes or helps, both of them necessary. Without the evidence of graces, it is not a safe nor a well-grounded assurance; without the testimony of the Spirit, it is not a plerophory or full assurance." And then he devoutly adds: "Therefore, let no man divide the things which God hath joined together."

These remarks of George Gillespie's will already suggest to us the function of this testimony of the Holy Ghost, as set forth by Paul as a co-testimony with the witness of our own spirit. It is not intended as a substitute for the testimony of our spirit—or, to be more precise, of "signs and marks"—but as an enhancement of it. Its object is not to assure a man who has "no signs" that he is a child of God, but to assure him who has "signs," but is too timid to draw so great an inference from so small a premise, that he is a child of God and to give him thus not merely a human but a Divine basis for his assurance. It is, in a word, not a substitute for the proper evidence of our childship; but a Divine enhancement of that evidence. A man who has none of the marks of a Christian is not entitled to believe himself to be a Christian; only those who are being led by the Spirit of God are children of God. But a man who has all the marks of being a Christian may fall short of his privilege of assurance. It is to such that the witness of the Spirit is superadded, not to take the place of the evidence of "signs," but to enhance their effect and raise it to a higher plane; not to produce an irrational, unjustified, conviction, but to produce a higher and more stable conviction than he would be, all unaided, able to draw; not to supply the lack of evidence, but to cure a disease of the mind which will not profit fully by the evidence.

We are here in the presence of a question which has divided the suffrages of Christian men from the beginning. The controversy has raged in every age, whether our assurance of our salvation is to be syllogistically determined thus: the promise of God is sure to those who believe and obey the Gospel; I believe and obey the Gospel; hence I am a child of God: or is rather to be mystically determined by the witness of the Holy Spirit in the heart. Whether we are to examine ourselves for signs that we are in the faith, or, neglecting all signs, are to depend on the immediate whisper of the Spirit to our heart, "Thou art a child of God." The debate has been as fruitless as it has been endless. And the reason is that it is founded on a false antithesis, and, being founded on a false antithesis, each side has had something of truth to which it was justified in clinging in the face of all refutation, and something of error which afforded an easy mark for the arrows of its opponents. The victory can never be with those who contend that we must depend for our assurance wholly on the marks and signs of true faith; for true assurance can never arise in the heart save by the immediate witness of the Holy Spirit, and he who looks not for that can never go beyond a probable hope of being in Christ. The victory can never be with those who counsel us to neglect all signs and depend on the testimony of the Holy Spirit alone; for the Holy Spirit does not deliver His testimony save through and in confluence with the testimony of our own consciences that we are God's children. "All thy marks," says Gillespie with point, "will leave thee in the dark, if the Spirit of Grace do not open thine eyes that thou mayest know the things which are freely given thee of God"; and again with equal point, "To make no trial by marks and to trust an inward testimony, under the notion of the Holy Ghost's testimony, when it is without the least evidence of any true gracious mark . . . is a deluding and an ensnaring of the conscience."

It is obvious that the really cardinal question here, therefore, concerns not the fact of the testimony of the Holy Spirit, not its value or even its necessity for the forming of a true assurance, but the mode of its delivery. It is important, therefore, to interrogate our text upon this point. The single verse before us does not speak very decisively to the matter; only by its conjunction of the testimony of the Spirit with that of our own spirit does it suggest an answer. But nowhere than in these more recondite doctrines is it more necessary to read our texts in their contexts; and the setting of our text is very far from being without a message to us in these premises. For how does Paul introduce this great assertion? As already remarked, as practically a subordinate clause to the preceding verse, with the virtual effect of a genitive absolute. He had painted in the seventh chapter the dreadful conflict between indwelling sin and the intruded principle of holiness which springs up in every Christian's breast. And he had pointed to the very fact of this conflict as a banner of hope. For he identifies the fact of the conflict with the presence of the Holy Spirit working in the soul; and in the presence of the Holy Spirit is the earnest of victory. The Spirit would not be found in a soul which was not purchased for God and in process of fitting for the heavenly Kingdom. Let no one talk of living on the low plane of the seventh chapter of Romans. Low plane, indeed! It is a low plane where there is no conflict. Where there is conflict—with the Spirit of God as one party in the battle—there is progressive advance towards the perfection of Christian life. So Paul treats it. He points to the conflict as indicative of the presence of the Spirit; he points to the presence of the Spirit as the earnest of victory; and on this experience he founds his promise of eternal bliss. Then comes our passage, introduced with one of his tremendous "therefores." "Accordingly, then, brethren,"—since the Holy Spirit is in you and the end is sure,—"accordingly, then, we are debtors not to the flesh to live after the flesh, but to the Spirit to live after the Spirit. . . . For as many as are being led" (notice the progressive present) "by the Spirit of God, these are sons of God, for" (after all), "the spirit that ye received was not a spirit of bondage, but a spirit of adoption, whereby we cry Abba, Father,—the Spirit Himself bearing witness with our spirit that we are children of God." "The Spirit Himself" bearing this witness? When? How? Why, of course, in this very cry framed by Him in our souls, "Abba, Father!" Not a separate witness; but just this witness and no other. The witness of the Spirit, then, is to be found in His hidden ministrations by which the filial spirit is created in our hearts, and comes to birth in this joyful cry.

We must not fancy, however, that, therefore, the witness of the Spirit adds nothing to the syllogistic way of concluding that we are children of God. It does not add another way of reaching this conclusion, but it does add strength of conclusion to this way. The Spirit is the spirit of truth and will not witness that he is a child of God who is not one. But he who really is a child of God will necessarily possess marks and signs of being so. The Spirit makes all these marks and signs valid and available for a true conclusion—and leads the heart and mind to this true conclusion. He does not operate by producing conviction without reason; an unreasonable conclusion. Nor yet apart from the reason; equally unreasonable. Nor by producing more reasons for the conclusion. But by giving their true weight and validity to the reasons which exist and so leading to the true conclusion, with Divine assurance. The function of the witness of the Spirit of God is, therefore, to give to our halting conclusions the weight of His Divine certitude.

It may be our reasoning by which the conclusion is reached. It is the testimony of the Spirit which gives to a conclusion thus reached indefectible certainty. It is the Spirit alone who is the author, therefore, of the Christian's firm assurance. We have grounds, good grounds, for believing that we are in Christ, apart from His witness. Through His witness these good grounds produce their full effect in our minds and hearts.

THE SPIRIT'S HELP IN OUR PRAYING

Rom. 8:26, 27:—"And in like manner the Spirit also helpeth our infirmity: for we know not how to pray as we ought; but the Spirit himself maketh intercession for us with groanings which cannot be uttered; and he that searcheth the hearts knoweth what is the mind of the Spirit, because he maketh intercession for the saints according to the will of God."

The direct teaching of this passage obviously is that the Holy Ghost, dwelling in Christian men, indites their petitions, and thus secures for them both that they shall ask God for what they really need and that they shall obtain what they ask. There is here asserted both an effect of the Spirit's working on the heart of the believer and an effect of this, His working on God. Even Christian men are full of weakness, and neither know what they should pray for in each time of need, nor are able to pray for it with the fervidness of desire which God would have them use. It is by the operation of the Spirit of God on their hearts that they are thus led to pray aright in matter and manner, and that their petitions are rendered acceptable to God, as being according to His will. This is the obvious teaching of the passage; but that we may fully understand it in its implications and shades it will be desirable to look at it in its context.

The eighth chapter of Romans is an outburst

of humble triumph on the Apostle's part, on realizing that the conflict of the Christian life as depicted in the seventh chapter issues in victory, through the indwelling of the Holy Ghost. Evil may be entrenched in our members; but the power of God unto salvation has entered our hearts by the Holy Ghost and by the prevalent working of that Holy Spirit in us we are enabled to cry Abba, Father; and being made sons of God are constituted His heirs and co-heirs with Jesus Christ. Not as if, indeed, we are to be borne without effort of our own into this glorious inheritance—"to be carried to the skies on flowery beds of ease." No! "Surely we must fight, if we would win." For, after all, the Christian life is a pilgrimage to be endured, a journey to be accomplished, a fight to be won. Least of all men was the Apostle Paul, whose life was in labours more abundant and in trials above measure, liable to forget this. It is out of the experiences of his own life as well as out of the nature of the thing that he adds, therefore, to his cry of triumph a warning of the nature of the life which, nevertheless, we must still live in the flesh. If "the Spirit Himself beareth witness with our Spirits that we are the Sons of God," and the glorious sequence follows, "and if children, then heirs, heirs of God and joint heirs with Christ," no less do we need to be reminded further of the condition underlying the victory—"if so be that we suffer with Him that we may also be glorified with Him." To share with Christ His glory implies sharing with Him His sufferings. "Must Jesus tread the path alone and all the world go free?" Union with Him implies taking part in all His life experiences, and we can ascend the throne with Him only by treading with Him the pathway by which He ascended the throne. It was from the cross that He rose to heaven.

The rest of this marvellous chapter seems to be devoted to encouraging the saint in his struggles as he treads the thorny path with Christ. The first encouragement is drawn from the relative greatness of the sufferings here and the glory yonder; the second, from the assistance in the journey received from the Holy Ghost; and the third from the gracious oversight of God over the whole progress of the journey. This whole section of the chapter, therefore, appears as Paul's word of encouragement to the believer as he struggles on in his pilgrimage—in his "Pilgrim's Progress"—in view of the hardships and sufferings and trials attendant in this sinful world on the life in Christ. It is substantially, therefore, an Apostolic commentary on our Lord's words, "If any man would come after me, let him deny himself and take up his cross and follow me;" "he that doth not take up his cross and follow after me, is not worthy of me." These sufferings, says Paul, are inevitable; no cross, no crown. But he would strengthen us in enduring the cross by keeping our eye on the crown, by assuring us of the presence of the Holy Spirit as our ever-present helper, and by reminding us of the Divine direction of it all. Thus he would alleviate the trials of the journey.

Our text then takes its place as one of these encouragements to steadfast constancy, endurance, in the Christian life—to what we call to-day "perseverance." The "weakness," "infirmity," to which it refers is to be taken, therefore, in the broadest sense. No doubt its primary reference may be to the remnant of indwelling sin, not yet eradicated and the source of all the Christian's weaknesses. But it is not confined to this. It includes all that comes to a Christian as he suffers with Christ; all that is included in our Lord's requirement of denying ourselves and taking up our cross. Paul's life of suffering for the Gospel's sake may be taken by us, as it, doubtless, was felt by him as he penned these words, as an illustration of the breadth of the meaning of the word. He who would live godly must in every age suffer a species of persecution; a species, differing in kind with the tone and temper and quality of each age, but always persecution. He who would follow after Christ must meet with many opposers. A strenuous life is the Christian life in the world; it is appropriately designated a warfare, a fight. But we are weak. And the weakness meant is inclusive of all human weaknesses in the stress of the great battle.

The encouragement which Paul offers us in this our confessed weakness, is the ever-present aid of the Holy Ghost. We are not to be left to tread the path, to fight the fight, alone; the Spirit ever "helpeth" our weakness, "takes our burden on Himself, in our stead and yet along with us," as the double compound word expresses. He does not take it away from us and bear it wholly Himself, but comes to our aid in bearing it, receiving it also on His shoulders along with us. In giving this encouragement of the ever-present aid of the Spirit in our weakness, the Apostle adds an illustration of it. And it is exceedingly striking that, in seeking an illustration of it, the Apostle thinks at once of the sphere of prayer. It shows his estimate of the place of prayer in the Christian struggle, that in his eye, prayer is really "the Christian's vital breath." Our weakness, he seems to say, is helped primarily by the Spirit through His inditing our prayers for us. Perhaps this will not seem strange to us if we will fitly consider what the Christian life is, in its dependence on God; and what prayer is, in its attitude of dependence on God. Prayer is, in a word, the correlate of religion. The prayerful attitude is the religious attitude. And that man is religious who habitually holds toward God, in life and thought, in act and word, the attitude of prayer.

Is it not fitting, after all, that Paul should encourage the Christian man, striving to live a Christian life—denying himself and taking up his cross and following Christ—by assuring him primarily that the Holy Ghost is ever present, helping him in his weakness, to this effect that his attitude towards God in his conscious dependence on Him, should be kept straight? For this it is to help us in prayer.

Nor can it seem strange to us that Paul adverts to our need of aid in prayer in the very matter of our petitions. It is worth noting how very vitally he writes here, doubtless, again out of his own experience. "We know not what we should pray for," he says, "in each time of need"—according, that is, to the needs of each occasion. It is not lack of purpose—it is lack of wisdom, that he intimates. We may have every desire to serve God and every willingness to serve Him at our immediate expense, but do we know what we need at each moment? The wisest and best of men must needs fail here. So Paul found, when he asked thrice that the thorn in the flesh might be removed and stayed not till the Lord had told him explicitly that His grace was sufficient for him. How often we would rather escape the suffering that lies in our path than receive of the grace of God! Nay, a greater than Paul may here be our example. Did not our Lord Himself say, "Now is my soul troubled; and what shall I say? Father, save me from this hour." Quick though came the response back from His own soul, "But for this cause came I unto this hour: Father, glorify thy name," yet may we not see even in this momentary hesitation a hint of that uncertainty of which all are more or less the prey? It is not merely in the recalcitrances of the Christian life—God knows we have need enough there!—but it is not only in the recalcitrances and the mere unwillingnesses of the Christian life that the Spirit aids us; but in the perplexities of the Christian life too. Under His leading we shall not only be saved from sins, but also from mistakes, in the will of God. And thus He leads us not only to pray, but to pray "according to the will of God."

And now, how does the Spirit thus aid us in praying according to the will of God? Paul calls it a making of intercession for us with groanings which cannot be uttered; making intercession for us or in addition to us, for the word could have either meaning. It is clear from the whole passage that this is not an objective intercession in our behalf—made in heaven as Christ our Mediator intercedes for us. That the Spirit makes intercession for us is known to God not as God in heaven, but as "searcher of hearts." It is equally clear that it is not an intercession through us as mere conduits, unengaged in the intercession ourselves; it is an intercession made by the Spirit as our helper and not as our substitute. It is equally clear that it is not merely in our natural powers that the Spirit speaks; it is a groaning of which the Spirit is the author and "over and above" our own praying. It is clear then that it is subjective and yet not to be confused with our own prayings. Due to the Spirit's working in our hearts we conceive what we need in each hour of need and ask God for it with unutterable strength of desire. The Spirit intercedes for us then by working in us right desires for each time of need; and by deepening these desires into unutterable groans. They are our desires, and our groans. But not apart from the Spirit. They are His; wrought in us by Him. And God, who searches the heart, sees these unutterable desires and "knows the mind of the Spirit that He is making intercession for the saints according to the will of God."

Thus, then, the Spirit helps our weakness. By His hidden, inner influences He quickens us to the perception of our real need; He frames in us an infinite desire for this needed thing; He leads us to bring this desire in all its unutterable strength before God; who, seeing it within our hearts, cannot but grant it, as accordant with His will. Is not this a very present help in time of trouble? As prevalent a help as if we were miraculously rescued from any danger? And yet a help wrought through the means of God's own appointment, that is, our attitude of constant dependence on Him and our prayer to Him for His aid? And could Paul here have devised a better encouragement to the saints to go on in their holy course and fight the battle bravely to the end?

ALL THINGS WORKING TOGETHER FOR GOOD

Rom. 8:28:—"And we know that to them that love God all things work together for good, even to them that are called according to his purpose."

THERE is a sense in which this verse marks the climax of this glorious eighth chapter of Romans. The whole chapter may properly be looked upon as the reaction from the depths of the seventh chapter. The key-note of that chapter is sounded in the despairing cry, "O wretched man that I am, who shall deliver me out of the body of this death." The key-note of this is sounded in the blessed shout, "If God is for us, who is against us?" In the seventh chapter Paul uncovers the horror of indwelling sin; in the eighth he reveals the glory of the indwelling Spirit. The Christian life on earth is a conflict with sin. And therein is the dreadfulness of our situation on earth displayed. But we are not left to fight the battle alone. The Christian life is a conflict of God—not of us—with sin. And therein is the joy and glory of our situation on earth manifested. As sinners we are in terrible plight. As the servants of God, fighting His battle, we are in glorious case.

The whole eighth chapter of the Romans is a

development of the blessedness which arises from the discovery of the Holy Spirit within us, as the real power making for righteousness which is in conflict with indwelling sin. It opens with the proclamation that the liberation of the sinner is effected by the presence in him of the "law of the spirit of life." It proceeds by dwelling on the blessings that are ours by virtue of this great fact of the indwelling Spirit. First, a new and unconquerable principle of life and holiness is implanted in us (1-11); next, a new relationship to God, as His sons and heirs, is revealed to us (12–17); still further, a new and unquenchable hope is made ours (18–25), which has respect amid whatever sufferings attend us here to the supreme greatness of the reward. Lastly, a new support in our present weakness is granted us (26–30).

The section from verse 26 to verse 30 is thus revealed to us as one of the grounds of the Christian's encouragement amidst the evils of life. It was not enough for Paul to paint the coming glory. Even in the present weakness we are not left without efficient aid. It is true that in this weakness—it is part of the very weakness—we cannot be sure what we need and cannot even pray articulately; we can only, like nature itself (vs. 22), groan and travail in pain, for we scarcely know what. But there is one who knows. In these very inarticulate groans the Spirit's hand is active; and the searcher of hearts according to whose appointment it is that the Spirit intercedes for saints, understands and knows. There is no danger, then, that we shall fail of the needed help. Maybe we do not know what we need—God does. He can and will read off our groans of pain and longing in terms of intelligence and of love. "For we know that with those that love God, God co-worketh in respect to all things unto good." There is nothing that can befall us which is undirected by Him; and nothing will befall those that love Him, therefore, which is not directed by Him to their good.

The fundamental thought is the universal government of God. All that comes to you is under His controlling hand. The secondary thought is the favour of God to those that love Him. If He governs all, then nothing but good can befall those to whom He would do good. The consolation lies in the shelter which we may thus find beneath His almighty arms. We are weak, we are blind; He is strong and He is wise. Though we are too weak to help ourselves and too blind to ask for what we need, and can only groan in unformed longings, He is the author in us of these very longings—He knows what they really mean—and He will so govern all things that we shall reap only good from all that befalls us. All, though for the present it seems grievous; all, though it be our sin itself, as Augustine properly saw and as the context demands (for is not the misery of the seventh chapter the misery of indwelling sin, and is not the joy of the closing verses of the eighth chapter the joy of salvation from sin?)—all, there is no exception allowed: in all things God co-operates so with us that it can conduce only to our good. Our eternal good, obviously; because it is throughout the good of the soul, the good of the eternal salvation in Christ, that is in evidence.

We say this is the climax of the eighth chapter of Romans. After this nothing remains but the pæan of victory that fills the concluding verses. If there is not only a power within us making for righteousness to which the final victory is assured; not only an inheritance far surpassing the present evil, awaiting us; but also everything that befalls us is so governed that it, everything, is for our good and befalls us only because it is for our good; why we certainly are in excellent case.

It is possible to say, indeed, that there is nothing revealed here which deserves to be thought of as the culmination of a specifically Christian encouragement. What, indeed, is here announced that devout souls have not always possessed? In what does this fervent declaration, for example, go beyond the philosophy of Joseph in the world's early prime—in the simple days of patriarchal faith—when, looking back on the fortunes of his own chequered life, on the plots of his brethren against his person when sold by them into Egypt, and the marvellous befallings which came to him there, he said to them at the last, "As for you, ye meant evil against me; but God meant it for good, to bring to pass as it is this day?" Did not Joseph already hold the secret of Paul's consolation—that God is Lord of all, that nothing comes to us except by His ordering, that therefore to those who serve Him, all that occurs to them, black as it may seem to their short vision, is meant for good and will bring to pass the peaceable fruits of joy and righteousness? Nay, did not that half-heathen Jew, the son of Sirach, who wrote the book of Ecclesiasticus, have adequate understanding of the whole matter, when he wrote, in a context which magnifies the all-reaching power of God, "For the good are good things created from the beginning . . . all these things are for good to the godly," adding on the other hand, that evil things are equally created for sinners and what is good for the godly is turned into evil for sinners?

Indeed, is there anything here to which the heathen themselves could not attain? Can we forget, for example, that beautiful discussion in the tenth book of the *Republic* in which Socrates reasons with Glaucon on the rewards of virtue? Must we not suppose, he urges, that the gods accurately estimate the characters of men, and know thoroughly both the just and the unjust? And must we not suppose that they look with friendly eye upon the just and with enmity upon the unrighteous? And must we not suppose, still further, that they will be good to those whom they recognize as their friends, and grant them every good—excepting, of course, only such evil as is the consequence of their former sins? "Then, this," Socrates continues, "must be our notion of the just man, that even when he is in poverty or sickness, or any other seeming misfortune, all things will in the end work together for good to him in life and death: for the gods have a care for anyone whose desire is to become just and to be like God, as far as man can attain His likeness by the pursuit of virtue." What is there in Paul's asseveration that goes beyond this calmly expressed conviction—the very language of which is so closely assimilated to Paul's—except a little characteristic fervency of tone?

Well, it is to be admitted at once that there is much in Paul's great statement which is not peculiar to it. The assurance of God's providential conduct of the whole complex of the universe that He has made; the conviction that in His control of the details of life He will not forget those who are specially well-pleasing to Him; the firm faith therefore that the path of happiness is to see to it that we are well-pleasing to God; that, as all that occurs is of God's ordering, so all that occurs to the friends of God will work out good to them—this is, of course, of the very essence of natural religion, and he who really believes in a personal

God clothed with ethical attributes, must needs believe it. All the more shame, then, when men who profess to believe in such a God—to be Theists—relax the height of this great and most fundamental faith, as many of the heathen have done; as some even of our modern Christian teachers have done, asking doubtfully or denyingly, for example, whether God sends trouble, as if trouble could come to one of God's beloved ones without His behest,—and totally failing to retain, we will not say Paul's height, but even the height of the higher heathenism, which could see that it is a higher as well as a truer view that trouble is an instrument of God's good to God's friends. Nevertheless, there is more in Paul's statement than was reached by the heathen sage; something more even perhaps than underlies the more enlightened and more penetrating view of Joseph.

We cannot stop to develop the differences in detail. But we may note briefly at least one of the most fundamental of them, one so fundamental that it transforms everything.

This is the difference in the ground of the assurance which is cherished. The ground on which the heathen sage founded his conviction was the essential righteousness of the expectation. God owes to those who love Him different treatment from that accorded to those who hate Him. Possibly we may think that the modern heathen rise a step higher when they substitute the idea of goodness for that of bare righteousness, and say that God will do good to those who love Him because He is essentially love and will do good to all men. The ground of Paul's assurance is something far higher. It is not merely an inference from a conception of God not obviously validated by a broad survey of His works. It is not even an inference from the ineradicable and thoroughly authenticated conviction that He is righteous. It is an express declaration of God's own. It is a "revelation from heaven" spoken by the lips of prophets and of the Son Himself.

To the heathen God is to bless His friends because they are His friends; to Paul they are His friends because God blesses them. The whole basis of the heathen's conviction is a judgment in righteousness; it is purely abstract; if a man is righteous then God must treat him as such. Granted. But, is a man righteous? I—am I righteous? If a man is righteous, God will, undoubtedly, treat him as such; God owes him good and not evil. But I—I myself—how will God treat *me?* Will that depend on whether I am now righteous? And on what my past sins deserve? Well, who is now righteous? And what do my past sins deserve? For the righteous man—who has no present and no past sins to come into consideration—this may be satisfactory enough. But where is that righteous man? This is what we mean by saying that the heathen's proposition is purely abstract. It is true enough; but it is of no personal interest to sinners.

Paul was thinking not of righteous men but of sinners. It is concerning sinners that he is talking, concerning those who had had and were having the experience of the seventh chapter of Romans. Essentially different, his good tidings to sinners from the cold deduction of reason which Plato offers to the just! And this is the exact difference: righteous men amid the evils of earth seek a theodicy—they want a justification of God; sinners do not need a theodicy—all too clear to them is the reason of their sufferings—they want a consolation, a justification *from* God. Paul's words are in essence, then, not a theodicy but a consolation. Such a consolation can rest on nothing but a revelation; and Paul founds it on a revelation which he represents as of immanent knowledge in the Church: "We know," says he, "that all things work together for good to them that love God." We bless God that we know it! For we are sinners, and what hope have we save in a God who is gracious rather than merely just?

MAN'S HUSBANDRY AND GOD'S BOUNTY

1 Cor. 3:5–9:—"What then is Apollos? And what is Paul? Ministers through whom ye believed; and each as the Lord gave to him. I planted, Apollos watered; but God gave the increase. So then neither is he that planteth anything, neither he that watereth; but God that giveth the increase. Now he that planteth and he that watereth are one: but each shall receive his own reward according to his own labour. For we are God's fellow-workers: ye are God's husbandry, God's building."

THESE verses form a natural section of this Epistle. The Corinthians had sent a letter to the Apostle, making inquiries on several important matters. But when the Apostle came to make reply, he had matters to speak to them about which were far more important than any of the questions asked in their letter. Trusty friends had reported to him the serious deterioration which the Corinthian Church was undergoing, the strange, as we may think them, and certainly outbreaking, immoralities into which they were falling. Chiefest of these, because most fundamental and most fecund of other evils, was the raging party spirit, which had arisen among them. Greek-like, the Corinthians were not satisfied with the matter of the simple Gospel, in whatever form, but had begun to clothe its truths (and to obscure them in the act) in philosophical garb and rhetorical finery; and had split themselves into factions, far from tolerant of one another, rallying around special teachers and glorifying, each, a special mode of presentation. So far had this gone that the rival parties had long ago broken the peace of the Church, and were threatening its unity.

Paul devotes himself first of all to the shaming of this spirit and the elimination of its results. In doing so he cuts to the roots. He begins with a rebuke of the violence of the Corinthians' party spirit, sarcastically suggesting that they had made Christ, who was the sole Redeemer of God's Church and in whom were all, a share; and so parcelled Him out to one faction—as if others had had Paul to die for them and had been baptized in his name, and so on. He then sets himself seriously to refute the whole basis of their factions and to place firmly under his readers' feet the elements of the truth. To do this, he first elucidates the relation of wisdom—philosophy and rhetoric, we would say now—to the Gospel; pointing out that the Gospel is not a product of human wisdom and is not to be commended by it; although, no doubt, it proclaims a Divine wisdom of its own to those who are capable of receiving it. Thus he destroys the very nerve of their strife. Then, with our present passage, he turns to the parallel occasion of their strife and explains the relation of the human agents through which it is propagated to the Gospel. This he declares to be none other than the relation of hired servants to the husbandry of the good-man of the farm. Proceeding to details, Paul and Apollos, he declares, are alike but servants, each doing whatever work is committed to him, work which may no doubt differ, externally considered, in kind, though it is exactly the same in this—that it is nothing but hired service, while it is God that gives the increase. There is no difference in this respect; not that the work is not deserving of reward; reward, however, not as if the increase was theirs but only proportioned to the amount of their work as labour. The harvest is God's; that harvest which they themselves are. They, the labourers, are fellow-labourers only, working for God. They, the Corinthians, do not belong to them; they are God's husbandry, God's building.

Thus the Apostle not only intimates but emphatically asserts that the Church of God is not the product of the ministry; no, nor is any individual Christian. Every Christian and the Church at large is God's gift. God sets workmen to labour in His vineyard; and rewards them richly for their labour, paying each all his wages. But these labourers, it is not theirs to give the increase, nor even to choose their work. It is theirs merely to work and to do each the special work which God appoints. The vineyard is God's and so is the increase,—which God Himself gives.

Now, looking at this general teaching of the

passage in a broad and somewhat loose way, we see that the following important truths are intimated.

(1) Christianity is a work which God accomplishes in the heart and in the world. It may even be said to be the work of God: the work that God has set Himself to do in this dispensation, and hence the second creation.

(2) Shifting the emphasis a bit, we perceive that the passage emphasizes the fact that Christianity is a work which is accomplished in the heart and in the world directly by God.

(3) Men are but God's instruments, tools, "agents" (ministers) in performing this work. They do not act in it for God, that is, instead of God; but God acts through them. It is He that gives the increase.

(4) All men engaged in this work are in equally honourable employment. If one plants and another waters and another reaps, it is all "one." They are all only fellow-labourers under God; equal in His sight and to be rewarded, not according to what they did, but according to how they did it. This would not be true if man made the increase; but the reaper no more makes the harvest than the sower. Nor would it be true if the reaper had the increase. But it is not the reaper's "field." He is a hired labourer, not an owner. It is God's field. Each gets his wages; little or much according to the quality of his work. Wages are

measured by labour, not results. And therefore it is all one to you and me, as labourers in God's field, whether He sets us to plough, plant, water or reap.

Looking at these truths in turn:

What an encouragement it is to the Christian worker to know that Christianity is, so to speak (in the figure of the text), the crop which God the great husbandman has set Himself to plant and to raise in this "season" in which we live. Therefore this dispensation is called "the year of salvation." And therefore, when pleading a little later with these same Corinthians to receive the grace of God not in vain, Paul clinches the appeal with the pointed declaration that now, this dispensation, is that accepted time, that day of salvation, at last come, to which all the prophets pointed, for which all the saints of God had longed from the beginning of the world. It is therefore again, leaving the figure, that this same Apostle declares that our Lord and Saviour has for the whole length of this dispensation assumed the post of the Ruler of the Universe, in order that all things may be administered for the fulfilment of His great redemptive purpose; in order that all things may, in a word, be made to work together for good to those that love Him. In a word, God is a husbandman in this season which we call the inter-adventual period; and the crop that He is planting and watering and is to reap is His Church.

No wonder our Saviour declared the Kingdom of Heaven like unto a sower who went forth to sow; who spread widely the golden grain, and reaped it too, a harvest of many-fold yield. For God's husbandry cannot fail. Other husbandmen are not in this wholly unlike their hired servants: they plant and water,—but they cannot compel life; and what may be the results of their labour they know not. The floods may come, the winds may blow, the sun may parch the earth, the enemy may destroy the grain. But God gives the increase. It is therefore that the Redeemer sits on the throne, that floods and rain and sun—all the secret alchemy of nature—may be in His control, that "all things shall work together for good to them that love Him." There, I say, is our encouragement. Christianity is the work of God, the work He has set Himself to do in this age in which we live. As we go forth as His servants to plant and water, we may go upheld by a deathless hope. The harvest cannot fail. When the sands of time run out and God sends forth His reapers, the angels, there will be His harvest thick on the ground—and the field is the world. The purpose of God stands sure. We may not be called to see the end from the beginning. But if God calls you and me to plant or to water, it is our blessed privilege to labour on in hope.

All this is just because the result is not ours to produce or to withhold. It is God that gives the increase. As Christianity is the work which God has set before Himself to accomplish in this age; so Christianity in the world and in the heart is a work which God alone can accomplish. It is not in the power of any man to make a Christian, much less to make the Church—that great organized body of Christ, every member of which is a recreated man. Why, we cannot make our own bodies; how much less the body of Christ! If in this work Paul was nothing and Apollos nothing, what are we, their weak and unworthy successors! This is the second great lesson our passage has to teach us; or, rather, we may better say this is the great lesson it teaches, for it was just to teach this that it was written. The fault of the Corinthians was that they had forgotten who was the husbandman, who alone gave the increase. Hence their divisions, making Christ only the share of one party, while others looked to Paul or Apollos or Cephas, just as if they stood related to the harvest in something of the same way as Christ. Nay, says Paul, Christ alone is Lord of the harvest. It is God alone who can give the increase.

Paul had reason to know this in his own experience. He knew how he had been gathered into the Kingdom. He was soon to acquire new reason for acknowledging it, in that journey of his from Ephesus to Macedonia, in which, while his heart was elsewhere, all unknown to himself God was leading him in triumph, compelling ever-increasing accessions to his train. Nor did he ever stint his declaration of it. Thus, take that passage (Eph. 2:10), where he, completing a long statement of God's gracious dealings with Christians in quickening them into newness of life, without obscurity or hesitation outlines the whole process as a creative work of God. "For it is by grace that ye are saved, through faith: nor is this of yourselves, it is God's gift; not of works, lest some one should boast. For we are His workmanship—creatures—created in Christ Jesus unto good works, which God hath afore prepared that we should walk in them." This is Paul's teaching everywhere: that as it is God who created us men, so it is God who has re-created us Christians. And the one in as direct and true a sense as the other. As He used agents in the one case—our natural generation (for none of us are born men without parents), so He may use instruments in the other, our spiritual regeneration (for none of us are born Christians where there is no Word). But in both cases, it is God and God alone who gives the increase.

Let us not shrink from this teaching; it is the basis of our hope. Though we be Pauls and Apolloses we cannot save a soul; though we be as eloquent as Demosthenes, as subtle as Aristotle, as convincing as Plato, as persistent as Socrates, we cannot save. And though we be none of these, but a plain man with lisping lips, that can but let fall the Gospel truth in broken phrases—we need no eloquent Aaron for our prophet. We need only God for our Master. It is not we who save, it is God; and our place is not due to our learning or our rhetoric or our graces, it is due to the honouring of God, who has mercy on whom He will have mercy, and whom He will, He hardens.

Hence we have the great consolation of knowing that the responsibility of fruitage to our work does not depend absolutely on us. We are not the husbandman; the field is not ours; its fruitage is not dependent on or limited by our ability to produce it. All Christian ministers are but God's "agents" (for that is the ultimate implication of the term used), employed by Him to secure His purposes; God's instruments, God's tools. It is God who plans the cultivation, determines the sowing and sends us to do it. Now this is to lower our pride. Some ministers act as if they owned the field; they lord it over God's heritage. More feel as if they had produced all the results; made, "created," the fruit. They pride themselves on the results of their work and compare themselves to others' disadvantage with their neighbours in the fruits granted to their ministry. This is like a reaper boasting over the sower or ploughman, as if he had made the crop it has been allowed him to harvest. Others feel depressed, cast down, at the smallness of the fruitage it has been allowed them to see from their work, and begin to suspect that they are not called to the ministry at all, because the work given them to do was not reaping. And herein is the consolation: just because we are not doing God's work for Him, but He is doing His own work through us; just because we do what work He appoints to us; not we but He is responsible for the harvest. All that is required of stewards is that they be found faithful.

Hence—and this is the final and greatest consolation to us as ministers—it ought to be a matter of indifference to us what work God gives us to do in His husbandry. Reaping is no more honourable than sowing; watering no less honourable than harvesting. Men disturb themselves too much over the kind of work they are assigned to, and can scarcely believe they are working for God unless they are harvesting all the time. But in the great organized body of labour it is as in the organized body to which Paul compares the Church later: if all were reapers, where were the sowing, where were the cultivating, where the watering? And if no sowing, and no watering, where were the reaping? It is not ours to determine what work we are to do. It is for us to determine how we do it. For none of us will fail of our wages and the wages are not proportioned to the kind of work, as if the reaper because he reaped would have all the reward. The field is not his, and the harvest is not his. He does not get the crop because he reaped it. He gets just what the planter and waterer get, his wages.

Wages, I say, not proportioned to the kind of work, but to the labour he does. Each one, says Paul, shall receive "his own reward" according to his own labour. The amount of labour, not the department of work, is the norm of our reward. What a consolation this is to the obscure workman to whom God has given much labour and, few results; reward is proportioned to the labour, not the results! And this for a very good reason. God apportions the work on the one hand and gives the increase on the other. But it is we that do the labour. And, of course, we are rewarded according to what is done by us, not God. Let us then labour on in whatever sphere God gives it to us to labour, content, happy, strenuous, untiring, determined only to do God's work in God's way; not seeking to intrude into work to which He has not appointed us, and not repining because He has given us this work and not that. Each one to his own labour, and God the rewarder of all!

COMMUNION IN CHRIST'S BODY AND BLOOD

1 Cor. 10:16, 17:—"The cup of blessing which we bless, is it not a communion of the blood of Christ? The bread which we break, is it not a communion of the body of Christ? Seeing that we, who are many, are one bread, one body: for we all partake of the one bread."

THERE are few injunctions as to methods of interpretation more necessary or more fruitful than the simple one, Interpret historically. That is to say, read your text in the light of the historical circumstances in which it was written, and not according to the surroundings in which, after say two thousand years, you may find yourself. And there is no better illustration of the importance of this injunction than the interpretations which have been put on the passages in the New Testament which speak of the Lord's Supper. Little will be hazarded in saying that each expositor brings his own point of view to the interpretation of these passages, and seems incapable of putting himself in the point of sight of the New Testament writers themselves. He who reads the several comments of the chief commentators, for instance, on our present passage, quickly feels himself in atmospheres of very varied compositions, which have nothing in common except their absolute dissimilarity to that which Paul's own passage breathes. If we are ever to understand what the Lord's Supper was intended by the founder of Christianity to be, we must manage somehow to escape from the commentators back to Paul and Paul's Master. Here then is a specially pressing necessity for interpreting according to the historical circumstances.

The allusion to the Lord's Supper in our present passage, it will be noted, is purely incidental. The Apostle is reasoning with the Corinthians on a totally different matter; on a question of casuistry which affected their every-day life. Immersed in a heathen society, intertwined with every act of the life of which was some heathen ordinance, the early Christian was exposed at every step to the danger of participating in idolatrous worship. One of the places at which he was thus menaced with what we may call constructive apostacy was in the very provision for meeting his need of daily food. The victims offered in sacrifice to heathen divinities provided the common meat-supply of the community. If one were invited to a social meal with a friend, it was to an idol's feast that he was bidden. If he even bought meat in the markets, it was a portion of the idol sacrifice alone that he could purchase. How, in such circumstances, was he to avoid idolatry?

The Apostle devotes a number of paragraphs in the first Epistle to the Corinthians to solving this pressing question. The wisdom and moderation with which he deals with it are striking. His fundamental proposition is that an idol is nothing in the world, and meats offered to idols are nothing after all but meats, good or bad as the case may be, and are to be used simply as such, on the principle that the earth is the Lord's and the fullness thereof. But, side by side with this, he lays a second proposition, that any involvement in idol worship is idolatry and must be shunned by all who would be servants of the One True God and His Son. Whether any special act of partaking of meats offered to idols involves sharing an idol worship or not, will depend mainly on the subjective state of the participant; and his freedom with respect to it is conditioned only by his debt of love to his fellow Christians, who may or may not be as enlightened as he is. The Corinthians appear to have been a heady set and the Apostle evidently feels it to be the more pressing need to restrain them from hasty and unguarded use of their new-found freedom. He does not urge them to treat the idols as nothing. He urges them to avoid entanglement with idolatrous acts. And our passage is a part of his argument to secure their avoidance of such idolatrous acts.

The argument here turns on a matter of fact which would be entirely lucid to the readers for whom it was first intended, but can be fathomed by us only by placing ourselves in their historical position. Its whole force depends on the readers' ready understanding of the nature and significance of a sacrificial feast. This was essentially the same under all sacrificial systems. The eating of the victim offered whether by the Israelite in obedience to the Divine ordinances of the Old Covenant, or by the heathen in Corinth, meant essentially the same thing to the participant. Therefore the Apostle begins the passage by appealing to the intelligence of his former heathen readers and submitting the matter to their natural judgment. He asks them themselves to judge whether it is consistent to partake in the sacrificial feasts of both heathen and Christian. This is the gist of the whole passage.

Participation in a sacrificial feast bore such a meaning, stood in such a relation to the act of sacrifice itself, that it was obvious to the meanest intelligence that no one could properly partake both of the victims offered to idols and of that One Victim offered at Calvary to God. To feel this as the Corinthians were expected to feel it, we must put ourselves in their historical position. They were heathen, lived in a sacrificial system, and knew by nature what participation in the victim offered in sacrifice meant. We may put ourselves most readily in their place by attending to what Paul says here of the Jewish sacrificial feasts, which he adduces as altogether parallel, so far, with the significance of the same act on heathen ground. "Consider Israel after the flesh," he says, "are not those that eat the sacrifices, communicants in the altar?" Here it is all in a nut-shell. All those who partake of the victim offered in sacrifice were by that act made sharers in the act of sacrifice itself. They—this body of participants—were technically the offerers of the sacrifice, to whose benefit it inured, and whose responsible act it was. Whether a Greek, sharing in the victim offered to Artemis or Aphrodite, or a Jew sharing in the victim offered to Jehovah, or a Christian sharing in that One Victim who offered Himself up without spot to God, the principle was the same; he who partook of the victim shared in the altar—in the sacrificial act, in its religious import and in its benefits. Is it not capable of being left to any man's judgment in these premises, whether one who shared in the One Offering of Christ to God could innocently take part in the offerings which had been dedicated to Artemis?

The point of interest for us to-day in all this turns on the implication of this argument as to the nature of the Lord's Supper in the view of Paul and of his readers in the infant Christian community at Corinth. Clearly to Paul and the Corinthians, the Lord's Supper was just a sacrificial feast. As such—as the Christians' sacrificial feast—it is put in comparison here with the sacrificial feasts of the Jews and the heathen. The whole pith of the argument is that it is a sacrificial feast. And if we wish to know what the Lord's Supper is, here is our proper starting point. It is the sacrificial feast of Christians, and bears the same relation to the sacrifice of Christ that the heathen sacrificial feasts did to their sacrifices and that the Jewish sacrificial feasts did to their sacrifices. It is a sacrificial feast, offering the victim, in symbols of bread and wine, to our participation, and signifying that all those who partake of the victim in these symbols, are sharers in the altar, are of those for whom the sacrifice was offered and to whose benefit it inures.

Are we then to ask, what is the nature of the Lord's Supper? A Babel of voices may rise about us. One will say, It is the badge of a Christian man's profession. Another, It is the bloodless sacrifice continuously offered up by the vested priest to God in behalf of the sins of men. History says, briefly and pointedly, it is the Christian passover. And, so saying, it will carry us back to that upper room where we shall see Jesus and His disciples gathered about the passover meal, the typical sacrificial feast. There lay the lamb before Him; the lamb which represented Himself who was the Lamb slain before the foundation of the world. And there was the company of those for whom this particular lamb was offered and who now, by partaking of its flesh, were to claim their part in the sacrifice. And there stood the Antitype, who had for centuries been represented year after year by lambs like this. And He is now about to offer Himself up in fulfilment of the type, for the sins of the world! No longer will it be possible to eat this typical sacrifice; typical sacrifices were now to cease, in their fulfilment in the Antitype. And so our Lord, in the presence of the last typical lamb, passes it by and taking a loaf, when He had given thanks, broke it and said, *This*—I hope the emphasis will not be missed that falls on this word, *this*—no longer the lamb but this loaf—is my body which is broken for you; this do in remembrance of me. And in like manner also the cup after supper, saying, This cup is the New Covenant in my blood; *this* do in remembrance of me; for as often as ye eat this bread and drink this cup, ye proclaim the Lord's death, until He come.

How simple, how significant, the whole is, when once it is approached from the historical point of view. The Lord's Supper is the continuation of the passover feast. The symbol only being changed, it is the passover feast. And the eating of the bread and drinking of the wine mean precisely what partaking of the lamb did then. It is communion in the altar. Christ our Passover is sacrificed for us; and we eat the passover whenever we eat this bread and drink this wine in remembrance of Him. In our communing thus in the body and the blood of Christ we partake of the altar, and are made beneficiaries of the sacrifice He wrought out upon it.

The primary lesson of our text to-day is, then, that in partaking of the Lord's Supper we claim a share in the sacrifice which Christ wrought out on Calvary for the sins of men. This is the fundamental meaning of the Lord's Supper as a sacrificial feast. The bread and wine of the Lord's Supper represent the body and blood of Christ; but they represent that body and blood not absolutely but as a sacrifice—as broken and outpoured for us. We are not to puzzle our minds and hearts by asking how His blood and body become ours; how they, having become ours, benefit us; and the like. We are to recognize from the beginning that they were broken and outpoured in sacrifice for us, and that we share in them only that, by the law of sacrificial feast, we may partake of the benefits obtained by the sacrifice. It is as a sacrifice and only so that we enter into this union.

A second lesson of our text to-day is, that in the Lord's Supper we take our place in the body of Christ's redeemed ones and exhibit the oneness of His people. The text lays special stress on this. The appeal of the Apostle is that by partaking of these symbols Christians mark themselves on the one hand off from the Jews and heathen, as a body apart, having their own altar and sacrifice, and, on the other hand, bind themselves together in internal unity, for "by all having a share out of the one loaf, we who are many are one body because there is (only) one loaf." The whole Christian world is a passover company gathered around the paschal lamb, and by their participation in it exhibiting their essential unity. When we bless the cup of blessing, it is a communion in the blood of Christ; when we break the loaf, it is a communion in the body of Christ; and because it is one loaf, however many we are, we are one body, as all sharing from one loaf. The Apostle very strongly emphasizes this idea of communion here; and it is accordingly no accident that we have so largely come to call the Lord's Supper the "Communion." It is the symbol of the oneness of Christians.

Another lesson which our text to-day brings us is that the root of our communion with one another as Christians lies in our common relation to our Lord. We are "many," says the Apostle; that is what we are in ourselves. But we "all" —all of this "many"—are "one"—one body, because there is but one loaf and we all share from that one loaf. Christ is one and we come into relations of communion with one another only through our common relation to Him. The root of Christian union is, therefore, the uniqueness, the solity of Christ. There is but one salvation; but one Christian life; because there is but one Saviour and one source of life; and all those who share it must needs stand side by side to imbibe it from the one fountain.

THE SPIRIT OF FAITH

2 Cor. 4:13:—"But having the same Spirit of faith, according to that which is written, I believed, and therefore did I speak; we also believe, and therefore also we speak."

THIS verse is a declaration on the Apostle's part of the grounds of his courage and faithfulness in preaching the glorious Gospel of Christ. The circumstances which attended his proclamation of this Gospel were of the most oppressive. In the preceding verses we have a picture of them which is drawn by means of a series of declarations which rise, one after another, to a most trying climax. He says that in the prosecution of his work he is in every way pressed, perplexed, pursued, smitten down. Here is a vivid picture of the defeated warrior, who is not only pressed by the foe, but put at his wits, ends,—not merely thus discouraged but put to flight,—not merely pursued but smitten down to the earth. A lurid picture of the befallings of Paul as a minister of Christ amid the spiritual conflicts on this side and that, in Galatia and in Corinth! Nevertheless things have not come to an end with him. Side by side with this series of befallings he places a contrasting series which exhibits the marvellous continuance of the Apostle in his well-doing, in spite of such dreadful happenings to him. Though he is in every way pressed yet he is not brought to his last straits; though he is in every way perplexed, yet he has not gone to despair; though he is pursued yet he is not overtaken; though he is actually smitten down he is yet not destroyed.

In the prosecution of Paul's work as a minister of Christ, there is thus a marvellous co-existence of experiences the most desperate and of deliverances the most remarkable. It is as if destruction had continually befallen him; yet ever out of destruction he rises afresh to the continuance of his work. In this remarkable contrast of his experiences the Apostle sees a dramatic re-enactment of Christ's saving work, who died that He might live and might bring life to the world. In it he sees himself, he says, ever re-enacting the putting to death of Jesus, that the life also of Jesus may be manifested in his body. As Jesus died and rose again, so he daily dies in the service of Christ and comes to life again; and so, abiding in life, he is ever delivered to death for Jesus' sake that the life also of Jesus might be manifested in his mortal flesh. Oh, marvellous destiny of the followers of Christ, in the very nature and circumstances of their service to placard before the world the great lesson of the redemption of Christ—the great lesson of life by death; to manifest thus to all men the life of Jesus and the life from Jesus springing constantly out of His death. Thus the very life-circumstances of Paul become a preached Gospel. They manifest Christ and His work for souls. They manifest it. For the dying is for Paul and the life for his hearers.

Now Paul gives a twofold account of those circumstances in which he preached the Gospel. He assigns them ultimately to the purpose of God. This great treasure of the glorious Gospel has been put into such earthen vessels for the very purpose of more fully manifesting its divine glory. In contrast with its vehicle, the power of the message is all the more discernible. It is just that the exceeding greatness of its power may be seen to be of God that it is delivered to men in vessels whose exceeding weakness may be apparent. On the other hand, that these earthen vessels are able to endure the strain put upon them in conveying these treasures, is itself from God. Paul attributes it to God's upholding power, operating through faith. That in the midst of such trials he is enabled to endure; that though smitten down continuously he is not destroyed; that though dying daily he still lives with a living Gospel still on his lips; it is all due to the support of his firm conviction and faith. "So then, it is death that worketh in us, but life in you, and having the same Spirit of faith, according as it is written, I believed and, therefore, did I speak; we also believe and therefore speak, since we know that He that raised up Jesus shall raise us up also with Jesus, and shall present us with you." Here are the sources of the Apostle's strength and of his courage. It is only because of his firm faith in the Gospel he preaches that he can endure through the trials into which its service has immersed him. With a less clear conviction and less firm faith in it, he would long ago have succumbed to the evils of his life and his lips have long ago become dumb. But he believed; and, therefore, though earth and hell combined to destroy him, he could not but speak. Let earthly trials multiply; beyond the daily deaths of earth there was an eternal life in store for him; and the more he could rescue from death to that life, the more multiplied grace would redound to increased thanksgiving and abound to God's glory. In the power of this faith the Apostle can face and overcome the trials of life.

There are many important lessons that may come to us from observing this declaration of the Apostle's faith.

Beginning at the remoter side we may be surprised to observe that he seeks the norm of his faith in the Old Testament saints. "Having the same Spirit of faith," he says, "according as it is written, I believed, and therefore did I speak"—referring for the model of faith back to the words of this hero Psalmist. Now we may not be accustomed to think of the Old Testament saints as the heroes of faith. The characteristic emotion of Old Testament religion, we are accustomed to say, was awe or even fear. The characteristic expression of it is summed up in the term, "The fear of the Lord." The New Testament on the other hand is the dispensation of faith. And if we have consideration only for the prevailing language of the Old Testament this is true enough. The word "faith" is scarcely an Old Testament word; it occurs but twice in the English Old Testament, and it is disputable whether on either occasion it fairly—or at least fully—represents the Hebrew. Even the word "to believe" applied to divine things is rare in the Old Testament.

But the word and the thing are different matters. And it may be doubted whether the conceptions of awe, fear, and of faith, trust, are so antagonistic as is commonly represented. Certainly reverence and faith are correlative conceptions. A God whom we do not fear with religious reverence, we cannot have such faith in as the Apostle's. And certainly the New Testament writers do always look to the Old Testament saints as the heroes of faith. This is the burden of one of the most magnificent passages in the New Testament, the eleventh chapter of Hebrews. And of others too. It is the faith of Abraham which is the standing model of faith to both Paul and James; and it is he who both in the subjective and objective senses of the word is represented to us as the Father of the Faithful. Let it be allowed that these heroes of faith lived in the twilight of knowledge; knowledge and faith stand in relation to one another, but are not the measure of one another. If there can be no faith where there is no knowledge, on the other hand it is equally true that the realm of dim knowledge is often the region of strong faith,—for when we walk by sight, faith has no place. No; he that believes in Jesus whom he has seen, must yield in point of heroism of faith and the blessedness promised to it, to him who having not seen yet has believed. Those great men of God of old, not being weak in faith, believed in the twilight of revelation, and waxing strong, died in faith; and we could wish nothing higher for ourselves than that we might be like them in their faithful faith.

It is observable next that the Apostle attributes the faith of the Old Testament heroes to whom he would direct our eyes as the norm of faith, to the work of the Holy Ghost. He felicitates himself not merely on having the same quality of faith with them. He looks deeper. The ground of rejoicing in their fellowship is that he shares with them the "same Spirit of faith." "Having the same Spirit of faith," he says. It may be doubted, once again, if we should have naturally spoken in this way. We may be accustomed to think of the Holy Spirit as an esssentially New Testament possession; and to conceive, in a more or less formulated manner, of the saints of the Old Testament as left to their own native powers in their serving of God. Heroes of faith as they were, it would be peculiarly difficult, however, to believe that they reached the height of their pious attainment apart from the gracious operations of the Spirit of God. Or shall we say that only in New Testament times men are dead in sin, and only in these days of the completed Gospel and of the New Covenant do men need the almighty power of God to raise them from their spiritual death?

Certainly the Bible lends no support to such a notion. Less is said of the gracious operations of the Spirit in the Old Testament than in the New, but to say less of it is one thing and its absence is quite another. And there is enough in the Old Testament itself—by prayer of Psalmist that the Holy Spirit should not be taken away from him, by statement of historian that through the Spirit God gave this one and that one a new heart, by assurance of prophet that the Spirit of God is the author of all right belief and of all good conduct,—to assure us that then, too, on Him depended all the exercises of piety, to Him was due all the holy aspirations and all the good accomplishments of every saint of God. And certainly the New Testament tells us in repeated instances that the Holy Spirit was active throughout the period of the Old Dispensation, in all the varieties of activities which characterize the New. The difference between the two lies not in any difference in the utter dependence of men on Him, or in the nature of His operations, but in their extent and aim with reference to the life of the Kingdom of God. Our present passage is one of those tolerably numerous New Testament ones in which the gracious operations of the Spirit in the Old Covenant are assumed. Paul here tells us that the faith of the Old Testament saints was the product of God's Holy Spirit; and he claims for himself nothing more than what he asserts for them. "Having the same Spirit of faith," he says. He is content—nay, he is full of joy—to have the same Spirit working faith in him that worked faith in them. He claims no superiority in the matter. If he has a like faith, it is because he is made by God's grace to share in a like fountain of faith. The one Spirit who works faith is the common possession of them and of him; and therein he finds his highest privilege and his greatest glory. What David had of the operations of the Spirit, that is what Paul represents as the height of Christian privilege to possess.

It may not be wholly needless to observe further the naturalness of Paul's ascription of faith to the working of the Holy Spirit—whether under the Old or the New Dispensation. He means to express the confidence he has in the glorious Gospel which he proclaims. He does not say, however, simply "having a confident faith." He says, "having the Spirit of faith," the same Spirit of faith which wrought in the Psalmist. So much was faith to him the product of the Spirit that he thinks of it in terms of its origin. Clearly to him, no Spirit, no faith. Faith is, therefore, most absolutely conceived by the Apostle as the product not of our own powers but of the Spirit of God, and it is inconceivable to him that it can exist apart from His gift.

We may sometimes fall short of the Apostle's conception and fancy that we can—nay, that we must—first believe before the Spirit comes to us. No, it is the Spirit who gives faith. Faith is the gift of God in its innermost essence; and the Apostle continually thanks God for it, as His gift. We find it enumerated in Gal. 5:23 among the fruits of the Spirit; in 1 Cor. 12:7 we find it among the gifts which the Spirit distributes to men. In our present passage it is emphasized as the work of the Spirit, by its being used as a characterizing description of the Spirit. We do not describe or define a thing by something which is common to it and others. The possession of a vertebral column will not define a man; and we should never use the designation of vertebrate as a synonym of man. That the Spirit is called the "Spirit of faith" means that faith does not exist except as His gift; its very existence is bound up in His working. Just as we call Him the Spirit of life, the Spirit of holiness, and the like, because all life comes from Him and all holiness is of His making, so, when Paul calls Him the Spirit of faith, it is the evidence that in Paul's conception all faith comes from Him.

It matters not where faith is found—under the Old Testament or the New—in Psalmist or in Apostle—or in the distant believers of the Twentieth Century,—it matters not what degree of faith is present, weak, timid faith which scarcely dares believe in its own existence, or strong faith that can move mountains,—it matters not what of divine things be its object, God as our Ruler and Governor, the Scriptures as His Word, Christ as our Saviour; if it exists at all, in any time, in any degree, the Holy Ghost has wrought it. He is the Spirit of faith and faith is His unique product.

Finally, it will be of interest to us who are charged with the same duty of proclaiming the Gospel of salvation with which the Apostle was charged, to take especial note that he attributes that supreme faithfulness and steadfastness which pre-eminently characterized his work in the Gospel to a Spirit-wrought faith in the Gospel which he preached. The secret, he tells us, of his ability to continue throughout his dreadful trials in the work to which he had been called; the secret of his power to faint not, that is, not to play the coward, but to renounce the hidden things of shame and refuse to walk in craftiness or handle the Word of God deceitfully; the secret of his power to preach a simple Gospel in honest faithfulness in the face of all temptations to please men, and to preach the saving Gospel in the face of all persecution—was simply that he had a hearty and unfeigned faith in it. When we really believe the Gospel of the Grace of God—when we really believe that it is the power of God unto salvation, the only power of salvation in this wicked world of ours—it is a comparatively easy thing to preach it, to preach it in its purity, to preach it in the face of a scoffing, nay, of a truculent and murdering world. Here is the secret—I do not now say of a minister's power as a preacher of God's grace—but of a minister's ability to preach at all this Gospel in such a world as we live in. Believe this Gospel, and you can and will preach it. Let men say what they will, and do what they will,—let them injure, ridicule, persecute, slay,—believe this Gospel and you will preach it.

Men often say of some element of the Gospel: "I can't preach that." Sometimes they mean that the world will not receive this or that. Sometimes they mean that the world will not endure this or that. Sometimes they mean that they cannot so preach this or that as to win the respect or the sympathy or the acceptance of the world. The Gospel cannot be preached? Cannot be preached? It can be preached if you will believe it. Here is the root of all your difficulties. You do not fully believe this Gospel! Believe it! Believe it! and then it will preach itself! God has not sent us into the world to say the most plausible things we can think of; to teach men what they already believe. He has sent us to preach unpalatable truths to a world lying in wickedness; apparently absurd truths to men, proud of their intellects; mysterious truths to men who are carnal and cannot receive the things of the Spirit of God. Shall we despair? Certainly, if it is left to us not only to plant and to water but also to give the increase. Certainly not, if we appeal to and depend upon the Spirit of faith. Let Him but move on our hearts and we will believe these truths; and, even as it is written, I believed and therefore have I spoken, we also will believe and therefore speak. Let Him but move on the hearts of our hearers and they too will believe what He has led us to speak. We cannot proclaim to the world that the house is afire—it is a disagreeable thing to say, scarcely to be risked in the presence of those whose interest it is not to believe it? But believe it, and how quickly you rush forth to shout the unpalatable truth! So believe it and we shall assert to the world that it is lost in its sin, and rushing down to an eternal doom; that in Christ alone is there redemption; and through the Spirit alone can men receive this redemption. What care we if it be unpalatable, if it be true? For if it be true, it is urgent.

NEW TESTAMENT PURITANISM

2 Cor. 6:11–7:1.—"Our mouth is open unto you, O Corinthians, our heart is enlarged. Ye are not straitened in us, but ye are straitened in your own affections. Now for a recompense in like kind (I speak as unto my children), be ye also enlarged. Be not unequally yoked with unbelievers: for what fellowship have righteousness and iniquity? or what communion hath light with darkness? And what concord hath Christ with Belial? or what portion hath a believer with an unbeliever? And what agreement hath a temple of God with idols? for we are a temple of the living God; even as God said, I will dwell in them, and walk in them; and I will be their God, and they shall be my people. Wherefore come ye out from among them, and be ye separate, saith the Lord, and touch no unclean thing; and I will receive you, and will be to you a Father, and ye shall be to me sons and daughters, saith the Lord Almighty. Having therefore these promises, beloved, let us cleanse ourselves from all defilement of flesh and spirit, perfecting holiness in the fear of God."

It is not easy to determine with exactitude the circumstances which gave occasion to this striking paragraph, which stands out so prominently on the pages of Second Corinthians as almost to separate itself from its context and form a whole of its own. Of two things, however, we may be reasonably sure. There was a party in the Corinthian Church which we may perhaps fairly describe as the party of the Libertines; and out of this party, too, there had arisen an opposition to the leadership of Paul, and a tendency to accuse him of insincerity and self-seeking in his work at Corinth. We must picture the Apostle, therefore, as compelled to defend himself and the purity of his ministry, in this Epistle, not only against a narrow Judaistic formalism, with its touch not, taste not, handle not, but also against a loose worldliness which was inclined to adapt its Christianity to the usages current in the heathen society about it. Differing in everything else, both parties agreed in unwillingness to subject themselves unreservedly to the guidance of Paul; and in defence of themselves represented him as acting towards the church from interested motives.

Bearing this in mind, we may readily understand how, when in the course of his self-defence the Apostle has been led to dwell upon the hardships he had suffered in the prosecution of his mission, he should break off suddenly with an appeal to his Corinthians to separate themselves from heathen practices and points of view, and themselves to walk worthily of the Gospel they professed. "See, O Corinthians," he exclaims, "how freely I am speaking to you, how widely open my heart is to you. You find no constraint on my part with reference to you; the only constraint there is between us lies in your own hearts. Give me what I give you—I am speaking as to my children; open wide your heart to me. Seek not your standards of life in the unbelievers about you. Remember who you are and what you should be as organs of the Holy Spirit; and be not content until you have attained that perfect holiness which becomes the children of God." So the Apostle transforms his defence of his ministry into an exhortation to his readers, in which he again exercises his ministry of love in a disinterested plea to them to walk worthily of the Gospel of holiness.

Dr. James Denney in his commentary on this Epistle, published in "The Expositor's Bible," heads the chapter in which he deals with this section, "New Testament Puritanism." On the face of it, this is a very good designation for it. The note of Puritanism, which is the note of separation, certainly throbs through the section. "Come ye out from among them and be ye separate, saith the Lord"—that assuredly expresses the very essence of Puritanism. Or, perhaps, we may more precisely say that it is exactly that conformity with the world which, above all things, Puritanism dreads, that Paul here declares, almost with indignation, to be inconceivable in a true Christian. "For what fellowship," he demands "is there between righteousness and iniquity? Or what communion is there for light with darkness? Or what concord of Christ with Belial? Or what part has a believer with an unbeliever? Or what agreement has a temple of God with idols?" Here certainly is Puritanism at the height of its expression.

Nevertheless we must be careful not to give the

Apostle's exhortation a turn which does not belong to it. The Apostle is not here requiring of Christians a withdrawal from the world, considered as the social organism; and most certainly he is not asking of them to segregate themselves into a community apart, between which and the mass of men there shall be no, or only the least possible, intercourse. On a former occasion, when addressing these same readers, he does indeed command them not to keep company with fornicators. But he immediately adds that he means this aloofness only as a disciplinary measure towards sinning brethren. If a man who is called a Christian be a fornicator, *Christian* fellowship must be withdrawn from him, that it may be brought home to him that a man cannot be both a Christian and a fornicator. But, says the Apostle, I do not mean that you should not associate with fornicators of the world; else you would need to remove out of the world—a thing, he implies, which would be manifestly impossible; and let us add, for the leaven which is placed in the world, grossly inconsistent with the prosecution of its function in the world, which is to leaven the whole mass. And if we will scrutinize our present passage closely we shall quickly see that the separation which the Apostle is urging here, too, is not separation from men but from evil—applying, indeed, to the Corinthians in the way of exhortation what our Lord prayed for in behalf of

His followers, not that they should be taken out of the world, but that they should be kept from the evil of the world. The exhortation: "Come ye out from among them and be ye separate, saith the Lord," is immediately followed by the explanation, "And touch no unclean thing." And the whole exhortation closes with a poignant prayer that they may "cleanse themselves from every defilement." It is not from their fellow-men that the Apostle would have Christians hold themselves aloof; it is from the sin and shame, the evil and iniquity, which stains and soils the lives of so many of their fellow-men. This is the Apostolic variety of Puritanism.

The opposite impression is perhaps fostered among simple Bible readers by the phrase which stands in the forefront of the exhortation in our English Bibles: "Be not unequally yoked together with unbelievers." This certainly appears at first sight to represent any commerce with unbelievers as indecorous and to forbid it on that account. This impression is wholly due, however, to the awkwardness of the rendering given to an unusual Greek phrase. This Greek phrase is an exceedingly awkward one to render; and I am not sure that it is possible to give it an English equivalent which will convey its exact sense. The figure which underlies it is, no doubt, the yoking together, in the bizarre way of the East, incongruous animals for labour, say an ox and an ass.

And the English version is a very creditable effort to bring the figure home to the English reader; for surely such a yoking of incongruous animals together is a very unequal one. Yet the English phrase fails to express the exact shade of meaning of the Greek term. This does not say: "Be not unequally yoked together with unbelievers" but rather, "Become not bearers of an alien yoke along with unbelievers"—or, in other words, "Take not on yourselves a yoke that does not fit you, in order to be with unbelievers." You see the point is very different from that which is often taken from the English phrase. What is forbidden is not that we should company with unbelievers; but that we should adopt their points of view and their modes of life. It is a question, in other words, not of intercourse, but of standards. What the Apostle is concerned about is not that his converts lived in social communion with their heathen neighbours; this he would have them do. What he is concerned about is that they took their colour from the heathen neighbours with whom they lived. He wished them to be leaven and to leaven the lump; they were permitting themselves rather to be leavened; and this made him indignant with them.

We see, then, that the Apostle's urgency here is against not association with the world, but compromise with the worldly. Compromise! In that one word is expressed a very large part of a

Christian's danger in the world. We see it on all sides of us and in every sphere of life. We must be all things to all men, we say, perverting the Apostle's prescription for a working ministry; for there was one thing he would on no account and in no way have us be, even that we may, as we foolishly fancy, win the more; and that is, evil. From evil in all its forms and in all its manifestations he would have us absolutely to separate ourselves; the unclean thing is the thing he would in no circumstances have us handle. Associate with the world, yes! There is no man in it so vile that he has not claims upon us for our association and for our aid. But adopt the standards of the world? No! Not in the least particular. Here our motto must be and that unfailingly: No compromise!

The very thing which the Apostle here presses upon our apprehension is the absolute conflict between the standards of the world and the standards of Christians; and the precise thing which he requires of us is that in our association with the world we shall not take on our necks the alien yoke of an unbeliever's point of view, of an unbeliever's judgment of things, of an unbeliever's estimate of the right and wrong, the proper and improper. In all our association with unbelievers, we, as Christian men, are to furnish the standard; and we are to stand by our Christian standard, in the smallest particular, unswervingly. Any departure from that standard, however small or however desirable it may seem, is treason to our Christianity. We must not, in any case, take the alien yoke of an unbeliever's scheme of life upon our necks.

Interesting to us as this exhortation itself is, and important beyond expression for the guidance of our lives, it, perhaps, yields in interest to the grounding which the Apostle supplies for it in an explanation of the essential springs of a Christian's life. This grounding he gives in a series of rhetorical questions, by means of which he sets forth the absolute contrariety of the Christian's and the unbeliever's points of view, sources of judgment and principles of conduct. The ordering of these questions is such that they begin by setting over against one another the obvious contradictions of righteousness and iniquity; and then proceed in a series of rapid and convincing antitheses until they end in setting the believer and the unbeliever over against one another as the embodiment respectively—at least in principle—of those contradictions, righteousness and iniquity. "What fellowship have righteousness and iniquity," the Apostle demands in support of his exhortation not to take on themselves the alien yoke of unbelievers, "or," he continues, "what communion has light with darkness? or what concord has Christ with Belial? or what portion has a believer with an unbeliever? or—

clinching the whole matter with a reference to the source of the entire contrast—what agreement has a temple of God with idols?"

The force of the appeal lies in the necessary—and inevitable—identification, as we go on through the series, of each pair with the preceding; so that with the fundamental "righteousness" is identified the light; and, of course, Christ; and because he is Christ's, the believer, who is the temple of the living God: and with the fundamental iniquity is identified the darkness, Belial, and the unbeliever, because he is the worshipper of idols and partaker of the idolatrous point of view. The reason, then, why a Christian must not take on himself the alien yoke of unbelievers is just because it is to him alien; he is in and of himself, because a believer in Christ and, therefore, a temple of the living God, a different, a contrary, an opposite kind of being from the unbeliever; and it is, therefore, incongruous in the extreme for him to put his neck in the same yoke with an unbeliever, seek to live on the same plane, or consent to order his life or to determine questions of conduct by his standards, in any degree whatever.

Now it is just in this contrast drawn by the Apostle between the believer and the unbeliever—in its firmness, its clearness, its extremity if you will—that we discern the most interesting, the most important, teaching of our passage. According to the Apostle, obviously, there are two kinds of men in the world, believers and unbelievers. And these two kinds of men stand over against one another in complete, not only contrast, but contradiction; as complete contradiction as righteousness and iniquity. There can be no compromise between them any more than between righteousness and iniquity. There may be intercourse—mutual action and reaction—but never compromise.

The Apostle is far from saying, of course, that in any given individuals this fundamental contradiction is fully manifested. It finds its complete manifestation only in the abstract—in the contrariety of righteousness and iniquity; and in the full concrete manifestation of righteousness and iniquity in Christ and Belial. Between Christians and unbelievers the manifested contradiction is only relative. Compromise there ought not to be—in principle there can not be—but compromise in fact there is. Christians are not, like Christ, pure embodiments of righteousness; they require exhortation not to admit iniquity into the governing principles of their life. Alas, alas, though they are temples of the living God, they are far, far from having no commerce with idols. The Apostle recognizes all this. On his recognition of it he founds the urgent exhortation of our passage. Nevertheless he founds this exhortation also on the fact that this contradiction exists in principle—that Christians, like Christ, their Lord, are in principle righteousness, and that unbelievers are, like Belial, their lord, in principle iniquity. It is because Christians are thus in principle holy and unbelievers are thus in principle unholy that he proclaims that it is incongruous that Christians should adopt their standards of life from unbelievers, who are not merely their opposites but their contradictories; so that there can be no mean between them but every one must be one or the other.

There are then, according to the Apostle, two kinds of men in the world, believers and unbelievers; and these two kinds of men stand in contradiction to each other. One may conquer and eliminate the other; but there can be no mixture between them. The ultimate source of the fundamental difference between them he finds in the indwelling in Christians of the Holy Ghost: "Or what agreement hath a temple of God with idols? For *we*"—emphatic here, in contrast with the unbelievers, "as for us, *we* are a temple of the living God." The influx of the Holy Spirit into the heart constitutes, then, a new humanity. Over against those who have not the Spirit, and who are, therefore, as another Scripture puts it, earthly, sensual, devilish,—the children of Belial, as this Scripture suggests,—those who have the Spirit are a new creation, with new standards and new powers of life alike. There can be no compromise between such opposites. It has become customary among theologians to speak of these two kinds of men as the men of nature and the men of the palingenesis; or as it is now becoming fashionable to call them, once born and twice born men. They who are born of the flesh are fleshly; and they only who are born of the Spirit are spiritual; and to the spiritual man belong all things. The message which Paul brings to us in this passage is, then, that we who are spiritual, because we are believers in Christ Jesus, have in principle the righteousness which belongs to Him, and though it may not yet appear what we shall be, we must in all our walk comport ourselves as what we are, the temples of the living God, having the powers and potencies of a new, even a Divine, life within us. The ultimate reason why the Christian man is not to compromise with the world is, because as a Christian man, he is a new creature, born from above, with the vigour of the Divine life itself moving in him and with an entirely new life-course marked out for him. Why should—how can—such an one put his neck incongruously within the yoke of worldly policy or self-seeking, or evil-living with unbelievers; and seek to deflect his Spirit-given powers to a life on this lower plane and for these ignoble ends? O, says the Apostle, O, Christian men, this is surely impossible to you; do you not see that in the power of your new life you are to—you must—take an utterly new course, directed to a new goal, and informed with new aspirations, hopes and strivings?

On the basis of this great declaration the Apostle erects, then, his exhortation. Nor is he content to leave it in a negative, or merely inferential form. In the accomplishment of the Spirit-filled life he sees the goal, and he speaks it out in a final urgency of exhortation into which he compresses the whole matter: "Having, therefore, such promises as *these* (note the emphasis), beloved," he says, "let us purify ourselves from every defilement of flesh and spirit and perfect holiness in the fear of God." It is perfection, we perceive, that the Apostle is after for his followers; and he does not hesitate to raise this standard before the eyes of his readers as their greatest incitement to effort. They must not be content with a moderate attainment in the Christian life. They must not say to themselves, O, I guess I am Christian enough, although I'm not too good to do as other men do. They must, as they have begun in the Spirit, not finish in the flesh; but must go on unto perfection.

What are they to cleanse themselves from? *Every* defilement—every *kind* of defilement—not only of the flesh but of the spirit. Aiming at what? At the completion of holiness in the fear of God! The Apostle does not tell them they are already holy—except in principle. They obviously were not already holy—except in principle. They were putting their necks in the alien yoke of unbelieving judgments. They were contenting themselves with heathen standards. They were prepared to say, O, the Lord doesn't ask all that of us; O, there is nothing wrong in this; O, I guess it will be enough if I am as good as the average man; O, you can't expect me to live at odds with all my neighbours; O, these things are good enough for me. Such compromises with the spirit of the world are wrong; and the Apostle tells his readers plainly that they are unworthy of them as Christian men. They were, if not born to better things, yet certainly born anew to better things. Let them turn their backs on all such inconsistencies and live on their own plane of life as believers, believers in Christ, Christ the Light, Christ our Righteousness. Let them remember they are temples of the living God and have no commerce with idols.

No, they were not perfect—except in principle. But in principle, they were perfect; because they had within them the principle of perfection, the Spirit of the Most High God. Let them walk in accordance with their privileges, then, on a level with their destiny. Hear God's great promise. And having these promises, cleanse yourselves; O, cleanse yourselves, the Apostle cries; cleanse yourselves from every defilement whether of flesh or spirit, and so perfect—complete, work fully out to its end—holiness in the fear of God. Let your standard be the holiness of the indwelling Spirit whose temples you are. Let your motive be, not merely regard to the good of others, much less to your own happiness, but joy in God's gracious promises. Let your effort be perfect sanctification of soul and body, cleansing from all defilement. Let your end be, pleasing God, the Holy One. In a word, says the Apostle in effect, here as elsewhere: O, ye Christians, work out your own salvation in fear and trembling, for it is God who is working in you the willing and the doing according to His own good pleasure.

We perceive, thus, in the end that the thing Paul is zealous for is the holiness of his followers. For in their holiness he sees the substance of their salvation. We are saved by Christ and only Christ; and Christ is righteous; both for us and unto us. For it is by grace that we are saved, through faith; and that not of ourselves, it is the gift of God—not out of works, lest we should boast, but unto good works, which God has afore prepared that we should walk in them. And if we walk not in them—are we, then, saved? Holiness of life is, I repeat, precisely the substance of salvation, that which we are saved to, that in which salvation consists. If then we are in Christ Jesus, shall we not live like Christ Jesus? "If we are in the Spirit, shall we not walk by the Spirit?" This is Paul's final exhortation to us; since we are

Christ's, and the Spirit dwells in us and we are the temples of the living God, let us be careful of good works; let us, remembering the great promises He has given us, cleanse ourselves from all defilement of body and soul; and let us perfect holiness in the fear of God, so that we approve ourselves His children and He will be to us as a Father and we shall be to Him sons and daughters.

PAUL'S GREAT THANKSGIVING

Eph. 1:3–14, especially 3—"Blessed be the God and Father of our Lord Jesus Christ, who hath blessed us with every spiritual blessing in the heavenly places in Christ."

If we would know how Paul felt about the gospel of the grace of God, by which he was saved, we could not do better than go to "the great thanksgiving" with which he opens the epistle to the Ephesians. The epistle to the Ephesians is, of course, not singular in beginning with a thanksgiving to God. That is Paul's customary method of beginning his letters. But it is, perhaps, singular in the marvellous richness and fervor of the thanksgiving with which it begins. And this is, perhaps, due to what we might have thought an entirely unimportant circumstance. The Apostle was accustomed to draw the theme of his thanksgiving from the special conditions and attainments of those he was addressing. But, unlike his other letters, this was addressed neither to an individual friend and fellow-worker, nor to a separate church with its special circumstances fresh in the Apostle's mind. There was in this case, therefore, no particular subject of thanksgiving, peculiar to the person or church addressed, pressing in on the Apostle's mind and requiring mention. He was thrown back on what was common to Christians to thank God for in behalf of his readers. And that is as much as to say he was thrown back on the great fundamental theme of the Gospel. Now, Paul's fervour always rises when he is face to face with the first principles of the Gospel.

What Paul returns thanks to God for here, is nothing less than the salvation in Christ. And with what magnificence of diction as well as depth of feeling and comprehensiveness of view he deals with it! The salvation in Christ involves, naturally, the saving action of the whole triune God: and it is easy to make out a trinitarian distinction in the parts of this long ascription of praise to God for His salvation. Many expositors have, therefore, so divided it. And in any event it is useful to note that there is described to us here the loving activity of God the Father in salvation (in verses 3–6), of God the Son (in verses 7–12), and of God the Holy Spirit (in verses 13–14). This successive adduction of the work of the persons of the trinity in salvation would seem, however, only an inevitable incident of any full description of the process of salvation; for in it all three persons of the trinity are, of course, concerned. And it is more useful to us, therefore, as an indication of the place which the doctrine of the trinity held in the mind of the Apostle, than as a principle of division of the thanksgiving before us. They gravely err who imagine that the trinity is only rarely or incidentally alluded to in the New Testament. On the contrary, it forms the underlying presupposition of the entire account of salvation given in the New Testament; and its elements are continually cropping out in the New Testament descriptions of the saving process. It lies in the very nature of the case, therefore, that a trinitarian suggestion should be visible through this description of the salvation in Christ.

The principle of arrangement in the present instance would seem, however, to be what we would call chronological, rather than economical. We would seem to be following more closely the natural lines of the development of the passage, if we note that Paul traces in it the salvation in Christ for which he blesses God, consecutively, in its preparation, execution, publication and application: in its preparation (verses 4–5), its execution (verses 6–7), its publication (verses 8–10), and its application (verses 11–16), both to Jews (verses 11–12) and to Gentiles (verses 13–14). Thus he brings before us the whole ideal history of the salvation in Christ, from eternity to eternity—from the eternal purpose as it formed itself in the loving heart of the Father, to the eternal consummation when all things in heaven and earth shall be summed up in Christ as under one head, and He shall be ready to restore the now perfected kingdom to the Father, that God may again be all in all. So looked upon, this splendid passage exhibits lucidly its true character as a compressed history of the kingdom of God in the world—an apostolic precis of human history conceived from the point of view of the Divine activity in the establishment and development and consummation of the kingdom.

Let us observe how the contemplation of the unrolling of this great historical process affects the Apostle's own mind and heart. This is revealed to us in the intense fervour that informs the whole passage—which is not a measured expression of the Apostle's thanks to God, but can be literally described as an inextinguishable burst of praise. Its keynote is struck in the opening word—"Blessed!" Note the reiteration of the term: "*Blessed* be God who hath *blessed* us with every spiritual *blessing!*" It is easy to perceive where Paul's mind and heart were when he was writing down these words. When a man's lips can frame only this one word—"Blessing, blessing, blessing!" we know what is in his heart. We should not fail to observe the ingenious, and more than ingenious, for it is the ingenuity of the heart, correlation of the term "Blessed" here, as applied to God, with the same term as applied to man. Paul blesses God because God has so highly blessed man: only, God blesses with deeds while man can bless Him only with words. But the thing to be especially observed is the joyful gratitude, the delighted wonder, the swelling praise that fills the Apostle's heart, as he contemplates what man has received in the salvation of Christ. He thinks and speaks of it as summing up in itself every conceivable good. Blessed be God! he cries. Why? Because He hath blessed us! How? With every possible blessing! For that is what this outburst of praise means. Every conceivable blessing, says Paul, is poured out on us in the salvation in Christ. And the form of the language shows that he means this to the uttermost.

As the Apostle goes on to describe the blessings received in the salvation in Christ, it would almost seem as if his pen had run away with him. Only it is not a matter of the pen, but of the heart: it is not a question of words, but of the feelings. But it must needs be confessed that the Apostle has so accumulated phrases at this point in the fervour of his emotions of gratitude and praise that it is very difficult to follow him in his heaped-up epithets. He is not content to say that in the salvation in Christ, God has blessed us with "every kind of blessing." He adds two further characterizations which seem to pile Pelion on Ossa and which distress us as we unavailingly strive to rise to the height of the great argument. "Blessed be God," he cries, "who hath blessed us—in every kind of spiritual blessing—in the heavenlies—in Christ." What are we to make of this chain of threefold enhancement?

No wonder the commentators are divided as to how the successive clauses are to be related to one another. When the heart speaks, there is such a fullness of meaning that the analyzing understanding stands sometimes aghast at the task set it. Are we, it asks, to take these clauses in one continuous string, each qualifying the immediately preceding? Or, are we to take them as parallel to one another, each further explaining, in the light of the preceding, the one matter of the nature of the blessing adverted to? In other words, is this what Paul praises God for—"that He has blessed us in the salvation in Christ with every kind of Spirit-given blessing that is in the heavenly places in Christ": so that he affirms that all the blessings that heaven contains are poured out on us by the Spirit, nay, that all the blessings deposited in Christ, Christ the exalted Conqueror of sin and death, seated now in heaven, clothed with all power in heaven and earth in behalf of His people, His body, His church, are lavished on us by His Spirit sent forth to minister to the heirs of salvation? Or is it rather this that the Apostle praises God for—"that He has blessed us with every possible kind of blessing that is given by the Spirit of God—that is to say with specifically heavenly things, supernatural things, those precious heaven-born gifts which are so much greater and more to be desired than any earthly things—that is to say, rather, with Christ himself, in whom are hidden not only all the treasures of knowledge and wisdom, but of blessing as well, and who is Himself so much greater than all His gifts that in Him are summed up all and more than all that we can mean by every kind of blessing"? One or the other of these things is what Paul seems to have meant. It is hard to say which: and it is probable that expositors will always differ as to which.

It does not seem to be of much importance, to be sure, after which fashion we analyze this great utterance of a full heart. For in either case, has not Paul said everything that could be said, to declare the blessing that has come to men in the salvation in Christ the supremest blessing man can conceive, nay, as "what eye hath not seen, nor ear heard, and what hath entered not into the heart of man, what God hath prepared for them that love him?" As he permits what God has prepared for them that love Him to display itself before his astonished eyes, Paul is overwhelmed with a sense of the blessing it brings to sin-laden men. What wonder if we are overwhelmed with his description of what he saw! What God has prepared for them that love Him! Ah! here is the key-note of the passage. It is all of God. It is not of our deserving: it is not of our doing. It is all of God. It is, therefore, that Paul blessed God for it all with such fervour of language. Were it of man, in any of its items, so far the voice of his praise would be stilled. And it is, therefore, that he simply sows his expressions of grateful praise with asseverations of the origin of all our blessings in Christ in God's gracious purpose, and with acclamations of praise to Him alone for its gift. The fundamental note in all Paul's praise is the note of "soli Deo gloria." All that comes to man in this salvation is of the grace of God alone, a grace prepared of God in eternity past, poured out on us now in the sovereign work of the Spirit, and to abide on us to the eternities to come in accordance with His gracious purpose—all to the praise of the glory of His grace. It is for this cause, says the Apostle, that when he heard that his readers now believed in Christ, he turned his eyes in thanksgiving to God—because to believe in Christ is of God, and he that believes in Christ is in the hands of His unutterable grace. It is obviously only another way of saying that "if God be for us, there is none who can be against us." And it is this thought that moves the Apostle with the deepest emotion of praise.

SPIRITUAL STRENGTHENING

Eph. 3:14–19, especially 16:—"That he would grant you, according to the riches of his glory, that ye may be strengthened with power through his Spirit in the inward man."

THIS certainly may be fairly called one of the great passages of the Bible. Note the series of great topics which are adverted to in it: the inward strengthening of the children of God by the Holy Ghost, the continual abiding of Christ in their hearts, their rooting and grounding in love, their enlargement in spiritual apprehension, even to the knowledge of the unknowable, their filling with all the fullness of God. Surely here is a catalogue of great things for God's people! These great topics do not lie on one level, however, set side by side as parallel facts, but are exhibited in special relations the one to the other. Paul is praying here for these high blessings to descend on the Ephesian Christians. But he does not pray for them simply as a bunch of blessings, arbitrarily selected to be on this occasion sought at the great Father's hands—the Father of these Ephesian Christians too, because He is the God of the Gentiles as well as of the Jews, and from Him every fatherdom derives its name. Here are rather a connected body of blessings which go naturally together, one being the ground and another the effect of the one great thing he craves for his readers.

The central thing he prays for is spiritual strengthening. "I bow my knees to the Father that He may give to you to be strengthened by His Spirit in respect to the inner man." Spiritual strengthening, then, that is the main thing that he prays for. By the mere term "spiritual strengthening" two things might be suggested to us. We might think of spiritual as distinguished from physical strengthening. Or we might think of strengthening by the Spirit as distinguished from some earthly agency. The Apostle's prayer includes both ideas. He prays that we may be strengthened in the inner man; that is, for the strengthening of our spirit, in distinction from the body. And he prays that we may be strengthened with respect to the inner man by God's Spirit; that is, for the Divine strengthening of our inward man. And this, I say, is the substance of his prayer—that we may be strengthened with respect to the inner man by the Spirit of God. All else is descriptive of this and tells us what it is, and what it results in; and so enhances our idea of what spiritual strengthening is.

First, Paul tells us somewhat further what it is. It is identical, he tells us, with the abiding of Christ by faith in our hearts. Of course it is not absolutely certain what the relation of this second clause is to its predecessor. It might express the aim or end of the spiritual strengthening, or (what comes to practically the same thing) its result, as well as (as we should take it), its more precise explanation. As it is followed by a series of expressly telic clauses, formally introduced by the proper telic particle, it would seem most natural to take it as epexegetical of the preceding clause. "I bow my knees to the Father, . . . that He may give to you, according to the riches of His glory, to be strengthened with might as to the inner man—to wit, that Christ may abide in your hearts by faith." To be sure, the sense would not be essentially different if we took it otherwise—to the end that, or so that, Christ may abide in your hearts by faith. In the one case it tells what the spiritual strengthening consists in—it is identical with the abiding of Christ in the heart; in the other, what it eventuates in,—it issues in the abiding of Christ in the heart. In either case the thing to be noted is that it is not the coming of Christ into the heart that is spoken of, but His abiding in the heart; and that it is just this idea that receives the emphasis in the sentence, the position of the words being such as to throw a strong stress on "abiding."

Two things result from this. The first is, that Christ is supposed to have already entered the hearts of those whom the Apostle is praying for. It is not a question of His coming but of His abiding. The Apostle is not praying that his readers should be converted; but, presuming their conversion, that they may be spiritually strengthened. The second result is that the spiritual strengthening is contingent on, or let us rather say, is dependent on the abiding presence of Christ in their hearts. The indwelling Christ is the source of the Christian's spiritual strength. This is, of course, not to set aside the Holy Spirit. But he has read his New Testament to little purpose who would separate the Holy Spirit and Christ: Christ abides in the heart by the Spirit. The indwelling of the Holy Ghost is the means of the indwelling of Christ and the two are one and the same great fact. We are strengthened in the inner man with might by the Holy Spirit, because by the operation of the Spirit in our hearts, Christ abides there—thus and not otherwise. And here we learn then the source of the Christian's strength. Christ is the ultimate source. His indwelling is the ground of all our strength. But it is only by the Spirit—the executive of the Godhead in this sphere too—that Christ dwells in the heart. It is the Spirit that strengthens us, and He so strengthens us that He gives us "might" in our inner man. The way He does this is by forming Christ within us.

The Apostle is one of the most fecund writers extant, and thus it happens that he does not leave the matter even there. It is by the Spirit that Christ dwells in us—that is the objective fact.

But there is a subjective fact too, and the Apostle does not fail to touch it—it is by our faith, too, that Christ dwells in us. "That Christ may abide in your hearts by your faith," he says. He does not say "by faith" merely, though he might well have said that, and it would have covered the whole necessary idea. But, in his habitual fullness of expression, he puts in the article, and thus implies that he recognizes their faith as already existent. They are Christians, they already believe, Christ is already dwelling in them by faith; he prays that He may abide in them by their faith. The stress is everywhere laid on continuance. May God strengthen your inner man, he says, by His Spirit. That is to say, he adds, may that Christ whom ye have received into your hearts by faith abide continuously in your hearts by that faith of yours. As much as to say, Christ is brought into your hearts by the Holy Ghost. He abides there by that Holy Ghost. May God thus continually strengthen your hearts by His Spirit, and that, even with might. I pray to Him for it, for it is He that gives it. But do not think, therefore, that you may lose hold on Christ. It is equally true that He abides in your hearts by your faith. When faith fails, so do the signs of His presence within: the strengthening of the Spirit and the steady burning of the flame of faith are correlative. As well expect the thermometer to stand still with the temperature varying as the height of your faith not to index the degree of your strength. Your strength is grounded in the indwelling Christ, wrought by the Spirit by means of faith.

Thus we have laid before us the sources of the Christian's strength. It is rooted in Christ, the Christ within us, abiding there by virtue of the Spirit's action quickening and upholding faith in us. And only as by the Spirit our faith is kept firm and clear, will Christ abide in us, and will we accordingly be strong in the inner man.

Such then is the nature and source of the Christian's strengthening. What does it issue in? How does it exhibit itself? Briefly, the Apostle tells us, in love and knowledge. "May God grant you," he says, "to be strengthened as to the inner man by His Spirit, that is, the abiding presence of Christ in your hearts, to the end that being rooted and grounded in love, you may be fully enabled to apprehend. . . ." The end of the prayer is, then, expansion of spiritual apprehension. May God grant that you may be strengthened with might . . . to the end that you may be full of strength to apprehend. The appropriate result of strengthening is that they may have full strength. The Apostle accumulates words expressive of strength to enhance the idea. He uses three separate words, but all impinging on the one idea, that he wishes his readers by the Holy Spirit's operations to be raised to the capacity of spiritual apprehension indicated. "God grant that ye may be empowered (relative and manifested power) with might (inherent general power), with which ye may have full strength (as your own endowment) to apprehend. . . ." This then is the proximate end of the prayer: Expansion of heart for the apprehension of spiritual things. "God grant that you may be strengthened with might by the Holy Spirit in the inner man, that you may have full strength to apprehend. . . ." These things to be apprehended are too great for man's natural powers He must have new strength from on high given him to compass them. He may by the Spirit be raised to a higher potency of apprehension for them. God grant it to you!

What are these things? The Apostle speaks quite generally about them. He says "that ye may have full strength to apprehend with all the saints, what is the breadth and length and height and depth. . . ." His mind is for the moment not on the thing itself but on the bigness of the thing. It is because the thing is so big that they need strengthening in the inner man before they have full strength to apprehend it. Yet it is not something for these special readers alone, but for all Christians. This strengthening the Apostle asks for is the heritage of the saints. The Apostle prays not that we may be expanded in spiritual apprehension by these great ideas, but up to them. This expanding is not to be done by them, but by the Holy Ghost. To enhance our conception of how big they are, he gives us a sample,—for that the last clause here is not adjoined as a parallel but as a subordinate clause seems indicated by the particle by which it is adjoined and as well by the concluding words "unto the whole fullness of God," which appear to return to a quite general idea: that ye may have full strength to apprehend with all saints what is the breadth and length and height and depth and to know the "knowledge-surpassing love of Christ."

Here is a sample of the broad and wide and high and deep knowledge to apprehend which we need to have our minds stretched: the quality of the love of Christ. It is too high for us; we cannot attain unto it. Do we wonder that the thing the Apostle prays for is that we should be strengthened in the inner man by the Spirit of God, that we may have full strength to apprehend this? Do we wonder that he speaks of this and such knowledge as too broad and wide and high and deep for us, not to be apprehended save by him in whose heart Christ abides? If, indeed, Christ be in us—then, possibly, we may know Christ without us. But surely in no other way. Here then is the gist of the matter, as to the end of our strengthening in the inner man. It is to give us full strength for the apprehension of these great and incomparable mysteries of our faith.

But in that fullness of the Apostolic speech to which we have already alluded, Paul does not content himself with simply saying this. He so says it as both to suggest an intermediate step in the attainment of this large spiritual apprehension, and to indicate a still higher goal. He suggests, I say, an intermediate step. He does not say simply, "God grant you spiritual strengthening, that you may have enlarged spiritual apprehension." He says, "God grant you spiritual strengthening that, having been rooted and grounded in love, you may have enlarged spiritual apprehension." Here then is an intermediate link between the strengthening by the Spirit and the enlargement of our spiritual understanding. It is "love." The proximate effect of the Spirit's work in empowering the inner man with might is not knowledge but love; and the proximate cause of our enlarged spiritual apprehension is not the strengthening of our inner man, but love. The Spirit does not immediately work this enlargement of mind in us; He immediately works love, and only through working this love, enlarges our apprehension. The Holy Ghost "sheds love abroad in our hearts." Love is the great enlarger. It is love which stretches the intellect. He who is not filled with love is necessarily small, withered, shrivelled in his outlook on life and things. And conversely he who is filled with love is large and copious in his apprehensions. Only he can apprehend with all saints what is the breadth and length and height and depth of things. The order of things in spiritual strengthening is therefore: (1) the working by the Spirit of a true faith in the heart, and the cherishing by the Spirit of this faith in a constant flame; (2) the abiding of Christ by this faith in the heart; (3) the shedding abroad of love in the soul and its firm rooting in the heart; (4) the enlargement of the spiritual apprehension to know the unknowable greatness of the things of Christ.

There is yet one further step, for even this spiritual apprehension is not its own end. "God grant," says the Apostle, "that you may be empowered with might by the Spirit, so to have full strength to apprehend the great things of God"—but he does not stop there. He adds "to the end that you may be filled unto the whole fullness of God." Here is the goal at last. And what a goal it is! We were weak—for it was "when we were without strength" that Christ died for us. We are to be strengthened, strengthened by the Spirit, by means of the constant indwelling of Christ, the source of all good. We are to be strengthened so as to know, to know the great things of God (read some of them in the parallel passage, Col. 1:11). But not that we may know for the mere sake of knowing. What good would such a bare knowing do us? We are to know that we may be "filled unto all the fullness of God." Look at this standard of fullness. "Unto"—not "with"—it is the standard, not the material. God's fullness is not to be poured into us; we are to be raised toward that standard of fullness, not in one particular but in all—unto the whole fullness of God. It may mean unto the fullness which God possesses; or it may mean unto the fullness which He provides. It may mean either that the enlargement of our spiritual apprehension is a means toward obtaining all the wonderful goods that God has in store for us; or it may mean that by it we shall be brought to a height of attainment comparable only to His attainments. No matter which it means. It is enough in either meaning for any Christian's hope. But there is no reason to doubt that it does mean the greatest thing: we shall be filled unto the whole fullness of God. We shall be like Him, and like Him only of all Beings in the universe. It is a giddy height to which our eyes are thus raised. No wonder we need spiritual strengthening to discern the summit of this peak of promise.

Of course it does not mean that we are to be transmuted into God, so that each of us will be able to assert a right to a place of equality in the universe with God. Of course, again, it does not mean that God is to be transfused into us, so that we shall be God, part of His very essence. It means just what it says, that God presents the standard towards which we, Christian men, are to be assimilated. We are to be made like Him, holy as He is holy, pure as He is pure. Our eyes, even in the depths of eternity, will seek Him towering eternally above us as our unattainable standard towards which we shall ever be ascending, but we shall be like Him; He and we shall belong to one class, the class of holy beings. We shall no longer be like the Devil, whose children we were until we were delivered from his kingdom and translated into the kingdom of God's dear Son. No more shall we be what we were as men in this world, still separated from God by a gulf of moral difference, a difference so great that we are almost tempted to call it a difference of kind and not merely of degree. Nay, we shall, perhaps, be more like God than even the holy angels are; in our head, Christ Jesus, we shall be in Him who in a pre-eminent sense is like God. The process of the "filling" may take long; it is but barely begun for most of us in this life; but that is the standard and that the goal—"we shall be filled unto the fullness of God"; and it shall never cease. Such is the goal of the spiritual strengthening spoken of in our text.

THE FULLNESS OF GOD

Eph. 3:14–19, especially v. 19:—"That ye may be filled unto all the fullness of God."

THE Epistle to the Ephesians is the poem among the Epistles. Its whole fabric is wrought in a grandeur of language, corresponding to the loftiness of its thought. The main subject of the Epistle is God's infinite and unspeakable mercy to the Gentiles, and the Apostle busies himself with two chief ends. These are (1) to beget in his readers an adequate sense of the immensity of their privilege, in the mercy of God, in that He has chosen them before the foundation of the world, redeemed them in Christ and called them by the Spirit out of their former Gentile darkness and alienation to be sharers in the glorious light of the Gospel, and to be admitted into the very household of God; and (2) to quicken them to a proper apprehension of the duties that grow out of their changed relation and life.

The noble prayer of the Apostle's, which the present passage constitutes, stands at the end of the first section of the letter. In that section he has described in the most lofty and glowing language the privileges which have been so freely granted his readers by God, in Christ. That section had been, it is true, closed at the end of the second chapter; and the Apostle begins the third chapter with a clause meant to make the transition to the second subject that weighed on his heart, the duties, arising from their very condition, pressing upon his readers. But he has no sooner begun the transition than he interrupts himself to give expression to a thought which struggled within him for utterance, concerning the relation of his own apostleship to the announcement of God's unsearchable riches to the Gentiles. Having unburdened his soul with praise to God for calling him to be the instrument in His hands for working out this glorious broadening of the boundaries of His Church, he resumes the sentence that had been broken off and makes the transition to the declaration of the duties of his readers, once more resumed, by means of a fervent prayer to God for their perfection in the Christian life.

This prayer is one of the most wonderful passages ever penned even by this wonderful Apostle. Look at it in its parts.

First, we observe to whom the prayer is offered. It is to "the Father," name of love and gratitude. But note how the Apostle expresses his sense of what this word "Father" means when applied to the all-merciful and all-glorious God. He calls Him not merely "the Father" but "the Father from whom every fatherhood in heaven and earth is named." His is not a figurative fatherhood;

He is not addressed as Father because we find some things in Him which remind us of the tenderness and love of our parents and so apply to Him, as in a figure, the name we have learned to love in them. On the contrary, His is the normal fatherhood; His is not derived by figure from theirs, but theirs is the poor and broken shadow of His. He is the Father of our Lord and Saviour Jesus Christ: the gloss, though a gloss, is a correct interpretation, and the closeness and intimacy and love of that relation is the norm from which every fatherhood in heaven and earth is named. What we know of fatherhood—dear as the name has become to us through our earthly relations—is but a faint shadow of what He, the true Father, first of Christ and then of us in Christ, is to His children. After his glowing outline of what God had done for his readers—Gentiles as they were, born in sin and hitherto living in sin—in receiving them into His very household and making them its members, not friends merely but His children, the Apostle's fervour cannot address Him in less full recognition of His glorious fatherhood than this: the Father of fathers, the normal, perfect, ideal father, of which all other fatherhood is but a broken and poor imitation,—"the Father, of whom every fatherhood in heaven and earth is named."

Next, let us observe the measure of the gifts prayed for: "according to the riches of his glory."

No earthly measure, but only according to the richness of that glory of the great God pictured in His majesty, power and love in all the preceding chapters. The gifts of Him who giveth to all men liberally, were according, not to their desert, not to their prospective usefulness, not even according to their needs which are greater than either, but away above all these, according to the riches of God's glory—the glory of the Father from whom every fatherhood in heaven and earth is named.

Next, observe the thing that is prayed for, in this marvellous prayer. And here there is a beginning and a middle and an end. The blessing which the Apostle craves for the Ephesians is nothing less than this: that they may be filled unto all the fullness of God, that is, that all of God's inestimable treasures of spiritual blessings —life, strength, love, holiness,—shall be poured out immeasurably unto them,—that they should be filled with all those spiritual perfections which assimilate them to the fullness of God.

The Apostle craves nothing less than that divine perfection which belongs to children of God, for his readers. But he knows that God does not deal magically with His children: there are means without which the end is not to be had. And this end of Christian perfection of life and heart, the being holy as God the Father is holy, the being perfect as God is perfect, is not to be had save in the path which God has marked out as leading to the goal. And the Apostle prays not for the goal but for the path which leads to the goal. Knowledge is in order to holiness and it is knowledge of the Gospel for which Paul prays for his readers, that they may by it be enabled to be "filled unto all the fullness of God." He prays that they may "apprehend with all the saints what is the breadth and length and height and depth," and that they may "know the love of Christ that passeth knowledge." It is this love of Christ that he has been speaking to them about for the whole of the Epistle, the love of Christ that led Him to immolate Himself for them before the foundation of the world, that led Him to come into the world and suffer and die for them in the fullness of time, that led Him now that He has been taken up to the Father's right hand to send forth the Spirit to call them inwardly, and the Apostle to call them outwardly. This love of Christ which the Apostle would have them know, in order that they may become holy, is briefly comprehended in the Gospel. And he prays for them to have an adequate apprehension of the riches of the "Gospel," the glad tidings of Christ's love, in order that they may be filled unto all the fullness of God.

But why pray for such knowledge? Is knowledge to be had by prayer, or by publication? Certainly not without publication, and Paul had published it in his long visits in Ephesus and his journeys through Asia; and he had just republished it in the whole of the former part of this Epistle. But such knowledge as he desires for his readers is not to be had by mere publication. It is not merely that they may hear the Gospel, not merely that they may be, in an intellectual and mechanical way, informed that nothing can account for Christ's work but love, love compelling Him to leave His glory behind Him in heaven and come to earth as a servant to save men, that he wishes for them. He wants them to understand, feel, and realize this; in the language of the present passage, to apprehend it in its height and breadth and length and depth: to have a realizing sense of it. For this, something more than mere informing is needed: even a preparation of the heart. Let the husbandman fling the seed never so widely and strew them never so thickly: if there is no prepared soil, how can he hope to have a harvest? So the knowledge which the Apostle desires for his readers is not merely external mind-knowledge, but the real knowledge of full feeling and apprehension; knowledge not of the mere head but of the heart. And for this, something more is needed than the mere proclaiming of the Gospel, which may be grasped in its propositions by the mere mechanical action of the intellect: even a new heart, Spirit-made and Spirit-determined.

Accordingly, this is not all that the Apostle prays for. As this is a means to the end sought, that they may be filled unto all the fullness of God, so there is a means even to this means—that the Spirit should prepare their hearts. And this also he prays for: "that ye may be strengthened with power, through His Spirit, in the inward man; that Christ may dwell in your hearts through faith." This is first. Then, this is to "the end that being rooted and grounded in love, ye may apprehend and know the love of Christ." This is second. Then, this knowledge is in order that we may be "filled unto all the fullness of God." This is the end of all.

We note then first of all, the comprehensiveness of this prayer. Is there any blessing not provided for in it? That our souls may be taken possession of by the Spirit and Christ may dwell in us by faith. That we may have a perfect and realizing knowledge of the Gospel. That we may be filled unto the very fullness of God. Is there any good thing lacking?

Next we note the significant order of the requests. First, the work of the Spirit in the heart; second, the realizing knowledge of the Gospel; third, the Christian life. Men sometimes seek other orders. We hear the cry around us daily of first the life, then the doctrine. Paul's order is, first the doctrine, then the life. We hear the cry around us of first know, then believe.

Paul's order is, first believe, then know. And as this is of theological importance to-day, as well as of practical importance in all days, observe it more closely. We have confined ourselves to broad outlines. Paul, however, writes with such rich fullness that every detail is counted in, in its proper place. What in detail is his order of salvation? Just this: first, the Gospel is proclaimed; secondly, there is the preparation of the heart by the Spirit; thirdly, then faith and Christ's indwelling through faith; fourthly, through this indwelling we grow strong to apprehend the truth of Christ's love; fifthly, by this apprehended knowledge we are enabled to live a Christian life. Search and look: and you will find the same order everywhere in Paul and in the New Testament.

We observe then, finally, that the prayer that Christ may dwell in our hearts by faith is the opening prayer to a series. This is not the end but the beginning: and just because it is a Divine beginning it is a beginning that has in itself the promise and pledge of the end. If we have this we will have all.

(1) It itself rests on a preparation of the heart by the Spirit: "That ye may be strengthened with power through the Spirit in the inward man." The idea here is a communication of power to the soul. We almost seem to be reading the Westminster Confession, for exactly what "power" here means is "ability." The soul then lacks

"ability" until moved upon by the Holy Ghost. The whole soul is there; the Spirit does not give it more faculties. But it is weak. The action of the Spirit is to strengthen it and the strengthening takes place by an infusion of "ability." Now the soul can exercise faith, and it exercises it. Faith lays hold of Christ. And so the enabled soul through faith obtains the indwelling of Christ. This indwelling of Christ is mediated by faith, and the exercise of faith is rendered possible by the strengthening of the soul by the Holy Ghost, by the infusion of "power," "ability."

(2) It consists in the constant presence of Christ in the soul. Presence is predicated of God wherever He manifests Himself, whether in the Temple by the Shekinah or in Israel or in the Church or in the individual. The indwelling of Christ is then the manifestation of Christ's power. The agent by which Christ manifests Himself to the soul is the Holy Ghost. So that the indwelling of Christ and the indwelling of the Spirit is one and the same. But the Spirit does not enter the soul to separate Christ and the believer but to unite them, and hence this indwelling draws Christ and the soul into communion. Christ dwells in us, that is, is present in us, quickening all our activities and making us but members of His body of which He is the directing Head.

(3) It issues hence into all Christian sentiments and activities. First the Apostle mentions

love; "being rooted and grounded in love" is the intermediate step to the apprehension of Christ's love. Love apprehends love. Out of this Christ-filled and Christ-led heart, we are able to see His love and to appreciate it. Hence, next, knowledge. And then, out of this knowledge, life.

Now, observe as to Christ's indwelling: (1) Christ may dwell in us; (2) He dwells in us through faith; (3) His dwelling in us is the source of all our knowledge of the Gospel and of all our Christian walk.

THE SEALING OF THE HOLY SPIRIT

Eph. 4:30:—"And grieve not the Holy Spirit of God, in whom ye were sealed unto the day of redemption."

IT is Paul's custom in his epistles to prepare for exhortation by the enunciation of truth; to lay first the foundation of fact and doctrine, and on that foundation to raise his appeals for conduct. The Epistle to the Ephesians is no exception to this rule. The former chapters of this epistle are a magnificent exposition of doctrine, a noble presentation to Paul's readers of what God has done for them in election and redemption and calling, and of the great privileges which they have obtained in Christ. To this he adjoins, according to his custom, a ringing appeal, based on this exposition of truth and privilege. This appeal to his readers is to live up to their privileges, or, in his own words, to walk worthily of the calling wherewith they were called. The whole latter or practical part of the letter is thus expressly based on the former or doctrinal part. And this is true of the exhortations in detail as well as in general. Paul wrote always with vital connectedness. There never was a less artificial writer, and none of his epistles bears more evident traces than the Epistle to the Ephesians of having been written, as the Germans say, "at a single gush." All here is of a piece, and part is concatenated with part in the intimate connection which arises out of—not artificial effort to obtain logical consecution—but the living flow of a heart full of a single purpose.

Take, as an example, the beautiful appeal of our text. The Apostle is not perfunctorily or mechanically repeating a set phrase, a pious platitude. He is making an appeal, out of a full heart, to just the readers he has in mind, in just their situation; and under the impulse of his own vivid appreciation of their peculiar state and condition. On the basis of the privileges they had received in Christ he had exhorted them generally to an accordant inner and outer conduct; and he had presented these general exhortations both positively and negatively. Now he has come to details. He has enumerated several of the sins to which they in their situation were liable, perhaps, in a special degree, sins of falsehood, wrath, theft, unbecoming speech. Shall they, they, the recipients of this new life and all these Divine favours, fall into such sins? He suddenly broadens the appeal into an earnest beseeching not so to grieve the Holy Spirit of God in whom they were sealed unto the day of redemption. That they, too, had this sealing, had he not just told them? Nay, had he not just pointed them to it as to their most distinguishing grace? It is not by a new or a merely general motive by which he would move their hearts. It is distinctly by the motive to which he had already adverted and which he had made their own. It was because he had taught them to understand and feel that they, even they, Gentiles according to the flesh, had been sealed with the Holy Spirit of promise, as an earnest of their inheritance, and could count on this being a living and moving motive in their minds—or rather it is because he himself felt this great truth as real and as a motive of power—that he adduces it here to move them to action.

If we are to feel the motive power in the appeal as Paul felt it and as he desired his readers to feel it, we must approach it as he approached it and as he desired them to approach it, namely, through a preliminary apprehension and appreciation of the fact underlying the appeal and giving it force. To do this we should approach the consideration of the text under some such logical analysis of its contents as the following. First, we should consider the great fact on which the appeal is based, namely, that Christians have been sealed by the Holy Spirit unto the day of redemption. Secondly, we should consider the nature of this sealing Spirit as the Holy Spirit, and the pain which all sin must bring to Him as the indwelling and sealing Spirit. Thirdly, we should consider the nature and strength of the motive thence arising to us, who are the recipients of His grace, to refrain from the sin which grieves Him, and to seek the life of holiness which pleases Him. Time would fail us, however, on this occasion fully to develop the contents of these propositions. Let us confine ourselves to a few brief remarks on (1) the nature of the basal fact on which Paul founds his appeal, as to our position as Christians; and (2) the nature of the motive which he seeks to set in action by his appeal.

The fundamental fact on which Paul, in the text, bases his appeal to a holy life is that his readers, because Christians, "have been sealed in the Holy Spirit unto the day of redemption." Now, "sealing" expresses authentication or security, or, perhaps, we may say, authentication and security. It is, then, the security of the Christian's salvation which is the fact appealed to; the Christian is "sealed," authenticated as a redeemed one, and made secure as to the completion of the redemption; for he is sealed unto the day of redemption.

The reference to Paul's teaching, in a former chapter, as to the grace given to his readers, will help us to understand the fact here adduced as a motive to action. There we have the fuller statement, that these Christians had had the Word of the Truth, the Gospel of salvation, preached to them; that they had heard it, and had believed it; and then, that they had been "sealed with the Holy Spirit of promise," in other words, the Holy Spirit who works out all the promises to us to fruition; "who," adds the Apostle, "is an earnest of our inheritance," an earnest being more than a pledge, inasmuch as it is both a pledge and a part of the inheritance itself. Then the Apostle tells us unto what we were thus sealed by the Holy Spirit of promise, who is Himself an earnest of our inheritance, namely, "unto the redemption of God's own possession" unto the praise of His glory.

Let us read these great words backwards, that we may grasp their full import. Christians are primarily the purchased possession of God: God has purchased them to Himself by the precious blood of His Son. But, the purchase is one thing, and "the delivery of the goods" another. Their redemption is, therefore, not completed by the simple purchase. There remains, accordingly, a "day of redemption" yet in the future, unto which the purchased possession is to be brought. Meanwhile, because we are purchased and are God's possession, we are sealed to Him and to the fulfilment of the redemption, to take place on that day. And the seal is the Holy Spirit, here designated as the "Holy Spirit of promise" because it is through Him that this promise is to be fulfilled; and the "earnest of our inheritance" because He is both the pledge that the inheritance shall be ours, and a foretaste of that inheritance itself. The whole is a most pointed assertion that those who have been bought by the blood of Christ, and brought to God by the preached Gospel, shall be kept by His power unto the salvation which is ready to be revealed at the last day.

The great fact on which Paul bases his appeal is, therefore, the fact of the security of believers, of the preservation by God of His children, of the "perseverance of the saints"—to use time-honoured theological language. We are sealed, rendered secure, by the Holy Ghost, unto the day of redemption: we are sealed by the Holy Spirit, the fulfiller of the promises, and the earnest of our inheritance, unto the full redemption of us, who are God's purchased possession. The fact the Apostle adverts to is, in a word, that our salvation is sure.

How is this a motive to holiness? Men say that security acts rather as a motive to carelessness. Well, we observe at least that the Apostle does not think so, but uses it rather as a motive to holiness. Because we have been sealed by the Spirit of God, he reasons, let us not grieve Him by sin. Men may think that a stronger appeal might be based on fear lest we fall from the Spirit's keeping; as if Paul should rather have said, Because you can be kept only by the Spirit, beware lest you grieve Him away by sinning. But Paul's actual appeal is not to fear but to gratitude. Because you have been sealed by the Spirit unto the day of redemption, see to it that you do not grieve, bring pain or sorrow to this Spirit, who has done so much for you.

It is not to be denied, of course, that the motive of fear is a powerful one, a legitimate one to appeal to, and one which in its due place is appealed to constantly in the Scriptures. It is, no doubt, a relatively lower motive than that here appealed to by Paul; but as Bishop Doane once truly said, most men are more amenable to appeals addressed to the lower than to those addressed to the higher motives. When men cease to be of a low mind, we can afford to deal with them on a higher plane. I have no sympathy, therefore, with the view, often expressed, that man must not be urged to save his soul by an appeal to his interests, by an appeal to the joys of heaven or to the pains of torment. You all know the old story of how St. Iddo, once, when he journeyed abroad, met an old crone with a pitcher of water in one hand and a torch ablaze in the other, who explained that the torch was to burn up heaven and the water to quench hell, that men might no longer seek to please God because of desire for one or fear of the other, but might be led only by disinterested love. History says that St. Iddo went home wondering. Well he might. For on such teachings as this he should have to forego the imitation of his Lord, who painted to men the delights of the heavenly habitations and forewarned men to fear him who has power after he has destroyed the body also to cast into hell, where, so He says, their worm dieth not and the fire is not quenched. The motives of fear of punishment and vision of reward, though relatively low motives, are yet legitimate motives, and are, in their own place, valuable.

But the Apostle teaches us in our present passage that the higher motives too are for use and in their own place are the motives to use. Do not let us, as Christian ministers, assume that our flocks, purchased by the blood of Christ, and sealed unto the day of redemption by the Spirit, are accessible only to the lowest motives. "Give a dog a bad name," says the proverb, "and hang him." And the proverb may be an allegory to us. Deal with people on a low plane and they may sink to that plane and become incapable of occupying any other. Cry to them, "Lift up your hearts" and believe me you will obtain your response. It is a familiar experience that, if you treat a man as a gentleman, he will tend to act like a gentleman; if you treat him like a thief, only the grace of God and strong moral fibre can hold him back from stealing. Treat Christian men like Christian men; expect them to live on Christian principles; and they will strive to walk worthily of their Christian profession.

So far from Paul's appeal to the high motive of gratitude here, then, being surprising, it is, even on the low ground of natural psychology, true and right. The highest motives are relatively the most powerful. And when we leave the low ground of natural psychology and take our stand on the higher ground of Christian truth, how significant and instructive it is. If the Holy Spirit has done this for me; if He in all His holiness is dwelling in me, to seal me unto the day of redemption, shall I have no care not to grieve Him? Fear is paralyzing. Despair is destruction of effort. Hope is living and active in every limb, and when that hope becomes assurance, and that assurance is recognized as based on the act of a Person, lovingly dealing with us and winning us to holiness, can we conceive of a motive to holiness of equal power?

Brethren, we must not speak of such things historically only. We are not here simply to observe how Paul appealed to the Ephesians, as he sought to move them to holy endeavor; nor to discuss whether or not this is a moving manner of dealing with human souls. His appeal is to us. The fact asserted is true of us,—we are sealed by the Holy Spirit to the day of redemption. He is in us too as the Holy Spirit whom sin offends, and as the loving Spirit who is working in us towards good. Do we feel the pull of the appeal? Shall we listen to and feel and yield to and obey Paul's great voice crying to us down through the ages: "Grieve not the Holy Spirit of God in whom ye were sealed unto the day of redemption"? Commune with your souls on these things to-day!

WORKING OUT SALVATION

Phil. 2:12, 13:—"So then, my beloved, even as ye have always obeyed, not as in my presence only, but now much more in my absence, work out your own salvation with fear and trembling; for it is God who worketh in you both to will and to work, for his good pleasure."

NOTHING could be more fundamental to Paul's conception of salvation than his teaching as to its relation to "works." He is persistently insistent that this relation is that of cause rather than of effect. The "not out of works, but unto good works," of Ephesians 2:9, 10, sounds the key-note of his whole teaching. In "good works," therefore, according to Paul "salvation" finds its realization: the very essence of salvation is holiness of life, "sanctification of the spirit." And equally in "salvation" "good works" find their only root: and it is only on the ground of the saving work of God that men may be hopefully exhorted to good works. As it is pregnantly stated in the passage from Ephesians we have already adverted to, God has prepared beforehand good works, to our walk in which we are introduced by a creative act on His part, in Christ Jesus (Eph. 2:10). Accordingly Paul's epistles (as is the whole New Testament), are full of particular instances of appeals to conduct based on the inception and working in us of the saving activity of God (e.g., 1 Thess. 2:12; 2 Thess. 2:13–15; Rom. 6:2; 2 Cor. 5:14; Col. 1:10; Phil. 1:21; 2:12, 13; 2 Tim. 2:19). Possibly in the words of our text we meet with the most precise expression of this appeal. Here the saint is exhorted to "work out his own salvation" just because "it is God who is the worker in him of both the willing and the doing, in pursuance of His good pleasure." If there is an antinomy involved in this collocation of duty and motive, it is in this passage certainly brought to its sharpest point. There are also many minor matters of interest in the language of the passage, which attract us to its study. Let us try to see briefly just what the Apostle says in it.

It will be useful to bear in mind from the beginning that the exhortation is addressed not to sinners but to saints: it is to "the saints in Christ Jesus" (1:1), that Paul is speaking. That is to say, this exhortation has reference not to entrance into Christian life but to the prosecution to its appropriate goal of a Christian life already entered into. This is already advertised to us by the very verb used. Paul does not say simply "work your salvation," but "work *out* your salvation"—employing a compound verb which throws its emphasis on the end, "bring your salvation to its completion." It is also involved in the contextual connection. This exhortation closes a paragraph which had begun (1:27) with the appeal, "Only let your manner of life be worthy of the gospel of Christ"; and it closes it with a reversion to the same dominant thought. These Philippian readers already stood with the Apostle in the fellowship of the gospel: his earnest desire for them was a complete realization in life of all that the gospel meant. They had entered upon the race; let them run it through to the goal. They had in principle received salvation in believing; let them work this salvation now completely out in life. At the opening of the letter Paul had expressed his confidence that, as God had begun a good work in them, He would perfect it until the day of Jesus Christ (1:6). He now exhorts them to strive to attain the same high end. "Work out your own salvation," i.e., work it completely out, advance it to its accomplishment, bring it to its capstone and crown it with its pinnacles.

Had it not been brought into doubt by some students of the passage, it would seem a work of supererogation to pause to assure ourselves that what Paul has in mind in his exhortation to "work out salvation" is primarily the attainment of ethical perfection. The eschatological reference of "salvation" must not, of course, be obscured. But neither must it be obscured that the pathway that leads to the eschatological goal of salvation is that walk in good works unto which Christians have been created in Christ Jesus, that "fruitage of righteousness" which is through Jesus Christ unto the glory and praise of God, with which the Apostle longs to see the Philippians filled "against the day of Christ" (1:10, 11). When he exhorts his readers at the close of this paragraph "to work out their own salvation," he obviously has the same thing in mind which he had at its beginning, when he exhorted them to "let their manner of life be worthy of the gospel of Christ"; and the same thing which he explains in the course of it to include steadfastness in testimony to the gospel, love to the brethren, humility of mind and the like Christian virtues. In the acquisition and cultivation of such graces they would be "working out their salvation," realizing in life in its ever-growing completeness what is involved in "salvation" as its essential contents.

The form and language in which the exhortation is cast are naturally coloured by the situation in which the writer found himself at the moment and the condition in which he conceived his readers to stand. For the Apostle was no abstract essayist, but wrote out of a burning heart, as a practical man to practical men, eager to meet the actually existent state of affairs. He had himself been interrupted in the midst of his work and cast into prison: he was labouring under deep anxiety lest his violent removal from the care of the infant churches should unfavorably affect their Christian development. He had, therefore, already described at considerable length how his imprisonment had not elsewhere injured the progress of the gospel (1:12 sq.), and had sought to separate the Philippians from dependence on his initiative (1:27). He very naturally reverts to the same consideration now and makes his absence from his hearers only a reason for redoubled exertions on their part, even hinting, perhaps, that they should know that, after all, each man must busy himself with "his own salvation," and the help he can obtain from others must be insignificant. This surely is, in part at least, the account to give of the emphatic pronoun—"work out *your own* salvation"—immediately connected as it is with the reference to the effect which his presence or absence should have on their activity: "not as if (you did so), only because I was present, but now much rather because I am absent, work out your own salvation." It is as much as to say, that the things that have happened to me fall out in your case, too, rather for the furtherance of the gospel: for if you have ever in any measure depended on me, my very removal should stir you up to increased effort—for after all it is *your own* salvation not my joy that is primarily at stake for you. It is possible meanwhile that this emphasis on "your own" may be, in part, due also to a reference back to the work of Christ so touchingly portrayed in the immediately preceding context: if Christ was willing to do and suffer all this for the salvation of *others*, should not you be willing to do and suffer in imitation of Him, for *your own* salvation? But in any case the main account of the emphasis thrown on the words would seem to be found in the reference to his readers' possible over-dependence on Paul's initiative.

One of the chief dangers in which the Apostle had found the Philippians to stand arose from a tendency among them to pride and high-mindedness, or, rather, perhaps, we should say, to party spirit, and to selfishness (2:1–4). It was, therefore, that he was led to devote the early part of this chapter to urging them to beware of faction and vainglory and to cultivate lowliness of mind: and it was on this account that he adduces for their imitation Christ's great example of self-humiliation for the good of others (2:5 sq.). Of course allusion to their most prominent ethical danger could not be absent from this closing exhortation, in which he sums up his desire for their ethical perfection. It is natural, therefore, that the Apostle, after his gracious conciliatory habit, should pause at the outset to recognize the general submissiveness of disposition which his readers had hitherto shown, in accordance with the example of Christ: for the back reference of the words, "even as ye have always submitted," to the "becoming submissive even unto death" of verse 8 is unmistakable. And it is due, doubtless, to the same clause that he throws so strong an emphasis, in the very exhortation itself, on the spirit in which they were to "work out their own salvation," namely, "with fear and trembling," that is to say, with due recognition of their humble estate in the sight of that God whose servants they were, and whose salvation they were now exhorted to use all diligence in realizing.

We must pause a moment on these words, "with fear and trembling." For the immense emphasis that is thrown upon them constitutes them, as has been convincingly pointed out by E. Schaeder, the hinge of the passage. The effect of this emphasis is that Paul does not here exhort his readers so much to "work out their salvation" as to work it out specifically "with fear and trembling." What he says in effect is, "Let it be with fear and trembling that you work out your own salvation." The whole force of the exhortation, in fact, accumulates on these words, "with fear and trembling." It is to the preservation of this state of mind in the working out of their salvation that the Apostle is really urging his readers. Now it is undeniable that there seems something strange in this. Why should the Apostle lay such stress on "fear and trembling" as the characterizing spirit of the Christian effort? Is Christianity, after all, even more than Judaism, which Hegel (though mistakenly) called the religion of fear *par excellence*, just the religion of slavish terror—every step in the cultivation of which is to be driven on by "fear and trembling"? What becomes then of that fundamental tone which resounds through every sentence and word and syllable of this very Epistle to the Philippians—that of "rejoice in the Lord" (3:1)? What harmony can exist between the two exhortations: "Let it be specifically with fear and trembling that ye work out your own salvation," and "Rejoice in the Lord always; again I will say, Rejoice" (4:4)? What union can there be between such carking anxiety and abounding joy, as twin states of heart characterizing the entire Christian walk? It is certainly puzzling to find the Apostle throwing the stress of his exhortation on these words; and it deserves our most careful scrutiny.

This puzzle is only increased when we observe, as we must observe at once on reading the exhortation itself—that is, the twelfth verse—in its context, that Paul's purpose is obviously to encourage not to frighten his readers, to enhearten not to dishearten them in their Christian walk. When we consider the inducements which he brings to bear on them to give force to his exhortation, we cannot believe that its nerve is fear lest they should after all not attain the end, but rather assurance that the end shall be certainly gained. For Paul places this exhortation between the two most powerful encouragements that could possibly be brought to bear upon a Christian's conduct—the example of Christ and the indwelling of the Holy Spirit. "*So then*, my beloved," he says, in introducing the exhortation. And this "so then" looks back upon and takes hold upon that marvellous exposition of the self-abnegation of Christ and His consequent great reward, which the Apostle had given in verses 5–11. "So then"—seeing then that you have this great example so plainly and so powerfully set before you, in imitation of it and inspired by its great lesson—do you "work out your own salvation." This exhortation is, to be sure, broadened beyond the specific application of the premise; the particular exemplary act adduced from Christ's great transaction is His self-abnegation, "accounting others better than Himself"; and the exhortation to the Philippians to "work out their own salvation" includes more than a recommendation of self-abnegation. The logical nexus, of course, lies in the fact that the special fault of the Philippians, fresh in the Apostle's mind as requiring eradication, as they advanced toward Christian perfection, was precisely that high-mindedness which was slow to look on the things of others as well as on their own things; and the special virtues they needed to cultivate in completing their salvation were just those virtues of self-abnegation to which the example of Christ would inspire them. Hence the fitness of this example to their case. But there seems no fitness in it to ground a specific appeal to "fear and trembling" as the proper state of mind in which they should prosecute their working out of their own salvation. Awe, reverence, humility, yes: these would be suitable frames of feeling for him who would work under the inspiration of such an example. But fear and trembling,—anxious dread lest failure after all should be the end of endeavour,—how could the example of Christ's great act of humiliation, issuing in so tremendous a reward, fitly call out such a state of mind?

The case is similar with the support which the Apostle brings to his exhortation from the other side. "Let it be with fear and trembling," says the Apostle, "that you work out your own salvation, *for*"—and this "for" looks forward to and takes hold upon the sharpest possible assurance of divine aid. "For He that worketh in you both the willing and the doing, in pursuance of His good pleasure, is none other than God." Surely this tremendous assertion of the implication of God Himself in the work he is exhorting his readers to prosecute, affords no reason why they should carry on that work in the grip of a dreadful fear lest they should after all fail. We must not neglect the emphasis that falls on the word "God" here—second only to that which falls on the words "with fear and trembling," so that in effect these two ideas are brought into sharp collocation, and each enhances the stress thrown on the other.

Nor should we neglect to notice, what has been well brought out by Kühl, that Paul is adducing here a general proposition—one in one form or another familiar to all readers of his epistles—the great truth central to his whole system of doctrine, that "it is God who in all matters of salvation, is the energizer in men of both the willing and the doing, in pursuance of His good pleasure." It is the same great fact that the Apostle planted at the root of the confidence of his Ephesian readers (1:11), when he traced all the blessings that had been brought them to the purpose "of Him who worketh all things after the counsel of His own will." It is the same great fact that rings out in the triumphant cry of Romans 8:31—"If God be for us, who can be against us." Surely, when he placed the Almighty Arms beneath them, the Apostle cannot have intended to instil into his readers a more poignant sense of the uncertainty of the issue of their labours, and to justify to them a demand that it shall be especially "in fear and trembling"—in doubt and terror as to the result—that they must prosecute their great task of "working out their own salvation." The great fact that he adduces is awe-inspiring enough. How solemnizing the assurance that God works in us all our good impulses! How fitted to teach us humility and beget in us a godly fear as we walk the pathway provided for us! But how little fitted to lead us to despair of the result, to live in dreadful uncertainty as to the outcome! "If God is for us, who is against us!"

The context, then, certainly lends no support to the emphatic words "with fear and trembling," if they be taken as an exhortation to an attitude of doubt and hesitation—to the presentation of a fear of failure as an incitement to diligence in labour. On the contrary, the context demands an encouraging, not a warning, note for the exhortation. This raises the suspicion that we may have mistaken the sense of Paul in the use of the phrase "with fear and trembling." And a closer scrutiny confirms this suspicion. The collocation of the two words "fear" and "trembling," it seems, had become something of a set formula with the Apostle, possibly grounded in the usage of the two together in such passages of the Septuagint as Genesis 9:2, Is. 19:16; and this formula seems no longer to have had the value to him of the two words in combination, but rather to have come to express little more than the proper reverence due to a superior. For example, in Ephesians 6:5, when the Apostle exhorts servants to be obedient to their masters "with fear and trembling," he can scarcely intend to recommend to servants a spirit of craven fear before their master's face. Did he not rather wish to commend to them an appropriate recognition of the distance between master and slave, and the respectful reverence befitting the relation in which they stood? So in 2 Cor. 7:15, when we are told that the Corinthians received Titus "with fear and trembling," we are surely not to understand that they received him with a vivid dread lest they should fall short of winning his favour, but rather simply that they received him with the respect and obedience due to his official position as one set over them in the Lord. Similarly, in 1 Cor. 2:3, the Apostle surely means only to say that he acted in his work at Corinth with due respect to his commission and subjection to the Spirit who accompanied his preaching with His power.

In a word, it is clear enough that in the phrase "with fear and trembling," we have to do with a set formula, which, in the Apostle's mind and lips, finds its reference to the attitude of dependence, reverence and obedience befitting an inferior, and is, therefore, especially related to the ideas of submissiveness and subjection. It owes its place in our present passage obviously to its correlation with the immediately precedent phrase, "As ye have always obeyed" (verse 12), which itself goes back to the obedience of Christ's great example (verse 8). If Chrysostom, therefore, is formally wrong in, without more ado, paraphrasing it by "with humility of spirit," he is not so far astray as might at first sight be thought in the substance of the matter. What the Apostle would seem to say, in effect is just this: "As ye have always hitherto been submissive, so let it be with the same submissiveness of spirit that ye bring your salvation to its completion, seeing that, as you know, the energizer who works in you both the willing and the doing is God, in pursuance of His good pleasure." It is to reverence, obedience, humility in their Christian walk in the consciousness of the same power of God operating in them, to which he exhorts his readers; not to terror and dread lest after all their labour they might yet prove to be castaways. It is not the difficulty of the task that he is emphasizing; but the solemnity of it.

It is under the encouragement of these two great facts, then, that Paul here stirs up his Philippian readers to the sacred work of advancing in the Christian walk steadily to the great end—the example of Christ and the interior working of God in their hearts. We have ventured to speak of the latter as the indwelling of the Holy Spirit. The Holy Spirit is not mentioned by name. But it is obviously His indwelling work that is adverted to; and accordingly the seventh chapter of Romans, with its sequel in the eighth chapter, really provides an extended commentary on this passage. The process which is there displayed to us, as the new power not ourselves making for righteousness is implanted in the heart, and from that vantage ground wages its victorious war against the sin still entrenched in the members, is here compressed for us into one sharp, crisp word of declaration. The Christian works out his own salvation under the energizing of God, to whose energizing is due every impulse to good that rises in him, every determination to good which he frames, every execution of a good purpose which he carries into effect. And in view of the great fact that this power within him making for righteousness is none other than God Himself, surely the only proper attitude for the Christian in working out His salvation is one of "fear and trembling,"—of awe and reverence in the presence of the Holy One, of submission and obedience to His leading, of dependence and trust on His guidance. This, in effect, seems to be the Apostle's meaning. It is, in a word, an uncovering of the sources of sanctification, and a reference of it as to its origin in every step to God's gracious activities.

We may then perhaps attempt a paraphrase of the passage. "So, then, my beloved, in view of Christ's great example of self-abnegation—even as ye have always obeyed, so now, not as if it were only because I was present, but much more just because I am absent, let it be in a spirit of reverent submissiveness that you carry your salvation to its completion. For remember that He that effects in you not only the willing but also the doing, is none other than God Himself. And He does it in pursuance of His good pleasure." Or more at large: "Under the inspiration of this great example that Christ Jesus has set us, an example of humble submission even down to death, and of His consequent reward, I may repeat and strengthen my exhortation to you. I gladly allow that you have never been failing in submissiveness of spirit. When I was present with you I saw it and rejoiced in it. I trust it was not due to my presence only that you were able to exhibit so Christlike a disposition. After all, it is not my pleasure but your own salvation that should primarily engage your thoughts. And if my presence were, indeed, useful to you, how much more effort should you make, now that I can no longer be with you and you are thrown on your own resources. Nay, let me not so speak. You are not in any case thrown on your own resources. Let it be with godly awe in your hearts and reverent fear of mind that you engage in this solemn work. For it is, you remember, none other than God Himself who prompts you to the effort,—whose it is to effect within you both the wish and the performance: and this He does in the prosecution of His blessed purpose of good towards you. It is in His hands that you are in this work: it is thus a holy work—in the prosecution of which you may, therefore, well put off the sandals from your feet. In devout submissiveness, then, carry it on, with all diligence, and depend on no creature's impulse or help: it is God who in it works in and through you and so fulfils His gracious will with respect to you."

THE ALIEN RIGHTEOUSNESS

Phil. 3:9:—"And be found in Him, not having a righteousness of mine own, even that which is of the law, but that which is through faith in Christ, the righteousness which is of God by faith."

"WHEN we attempt to gain an apprehension of Paul's doctrine of salvation on the ground of an alien righteousness," remarks Professor George B. Stevens, "we must bear in mind that Paul was waging an intense polemic—the great conflict of his life." The remark is true enough in itself, but will scarcely warrant Professor Stevens' inference from it, namely, that we must be careful therefore not to take Paul's statements in this matter *au pied de la lettre;* that we must expect (and will find) a certain exaggeration in his language at this polemic point, a certain one-sidedness in his assertions; and be, therefore, prepared to tone down the extremity of his statements to more reasonable proportions. From this warning of Professor Stevens' we may, perhaps, learn this much, however: that Paul's statements at this point are radical and leave little room for that nice balancing so dear to the hearts of so-called "moderate" thinkers, by which they would fain retain some room for glorying in the flesh while yet joining in the universal song of the saints of God, Gloria Deo Soli.

It is clear, at once, that the forms of Paul's language at least do not easily lend themselves to the notion that, though Divine aid is requisite to salvation, yet the fundamental movement thereunto must be of man's own making; or even that, though salvation is predominatingly from God, yet this is not to the exclusion of the necessity on man's part of at least assent and consent to the Divine working; that if the basis of the Divine acceptance of man is to be found in the work of Christ, at least faith is demanded of man as the condition on the performance of which alone will this acceptance be accorded to him. It is something like this that Professor Stevens wishes to reserve to man as his part in salvation. And it is in his effort to rescue this to man from the obviously unwilling hands of Paul that he is led to remark that Paul's language must be interpreted as that of a headlong controversialist, who in his zeal falls into "a certain one-sidedness" in his representations, and keys his reasonings so high that they must be taken rather as "purposely one-sided *argumenta ad hominem*" and do not fairly set forth perhaps Paul's whole thought on the subject. Whence, we say, it seems perfectly clear that the language of Paul, taken as it stands, excludes even so much of a human element lying at the basis of salvation. What he says—whatever he means—is obviously that our own righteousness—in every item and degree of it—is wholly excluded from the ground of our salvation; and the righteousness provided by God in Christ is the sole ground of our acceptance in His sight. According to his express statements, at least, we are saved entirely on the ground of an alien righteousness and not at all on the ground of anything we are or have done, or can do,—be it even so small a matter as believing.

For the rest, true as it is that in this matter Paul was involved in an ineradicable conflict with the Judaizers—in what may be with good right called indeed "the conflict of his life"—it is very easy to press beyond the mark in our estimate of the effect of this conflict upon his thought or even upon his language. After all, Paul's interest in the ground of human salvation was a positive one, rather than a negative one. In the providence of God he was led to develop his doctrine of salvation for the benefit of his disciples in conflict with Judaizers; and we view it to-day in the forms of statement given it under the necessities of that controversy. But there is no reason to believe that he would not have taught precisely that same doctrine of salvation, though, doubtless, in different forms of statement, had he been required to meet erroneous teaching of a totally different kind, proceeding from a wholly different quarter—that is, if we really believe that the essence of his doctrine is the truth of God, given him by revelation, and not merely his personal position assumed to hold standing ground for himself as a determined opponent of the old Jewish party in the Church. In other words, the conflict with the Judaizers was not first with Paul and his doctrine of salvation second, either in time or importance; but, on the contrary, his doctrine of salvation was first and his controversy with the Judaizers both subsequent and consequent to it. He did not hold this doctrine of salvation because he polemicized the Judaizers, but he polemicized the Judaizers because he held this doctrine of salvation. He did not attain this doctrine of salvation then in controversy with the Judaizers, but he controverted the Judaizers because their teaching impinged on this precious doctrine. Though, therefore, the forms in which he states the doctrine in these epistles take shape from the fact that he is rebutting the assaults on it and the subtle undermining of it derived from the conceptions of the Judaizers, the doctrine stated is prior in the order of time and thought in his mind to the rise of the danger to it which he is repelling in these expressions. The interest and importance of this to us is that it thereby is brought to our clear consciousness that Paul's fundamental interest in this matter turns not on the violence of his conflict with the Judaizers but on the profundity of his conviction of the truth of his position. Whenever he replies to the Judaizers' assault in whatever sharpness of rebuke and keenness of polemic thrust, his primary interest is not in silencing his opponents but in upholding his teaching.

We could not have a better illustration of this than in the passage now before us. The whole of it is suffused with an emotion which is far deeper and far purer than polemic zeal. Nowhere do Paul's polemics burn more fiercely. Nowhere is his language sharper or his expressions more "extreme." But nowhere is it clearer that his heart is set on higher things than on the refutation of errorists whom he would correct; and nowhere is it less legitimate to pare down his expressions to the level of mere controversial violence. The Apostle as he opened the third chapter of this Epistle was contemplating drawing it to a close. "Finally, my brethren," he says, using the familiar formula for introducing the concluding words,—"finally, my brethren," he says, closing the letter, as is his wont, with some striking fundamental thought that would abide in the mind of his readers as a last message to their souls,—"finally, my brethren, let your joy be in the Lord." This is no mere formula of farewell, as some, misled by the "rejoice"—which is to be sure an ordinary formula of epistolary salutation—have imagined. The conception of Christian rejoicing is a fundamental note of this letter, and here it has all the emphasis that this gives it. And it is not merely the idea of rejoicing that is here emphatic, but the added idea of rejoicing "in the Lord." "Finally, my brethren," says the Apostle, "let your joy be in the Lord." Ah, this is where the Apostle's heart is as he opens this paragraph—this is the thought he would leave with his readers. "Let your joy be in the Lord"—not in yourselves, but in the Lord. We should say, perhaps, rather, Let your boast be in the Lord; let your glorying be only in the Lord. It means fundamentally the same thing. The Apostle would bring his letter to a close by reminding his readers of the very core of the saving proclamation. They are saved—not self-saving souls. Let them rejoice, let them continually joy, in the Lord!

This is not a new theme with the Apostle. It is rather one of his favourite subjects, this of boasting in Christ Jesus. He is conscious that he harps on it. But he is not ashamed of harping on it; it is the heart of the Gospel and he is not ashamed of the Gospel of Christ. But he makes a quasi-apology for so harping on it. "I know this is repetitious," he says at once, "but I like to say it, and it may be useful to you." "To write the same things to you, to me on the one hand is not irksome, but to you on the other it is safe." It is a joy to Paul to cry over and over and over again, "Let your joy be in the Lord"; in Him only put your boasting; in Him alone do your glorying; and it is a safe thing to impress on his readers. At the mention of this, the floods of polemics rush in. Paul remembers those who were endangering the purity of this attitude of dependence on the Lord alone in his flocks, and remembering them, what can he do but burst out with renewed warnings?

So the letter does not close, after all, at this point, but instead, we have the sharp exhortation, "Mark ye the dogs! Mark ye the evil workers! Mark ye the concision!" Why does his polemic burn so hotly against these men? Simply because they endangered that attitude which he was impressing on his readers, and in which the whole Gospel consisted for him—the attitude of entire dependence on Christ to the exclusion of everything in themselves. Accordingly his rapid and clearly cut speech leaps at once into the reason: "Mark ye the concision,—the concision I say, the mere imitation; for we are the circumcision, the real sealed ones to God, who worship by the Spirit of God and boast in Christ Jesus, and put no confidence in the flesh."

We do not need to follow the subsequent turns of the polemic into which the Apostle here enters. It is enough for us to note that the language abundantly confirms the interpretation of the drift of the paragraph and the intent of its opening words on which we have insisted. Paul exhorts his readers "to let their joy be in the Lord," and he repudiates the concision on the express ground that their claims are antagonistic to a purely spiritual worship, to boasting in Christ Jesus alone and the withdrawal of all confidence from the flesh. This is that to which the Apostle is engaged in exhorting his readers therefore—boasting in Christ Jesus alone and the removal of all confidence in the flesh. We all know how richly he develops this idea in the following words—enumerating his own high claims in the flesh and asserting roundly that all of them are but as refuse to him in the matter of salvation. Christ Jesus is all. The language of our text is but the elaboration of this vital idea in other and more precise language. All that he is, all that he has sought after, all that he has done,—though from a fleshly point of view far superior to what most men can appeal to—all, all, he counts (not merely useless but) loss, all one mass of loss, to be cast away and buried in the sea, "that he may gain Christ and be found in Him." On the one side stand all human works—they are all loss. On the other hand stands Christ—He is all in all. That is the contrast. And this is the contrast re-expressed more formally in our text: "not having my own righteousness that is out of law, but that which is through faith in Christ, the righteousness that is from God on faith."

The contrast is between the righteousness which a man can make for himself and the righteousness that God gives him. And the contrast is absolute. On the one, in the height and the breadth of its whole idea—we cannot exaggerate here—Paul pours contempt, as a basis or, nay, even the least part of the basis, of salvation. On the other, exclusively, he bases the totality of salvation. The outcome is, that not merely polemically but fundamentally, he founds salvation solely on an alien righteousness, with the express exclusion of every item of our own righteousness. The whole contents of the passage demands this as Paul's fundamental thought.

Now, it is not necessary for us, on this occasion, to stop to analyze in its details Paul's thought; to show by detailed exposition how utterly the righteousness rejected by him is rejected and how exclusively the righteousness laid hold of by him is trusted in, and how completely the ground of our trust is cleansed by Paul from every scintilla of human works. It will suffice for the present to accept the discrimination he makes in the large and to try to realize how fully to him the totality of the Gospel lay just in this discrimination. The Gospel, to Paul, consists precisely in this: that we do nothing to earn our salvation or to secure it for ourselves. God in Christ does it all.

It is easy, of course, to brand such an assertion as immoral. Men were not slow to brand it as immoral in Paul's day, and men are not slow to brand it as immoral ("unethical" is their way of phrasing it) to-day. "What," they say, "we are to do nothing! Christ does it all! Nothing depends on us! Not even our believing! Then, let us eat, drink and be merry!" They do not stop to consider that the repetition against those who draw this doctrine from Paul's teaching, of precisely the same charge that was urged against Paul, is the last thing which could be needed to prove that Paul has not been misunderstood when he is interpreted as advancing by set purpose just this doctrine. Paul does not meet the charge by explaining that he wishes his words concerning the exclusion of all our righteousness from the ground of salvation to be taken *cum grano salis;* but by explaining that, being saved not indeed "out of works" but certainly "unto good works," we cannot walk in sin and yet be saved. This positing of a new antithesis, not out of works but unto good works, clinches the essence of his doctrine, and may be adopted by us as the sole defence it needs against the accusations of men.

You remember how Mr. J. A. Froude in a famous essay adduced as a speaking evidence of the "immorality of Evangelicalism," the well-known revival hymn beginning:

> "Nothing either great or small,
> Nothing, sinner, no;
> Jesus did it, did it all,
> Long, long, ago."

What was particularly offensive to him was the assertion that

"Doing is a deadly thing,
Doing ends in death";

and the consequent exhortation

"Cast your deadly doing down,
Down at Jesus' feet,
Stand in Him, in Him alone,
Gloriously complete."

It is, nevertheless, the very *cor cordis* of the Gospel that is here brought under fire. The one antithesis of all the ages is that between the rival formulæ: Do this and live, and, Live and do this; Do and be saved, and Be saved and do. And the one thing that determines whether we trust in God for salvation or would fain save ourselves is, how such formulæ appeal to us. Do we, like the rich young ruler, feel that we must "do some good thing" in order that we may be saved? Then, assuredly, we are not yet prepared to trust our salvation to Christ alone—to sell all that we have and follow Him. Just in proportion as we are striving to supplement or to supplant His perfect work, just in that proportion is our hope of salvation resting on works, and not on faith. Ethicism and solafideanism—these are the eternal contraries, mutually exclusive. It must be faith or works; it can never be faith and works. And the fundamental exhortation which we must ever be giving our souls is clearly expressed in the words of the hymn, "Cast your deadly doing down." Only when that is completely done is it really

Christ Only, Christ All in All, with us; only then, do we obey fully Paul's final exhortation: "Let your joy be in the Lord." Only then do we renounce utterly "our own righteousness, that out of law," and rest solely on "that which is through faith in Christ, the righteousness of God on faith."

PEACE WITH GOD

Phil. 4:7:—"And the peace of God, which passeth all understanding, shall guard your hearts and your thoughts in Christ Jesus."

THE exact phrase which we have given as the subject of our reflection this afternoon, though one of the most familiar phrases in our religious speech, has a very slender claim to be looked upon as Biblical. It occurs but once in the Bible (Rom. 5:1), and then, as it seems to me (though on this the commentators differ), not in its fundamental sense, or in the sense in which it is probably most prominent in the minds of most of us here this afternoon, but in its subjective sense of consciousness of peace with God. The thing denoted by the phrase is of course a frequent and basal idea in Scripture, though not expressed by the exact phrase now before us. The correlated terms "enmity," "reconciliation," "peace," occur with sufficient frequency and express what may properly be called a fundamental idea of the Gospel.

We are told that we are naturally "enemies" of God, that God looks upon us as such, and that we cherish the feelings appropriate to that condition—being enemies in our minds by wicked works, and because of a carnal mind necessarily at enmity with the Holy God. This enmity we are told Christ has "abolished," "slain" on His cross, "reconciling" us with God by His propitiatory work. As a result of this "propitiation," we are told, He has made "peace" (Eph. 2:18); and, therefore, He is called "our peace," and His Gospel, "the Gospel of peace" (Rom. 10:15; Eph. 6:15). His whole work was "that we might have peace in Him" (Jno. 16:33), and His gospel consisted in "preaching peace by Jesus" (Acts 10:36). Even in the Old Testament prophecy, He is promised as the "Prince of Peace" (Isa. 9:6), and it is clearly perceived that He is such because the "chastisement of our peace shall be on Him" (Isa. 53:5); in other words, because that punishment by which our sins are expiated and we are reconciled with God should be borne by Him.

There is no lack, therefore, of the most explicit enunciation in Scripture of the fact which our phrase expresses; it is rather one of the pervading representations of Scripture that we are at enmity with God and can have peace with Him only in the blood of Christ. Only it so happens that the connection in which the word "peace" occurs most frequently in Scripture is one which raises our eyes rather to God as the giver of peace than emphasizes the fact that it is with Him that the peace is established. "Peace from God" happens, therefore, to be a commoner Scriptural locution than "peace with God." "I will give unto him my covenant of peace" (Numb. 28:12), though not spoken with this broad implication may almost be represented as the primary promise of the Old Covenant, under which the longing of God's people expressed itself in the assurance that "He would speak peace with His people and to His saints" (Psa. 85:8). Wherefore that Old Covenant saint upon whose glad eyes the dawn of salvation had fallen, expresses his joy that the coming of the Day-spring from on high was a promise that now, at length, the feet of God's people should be guided in the way of peace (Luke 1:79). Accordingly Jesus represents the result of His work as giving peace to His followers (Jno. 16:33)—"My peace I leave with you, my peace I give unto you" (Jno. 16:27), and His disciples going everywhere "preached peace by Jesus" (Acts 10:36). It is the "peace of God" that passeth all understanding, that the Apostle would have rule in the hearts of His converts (Phil. 4:7); and the prayer that "peace from God" should be on them became the fixed form of Apostolic benediction (Rom. 1:7).

This pervading longing for peace and promise of it as one of the most precious gifts of God, certainly enhances our sense of its value. Perhaps we may say that the chief difference in the feeling of the two terms "peace from God" and "peace with God" is that the primary emphasis in the former falls naturally on subjective peace—

though by no means to the exclusion of objective peace; while, with the latter the reverse is the case. When we speak of "peace from God" coming upon us, of the peace of God that passes all understanding "sentrying" our hearts and thoughts, of the peace of Jesus which He left with us, when He added: "Let not your heart be troubled, neither let it be fearful," we necessarily think first of all of the deep sense of inner peace and satisfaction which pervades the hearts of none in the world who have not "found their peace" as we say, in Christ. On the other hand, when we speak of "peace with God" our thoughts go primarily back to that great transaction on Calvary when He who is our peace reconciled us to God by His cross, having slain the enmity thereon; and we who were alienated in our wicked minds from Him were brought nigh in the blood of Christ. We cannot think of the one, indeed, without thinking of the other; nor can one exist apart from the other. We cannot have peace of heart, until our real and actual separation from God is bridged by the blood of Christ. We cannot have the breach between God and us healed without a sense of the new relation of peace stealing into our hearts. And possibly we cannot do better to-day than just to realize how interdependent the two are and how rich the peace is which we obtain in Christ Jesus.

To this end, let us consider (1) the utter lack of

peace which man suffers by nature; (2) the fullness of peace brought to us by Jesus; and (3) the process by which this peace is made the possession of the mind and soul.

It is a curious thing if you look at it, how little peace man out of Christ, that is, apart from God and His right relation to him, has in the world; how utterly out of joint he is—at war, in fact—with even his physical environment. Every other creature finds a place for itself in nature; nature cares for them all. "She spreads a table for the tiger in the jungle, for the buffalo on the prairie, for the dragon-fly above the summer brook." But she spreads no table for man. Foxes may have holes and the birds of the air, nests; but like his Lord, man has no place in nature where he can safely lay his head. As a mere animal, he is the weakest and most helpless of all, with no natural covering to keep him warm, with no natural weapons to protect himself, with no speed for escape, and no cunning for hiding. The sun burns him and the winter freezes him. A brilliant writer, upon whom I am drawing very freely in these paragraphs, calls him justly, the step-child of time. Revelation accounts for it by the fall. Man stood at the gate of Eden, an exile, facing a wild world, a world of briers and thorns, of hostile fears, of death. What man out of Christ thinks of it, the myths he has invented tell us; from the shrinking terror of the fetish worshipper at every old bone or bit of stick, to the weird shapes and glowing myths of our own Scandinavian fathers. Man knows himself to be at war with the world.

It is much if he can get his food. Most do not. But food does not satisfy him. "Put an ox in a fat pasture beside a clear stream and the ox is as happy as an ox can be. The hungry tiger with reeking jaws, tearing the slaughtered buffalo, is happy to the utmost limit of tiger nature." But after man has conquered nature, he is still not at peace with her. He is no happier in the palace than in the hut.

> "In the cool hall with haggard eyes
> The Roman nobly lay;
> Then rose and drove in furious wise
> Along the Appian Way.
>
> He made a feast, drank fierce and fast
> And crowned his head with flowers,
> No easier and no swifter passed
> The impracticable hours."

Man assuredly is at odds with nature; but not only with nature, there is something deeper than that. Man is at odds with himself. So that, even though he were not the stepchild of nature and all that is external to him existed only to do his pleasure, so that like the lotus-eaters he could merely lie and be happy; man would not be happy. The deep unrest of his nature has a deeper cause than merely his lack of physical adjustment to his environment. He is out of joint with himself. He has a conscience and knows the right. But he also knows what is not right. And this sense of sin, ineradicable instinct in every soul, is the source of a restless uneasiness which knows and can know no peace. His very disquietedness with nature receives half its terror from it. If man merely felt that he must manipulate nature for his comfort, he might, at least, be inwardly easy or troubled only by those natural anxieties for the future that cluster around the questions, What shall I eat, and what shall I drink, and wherewith shall I be clothed. But his inward unrest clothes nature with a thousand terrors; her forces become avenging furies, her thunders the voice of an accusing God, her lightnings and tornadoes—her quietly working poisons of miasma and disease—become the tools of God's anger. Because he is a sinner, man's inward war is inflicted on his outward environment. And his conscience it is that will give him no peace.

But neither is conscience the ultimate fact. As the terrors of nature are due to the fact that they are not ultimate but point upwards and inwards to the war in the heart, so the terrors of conscience are due to the fact that they, too, are not ultimate but point upwards to a higher Power. Conscience is the voice of God proclaiming war in man; and through it man knows that he is not at peace with God. Hence its pain and terror.

Everywhere, man knows that because he is a sinner, he is at enmity with God. Man's sense of enmity with God is the source of all his terror, all his unrest, all his misery. It is ineradicable and universal. It must abide so long as man knows he is a sinner. But so long as it abides, he cannot be other than miserable.

Now the Apostle, in the text, recognizing this state of things, promises us as if it were the fundamental blessing, the peace of God. And he promises it to us in language which exhibits his high appreciation of its nature. He calls it, a peace that passes all conception. And he promises it as something that will guard or "sentry" our hearts and thoughts—as if it were able to keep us pure and holy as few things can. Let us note then in opposition to the restlessness of man's heart by nature the surpassingness of God's peace.

And here, note especially, the universality of this peace of God; how it supplies the whole lack of peace in which we are by nature.

It is fundamentally peace with God. "But now in Christ Jesus ye that once were afar off are made nigh in the blood of Christ. For he is our peace, who made both one, and broke down the middle wall of partition, having abolished in his flesh the enmity, even the law of commandments and ordinances, that he might create in himself of the twain one new man, so making peace; and might reconcile them both in one body unto God through his cross, having slain the enmity thereby." Christianity does not come crying peace, peace, when there is no peace, and when we know there is no peace. It does not come crying that God is love and nothing but love, and the Father of all, not at enmity to us, not needing any reconciliation. It comes recognizing the enmity and laying an adequate foundation for peace. It recognizes our sin and guilt and offers an atonement for it. It recognizes our condemnation and makes provision for its reversal. It institutes peace out of war, and that by a method which commands our assent as complete, availing, effective. Thus it makes peace between us and God.

And just because it does not talk of a peace already existing when our hearts know there is war, it relieves also our unrest of conscience and brings us to peace with ourselves. Looking upon the satisfaction of Christ, the heart can comfort itself in the knowledge of a reconciled God and receive His promises that on the basis of that atonement the Spirit shall come and work peace in the soul.

And once again, this peace of soul mightily works to produce peace in our environment, for now the soul no longer looks upon the external world as its enemy and no longer on the laws of nature as purely natural forces, grinding out evil for it. It sees that in nature and above nature a Father sits—truly a Father, now, that He is reconciled to us in Christ, and that all Providence is in His hands, touching us. In nature itself—in history—the reconciled soul meets God and perceives everywhere the hand of One who loves him and cares for him. Amid all happenings he is peaceful and serene; he knows nothing can harm him now; he knows nothing can take away his peace; he knows that all things shall work together for good to him. The external world is no longer his enemy, but his friend.

In our absorption with the weightier matters of the fundamental reconciliation of the soul with God in Christ and the operation of the Spirit working peace in us, we are apt to neglect this element of peace, in which we are ourselves at peace in the world, no longer orphans but communing with God in all our happenings. How important an aspect of the matter it is may be advertised to us by the comfort which the theologians of the school of Ritschl find in it, the only form of communion with God they acknowledge, and how it fills their hearts to be able by the revelation of Christ to look on the world as God's Kingdom in which His children are not orphans but sons of a living God.

The inestimable value of the peace of God is apparent next from the reasonableness and surety of this peace. There may be a peace which is not reasonable; a peace which is not assured. The worldly man's peace on which he strives to stay himself is of this kind; the peace of a drunkard in a house on fire, the peace of a lunatic who fancies himself a king, the peace of a fool who cries Peace! Peace! when there is no peace. Such a peace can be maintained only by shutting our eyes to what we are and where we are and the relations that actually exist about us and between us and God. Any accident that calls us to ourselves destroys it. Any ray of true light arising in our conscience extinguishes it. And when evil and death come, where is it then? But God's peace is a rational peace, and a stable peace. It arises not from shutting our eyes to our real state, but from opening them to it, and the more our eyes are open and the more we realize our real condition, understanding what Christ is, what we are, and what He has done for us, the more peace flows into our hearts. The more searching the light we turn on the scene, the more glorious the prospect. Light turns a false peace into torment. Light awakes in the countenance of the true peace, happy smiles.

Is this peace ours? How can we obtain it? Whence obtain it? We must distinguish. It is not our peace; it is God's. We do not make it; He makes it. But we can by God's grace enjoy it more and more.

(1) Its foundation is, of course, in Christ and Christ's work. It can be had on no other basis, in no other way. "Being justified by faith, we have peace with God." We cannot go about to

establish it; we should be doomed to utter failure. We are by nature at enmity with God. No peace can be found until that enmity is removed. It cannot be removed by aught but a perfect sacrifice, a perfect righteousness. Christ alone can do it. For the inestimable peace of God, therefore, we must look to Christ. It can have no other foundation than His perfect work.

(2) Its formation in us is, of course, by the Holy Ghost. We cannot produce it for ourselves, even on the basis of Christ's work. A fountain cannot rise higher than its source and a sure and stable peace—an everlasting peace—an infinite and perfect peace—must be the work of Him who is Himself all this. "Now the works of the Spirit are love, joy, peace."

(3) But the cultivation of it is placed by God's grace in our hands. Christ may have died for us; the Spirit may have applied that death savingly to us; and yet we may still hold back from the full consciousness of our safety; wrong thoughts and feelings may stand in our way. We are at peace with God; our conscience knows it. But we may so seldom look to Him who is our Peace, and so much to ourselves, that we fail to take the true comfort and joy of our changed position.

Hence a good old writer (William Bridge) draws two useful distinctions: a distinction between Fundamental Peace and Additional Peace; a distinction between Dormant Peace and Awakened Peace,—peace in the seed and peace in the flower. Fundamental Peace, he tells us, is that peace which naturally and necessarily arises from our justification; those who are justified by faith have peace with God. We cannot cultivate this, we have it; it cannot be less true or be made more true. But it is objective. There is, then, the subjective peace, founded on this: the additional peace that arises from the sense of our jusfication. This we may neglect to cultivate; it may be lost for a time. As the thief breaking in at night can steal the accumulated income hoarded in the safe, but cannot steal the capital invested in the land; so the great thief of the universe, Satan, may take away our additional peace but never the fundamental. So we may also speak of Dormant peace—a peace we have ever in heart but do not realize always; and Awakened peace, which manifests itself to the soul.

On the one hand, the wicked man may give himself great comfort till the day of death comes, but when trouble breaks forth upon him, he is at length awake. The sin and guilt were in his heart always; they lay sleeping there, but now they are awakened. So the German poet sings:

The heart hath chambers twain,
  Which inhabit
Sweet joy and bitter pain:
Oh joy, take thou good heed!
  Tread softly,
Lest pain should wake indeed!

Just so, on the other hand, men may have a great reservoir of true peace within them, and yet have never drawn on it for the supply of their needs. After a while the need arises that breaks the retaining wall and the whole soul is flooded with peace. This is peace indeed! O, that we may have this peace! Not merely Fundamental peace—though that is the main thing—but Additional peace; not merely Dormant peace, but Awakened peace—the sense of being at peace with God.

THE HERITAGE OF THE SAINTS IN LIGHT

Col. 1:12:—"Giving thanks unto the Father who made us meet to be partakers of the inheritance of the saints in light."

OUR passage is one of those fervent descriptions of the blessed state of the saved soul in which the writings of Paul abound. It occurs in the midst of the prayer which he says he has been offering for the Colossians ever since their conversion. The Colossians were not brought to Christ by his own preaching, but by that of his faithful minister in the Gospel, Epaphras. And when Epaphras brought him the good news of the turning of the many at Colossæ from darkness to light, the heart of the Apostle overflowed with thanksgiving. From that day, he says, he has been continually thanking God for the Colossian Christians, and mingling with his thanks earnest petitions for their Christian walk.

The gist of his petition is that they—so lately brought to Christ and so surrounded by danger—should be filled with the knowledge of God's will in all wisdom and spiritual understanding, so that they might walk worthily of the Lord unto all pleasing. Two points are to be noted here.

The thing which Paul desires for the Colossian converts is that they may, in their walk and conversation, be well pleasing to Christ. This is expressed by means of a term of rather startling strength; a term which in its classical usage bore an implication of cringing subjection to the whims of another and was applied to the sycophant and the flatterer. Of course, the nobler association with Christ voids it of its unworthy suggestions, but there is left on the mind a strong impression of the fullness of the devotion which the Apostle would fain see in the lives of Christians to their Lord. External service—eye service—is not enough; our thoughts must run ahead of the command and all our lives be suffused with this principle—that we may be well pleasing to Christ. This is what the Apostle asks in behalf of the Colossian converts.

The second thing to be noted is that Paul expected this perfection of service to be mediated by perfection of knowledge. What he directly asks for is that these converts may be filled with the knowledge of God's will in all wisdom and spiritual understanding—and the word used here for "knowledge" is the term for precise, full, accurate, profound knowledge. He prays directly that they may have the knowledge—in order that they may walk worthily of their Lord unto all kinds of pleasing. Obviously it seemed to the Apostle that the pathway to a right life lay through a right knowledge. It was only as they knew the will of God that they could hope to please Christ in action. Knowledge comes thus before life and is the constructive force of life. Thus the Apostle teaches us the supreme value of a right and profound and exact knowledge of Divine things. Not as if knowledge were the end—life, undoubtedly, is the end at which the saving processes are directed; but because the sole lever to raise the life to its proper height is just right knowledge. It is life—the right life—that the Apostle is praying for in behalf of the Colossians: but he represents knowledge—right knowledge—as possessing the necessity of means to that life.

The nature of this right life is perhaps sufficiently outlined in the single phrase in which Paul gives expression to his longing. He says that he is asking that the Colossians may walk worthily of the Lord in every kind of pleasing. It is a Christ-pleasing life that he wishes for them. But it is not the Apostle's way to content himself with broad phrases. And he proceeds at once to suggest more fully what kind of a life he conceives a Christ-pleasing life to be. There are three characteristics which he throws into emphasis. It must be a fruitful life. It must be a stable life. It must be a thankful life. Here is the way he develops its idea. That ye may walk worthily of the Lord unto every kind of pleasing, he says—(1) by bearing fruit and yielding increase in every good work, through the knowledge of God; (2) by being strengthened in every sort of strength according to the might of His glory, unto all obedience and long-suffering; (3) by joyfully giving thanks to the Father, who has qualified us for our share in the lot of the saints in the light. Abounding fruitfulness in good works; strong patience in the trials of life; joyful thankfulness for the blessings of salvation; these are the traits of the Christian walk which shall be worthy of the Lord unto all pleasing; these are the marks of that life on which our Saviour will smile.

Now it is particularly to the third of these traits of a Christ-pleasing life that our text draws our attention to-day. It is one of the marks of right Christian living when we are joyfully thankful to the Father of our Lord and Saviour Jesus Christ for our introduction into the blessings of the Christian life. For, more accurately speaking, that is the substance of the thanksgiving which the Apostle desires to see illustrated in the Colossian Christians. The terms in which he expresses it are worth our careful consideration. "With joy, giving thanks to the Father," he phrases it, "who made us sufficient for a share of the lot of the saints in light." The ground of the thankfulness which he would fain find in them is that supernal act of the Father of our Saviour by which he has introduced us into the company and endowed us with the heritage of the saints. Of course, the reminiscence of our primal estate as aliens from the household of God underlies the thought; but it is not explicitly adverted to until the next verse. What is emphasized here is the wonder of the act by which we were transformed into fellow-citizens of the saints, and fellow-heirs with them of God. That, says the Apostle, is the ground of a thanksgiving on our part which should transfuse our whole life and by which our life will be characterized as a Christian one.

For the development of the thought, let us emphasize in turn the four chief elements which seem to enter most prominently into it. These words of the Apostle would seem to advise us, then, of at least these important facts:

1. That the saints have a heritage.
2. That the heritage of the saints is "in the light."
3. That it is God and God alone who has the power to introduce men into this heritage.
4. That it is a matter of profound thanksgiving to men, therefore, when they find themselves invested with this heritage—a thanksgiving which should transform their whole lives and make them conscious debtors to God to such an extent that henceforth they should live to Him and His glory should be their one pursuit—in a word, that they should walk worthily of the Lord unto all pleasing.

That the saints have a heritage is obviously the central implication of the passage. What Paul wishes his readers to be thankful for is their capacitating by the Father for their share "in the inheritance of the saints." Our term "heritage" may indeed be misleading in this connection. The Greek term may not naturally emphasize the same connotations, possibly may not contain all that we are accustomed to think of in connection with it. It may be better to use the word "lot," for example, and speak of "the lot" of the saints. The main implication is that of a possession which becomes ours, not by our earning it but by gift from another. What the saints obtain is not merited by them, is not theirs by right and their own desert; it is allotted to them. The language is founded on and is reminiscent of the allotment of Canaan to the Tribes which composed the ancient people of Jacob. As in that typical transaction the whole land was the gift of God to the people and was allotted to the several tribes and families, each having his own portion, so, in the antitype, the saints are conceived as having in possession their allotted heritage, in which each has his specific portion which is to be his indisputably and his forever. As under the Old Testament, so under the New, there remains a land, a country, an abiding home, for the people of God, into which abode the true Joshua leads them to their rest. And this, I say, is the fundamental implication of the passage.

The designation of this country of the saints as "in the light" follows a symbolism which pervades the whole Bible, and the grandeur of which is, perhaps, liable to be missed by us through our very wontedness to it. Throughout the Scriptures "light" is used as the designation of all that is of consummate and unapproachable perfection, whether in the physical, intellectual, moral or spiritual spheres. In contrast with the darkness of sorrow and peril we have the light of joy and safety; in contrast with the darkness of death we have the light of life; in contrast with the darkness of error we have the light of truth; in contrast with the darkness of sin we have the light of holiness; in contrast with the darkness of destruction we have the light of salvation. Physically, intellectually, ethically, spiritually, savingly, "light" is all that is pure and true, bright and holy and blissful. And light is the heritage of the saints. It is the sphere in which God lives, for we are to walk in the light as He is "in the light." It is the glorious city built foresquare of luminous stones, in which the saints have their real citizenship and the "light" of which is God Himself. God Himself is "light" and we, as His children, are the "children of light." In Him is no darkness at all, or as the strongly emphatic language of John seems to say, "Darkness is not in Him; no not in any way"—not in the way of physical infirmity, of intellectual error, of moral fault, of spiritual stain, or of sullied blessedness. In Him and in Him only, who dwelleth in light inaccessible, is there no darkness,—no, not in any way.

Meanwhile we fairly wallow in darkness. But for the saints there is a heritage "in the light" that streams out from the Throne of God, that light which is the source and condition of all life, and health, and strength, and all knowledge and righteousness, holiness and bliss. There lapped in the actinic rays of the "light of life," dwell the saints. There each has his appointed portion, his home. There each obtains his own higher qualities of knowledge, righteousness, holiness and bliss; and becoming thus luminiferous is made himself a "light bearer" in the world. All this and more is meant by the Apostle when he tells us of the "heritage of the saints in light."

Now he tells us further that it is God and God alone who can introduce men into this glorious region of "the light." It is God who is light and all the light that is in the world streams from Him. We, on our part, are under the dominion of "darkness," and darkness has filled our hearts. How can we be rescued from the rule of darkness and translated into the kingdom of the Son of God's love? Obviously it is only by an act of God, the Light, Himself shining into our darkened heart. And so the Apostle tells us, declaring that it is God who has made us meet for a share in the heritage of the saints. Our English word "meet" probably only brokenly represents the Greek word which he employs. In the Greek word the idea of sufficiency, adequacy, ability, is more prominent than that of worthiness, suitability. The notion conveyed is, perhaps, not so much that God has made us fit, worthy, to be in the Kingdom of light—though that in any event is included, and as to the thing itself is not inharmonious with the Apostle's main intention; but that He has made us able to enter into this state. Immersed in the kingdom of darkness, or worse than that, with the kingdom of darkness within ourselves, we were incapable of entering the kingdom of light. We needed to be made "sufficient," "competent," "adequate," "capable," to be "qualified," "capacitated" for entering into our portion in the allotment of the saints. There was no power in us for entering these light-sown regions; our natural home was elsewhere. Only by a creative act of God were we able to enter upon their sacred precincts.

You see the idea is not that we had the power to enter but not the fitness to abide there; it is that we had no power to enter—the light striking us in the face drove us away because we were of the darkness and incapable of the light. It was God and God alone who made us able to receive a portion in the inheritance of the saints in light; He alone who delivered us from the authority (we were under its authority) of darkness and translated us into the kingdom of the Son of His love. And we will utterly fail to catch Paul's real meaning unless we feel profoundly how entirely he ascribes the totality of the transaction by which we are vested with a heritage among the saints "in the light" to God and to God alone. It is to God and not to ourselves—not to our fellow-men, nor yet to angels,—to God and to God alone, that we owe it that our part is with the saints in the light. It is He that has qualified, capacitated, competentized, sufficientized us, for our part in the lot of the saints.

And it is just on this basis that He calls on us to spend our lives in one long thanksgiving to God, as the one who has enabled us for our share in the heritage of the saints in the light. Thanksgiving presupposes indebtedness. The nature of the indebtedness is already enshrined in the one word "who made us competent," but it is richly developed in the subsequent verses. We were held under the power of darkness; we have been delivered from it and translated into the Kingdom of the Son of God's love. We were under the curse of sin; we have received in Him redemption, even the forgiveness of sins. In this great rescue we have been made sufficient for both things. There is obviously an objective and a subjective side to it; an ideal and an actual possession involved. But the upshot of it all is—that God has taken us out of darkness with all that that involves and placed us in the light, with all that that involves. And as children of the light we must rejoice in the light—which light God is.

THE HIDDEN LIFE

Col. 3:1–4, especially 3:—"Your life is hid with Christ in God."

We cannot hope to empty so great a text as this into our minds and hearts in the course of a quarter of an hour's study of it. It is a great fountain filled with refreshment. But we may like to sip a little of its strengthening waters. To do so, let us in a very simple way just glance at its contents.

And first we observe that the text assumes a fact. Its opening words, "If then ye were raised together with Christ" posit a fact beneath all that it has further to say. And the resurrection here adverted to implies a previous death; and looking back to the preceding chapter, we find it also mentioned. Here, then, are the two wings of the fact assumed: "If ye died with Christ from the rudiments of the world"; "If then ye were raised together with Christ." At the bottom of all, then, lies this great fact, the fundamental fact of the Christian religion: that Christ died and rose again. On this great fundamental fact everything in our present passage is based. But not upon it as a bare fact, without further significance than that it happened. For it is no more a fact that Christ died than that He died for our sins; and no more a fact that He rose again than that He rose again for our justification.

This then is the fact assumed in our text, that Christ died for our trespasses and was raised again for our justification. But if He died for our sins, He died to take them away, and His death did take them away. All those for whose sins Christ died, died then with Him in the death which He accomplished on the cross; died with Him to sin, that they might no longer be sinners. And if He was raised again for our justification, He rose again to usher us into acceptance with God and into all that is involved in that great word, life, and His resurrection has brought us into God's favour and into life indeed. All those for whom He rose again, rose again with Him, therefore; rose again with Him to life that they might live again to God. And here now is the great fact in its fullness which Paul assumes and lays at the base of our present passage: the great fact of the participation of Christians in Christ's death and rising again.

If we be Christians at all, we are such only in virtue of the fact that when He died, He died for us, and we, therefore, died as sinners with His death; and that when He rose again for our justification, we rose again into newness of life with Him,—the life that we now live is a new life, from a new spring, even the Spirit of Christ which He as the risen Lord has sent down to us. This is the great fact of participation in the saving work of Christ, with all that it involves. And what we have here is an assertion that such a participation involves seizing of us bodily and lifting us to another and higher plane. We were sinners, and lived as sinners; we lived an earthly life, in the lowest sense of that word. But now we have died with Christ as sinners and can live no more as sinners; we have been raised together with Him and can live only on the plane of this new life, which is not in sin, not "in the earth," but in heaven. In a high and true sense, because we have died to sin and been raised to holiness, we have already passed out of earth to heaven. Heaven is already the sphere of our life; our "citizenship is in heaven"—we are citizens of the Kingdom of Heaven, and have the life appropriate thereto to live.

And now we observe, secondly, that on this fact the Apostle founds an exhortation. "If then ye were raised together with Christ, seek the things that are above." The exhortation is simply to an actual life consonant with our change of state. If we have participated in Christ's death for sin and rising again for justification; so that with Him we died to sin and rose again unto holiness; live accordingly. If we have thus died as sinners, as earth born, and earth confined crawlers on this low plane, and been raised to this higher plane, even a heavenly one, of living—show in walk and conversation that the change has been a real one. It is an exhortation to us to be in life real citizens of the heavenly kingdom to which we have been transferred; to do the duties and enter into the responsibilities of our new citizenship. It is just as we might say to some newly enfranchised immigrant: You have left that country of darkness in which you were bred, where no liberty of action or of worship existed; you have been received into our free America, and have been clothed with the rights and duties of citizenship in this great Republic; now live worthily of your new citizenship; be now in life and thought no longer a serf but a freeman. So, Paul says in effect, you have passed out of the realm of sin and death, out of the merely earthly sphere; you have been made a citizen of the heavenly kingdom; do the deeds and live the life conformable to your great change.

And we observe, again, that the Apostle describes to us the nature of this heavenly life to which we are committed, by passing out of the earthly into the heavenly sphere through participation in the death and rising again of Christ. "Seek the things that are above." "Set your mind on the things that are above, not on the things that are upon the earth." What is meant by seeking the heavenly things rather than the earthly? We may, at least, say that the following is meant.

To seek the things that are above, in distinction from those that are upon the earth, means primarily to seek what is good and refuse what is evil. It is an exhortation to a moral life as opposed to an immoral one. It is an exhortation to a life of purity and holiness as opposed to a life of sin. This at least is made evident to us by the immediately succeeding context. For just after giving the exhortation to seek the "things that are above and not the things that are upon the earth," the Apostle explains what the things that are upon the earth are which we are to refuse. "Mortify, therefore," he adds, at once, "your members that are upon the earth; fornication, uncleanness, passion, evil desire and covetousness." And he proceeds also to explain what the heavenly things are which we are to seek: "Put on, therefore, as God's elect, holy and beloved, a heart of compassion, kindness, humility, meekness, long-suffering" and the like. These, then, are "the things that are above" which we are to seek: and those "the things that are upon the earth" that we are to keep ourselves free from, and, when they are already in us as members, which we are "to mortify," to "slay." But this is as much as to say that the heavenly life which, as those who have shared in Christ's death and resurrection, we are to live, is, first of all, a moral life, or better, a holy life, a life of purity and virtue, as distinguished from a life of sin. And this, indeed, follows from its very conception, for our death with Christ was a death to sin and our rising with Him was a rising out of sin,—which is the death of the soul,—to a new life, spiritual life, which in its very idea is holiness. Before all else, this, then, is to seek the things that are above: to put aside the sin that so easily besets us and to live holily as becomes saints.

But this fundamental conception—and all inclusive conception, too, when rightly understood—hardly exhausts, when only thus broadly stated, the matter as it lies in the Apostle's mind here. On closer observation we see that the Apostle has also a special application of it in mind, and we need to note it. Let us say, then, that the seeking of the things that are above, means here also this: the seeking of the things that are really good in contradistinction to those that are apparently good. For if the subsequent context is the professed explanation of the fundamental meaning of the exhortation, the preceding context, furnishing the occasion of the special form which the exhortation takes, is the explanation of this. "If, *therefore*, ye were raised together with Christ." Now, in this preceding context, the Apostle was attempting to save his readers from a grave heresy which had shown itself in their region. The characteristic of this heresy was that, along with certain speculative errors, a specific moral teaching was offered: a moral teaching of apparently high and lofty nature. The Apostle does not deny that the principles thus pressed upon his converts as a rule of life had the appearance of goodness, and of wisdom: "which things have a show of wisdom in severity to the body." He does not deny that there were real evils to be met. There were gross indulgences of the flesh to which men were prone: intemperance, impurity and all the catalogue of such evils. How apparently wise and right to preach: Handle not, nor taste, nor touch! Should Christian men fail to join in this great cyclone of moral reform? If they did, were they not open to the charge of indifference to morality itself—the very mark and sign of their profession of having died to sin and been raised again to righteousness?

Paul's deliberate judgment is that all such precepts are precepts of men; that their tendency is to enslave men again under the yoke of legalism—men who had become free in Christ. And his deliberate exhortation is, to keep to the path of seeking the really good instead of these apparent goods. His exhortation becomes thus an exhortation to seek what we call the religious, rather than the moral way to reform man and the world. When men come saying, Touch not, taste not, handle not, Paul says they are offering you an inoperative mode of saving the world from sin; they are offering you law which only condemns, not grace in which alone is saving power. He says, reject such human commandments, and be content to hold fast to the Head—that Christ who has created all these things, whose they are, and who has given them to you for use, though, of course, not for abuse. He says, you are living on a higher plane than this earthly one of precepts and prohibitions; see that you live on this higher plane; seek the real good even if you are evil-spoken of, because you refuse a path of apparent good, one which has a show of wisdom, indeed, but is no real "specific" against the evils of the flesh.

But there is yet another special aspect of the exhortation, growing immediately out of these facts, which we must notice. Just because the seeking of the really good as over against the apparent good will necessarily bring misunderstanding, and even misrepresentation (for they that called the Master Beelzebub are not likely to mince matters in speaking of his followers), Paul represents the seeking of the things above, as a seeking of the hidden good, as distinguished from the open, publicly recognized good. This life of ours is a hidden life; hid with Christ in God. God, not the world, is the sphere in which it is passed. Christ is it itself. And Christ is now with God. The Christian in seeking heavenly things must not seek to be known of the world to be good, but only to be seen of God. It belongs to the Pharisee, not to the Christian, to do good to be seen of men. It is a hidden life he leads; and he must be content to be misunderstood and misrepresented, even persecuted for righteousness' sake; for him it is not appearances, or even appearance that he seeks; it is only the good. Not that his good shall always be unrecognized. There comes a day of manifestation; "When Christ is manifested, then shall ye be manifested with him, in glory." For that day of the revelation of all, he can afford to and he must wait.

But there is more in this hidden life than this. Here is an intimation of the quiet of the Christian life; here is also an intimation of its perfection. It is better than men know or even dream. The Christian is to refuse men's commands of "Touch not, taste not, handle not," not because he is indifferent to morality, but because he has a better morality and a better way. He is not to fall behind human morality; he is to transcend it. He seeks not law but grace; he seeks not to make the outside of the platter clean—how diligently men are willing to work at that!—but to make the heart clean. His remedy for the world's ills, as for his own, is—a life hid with Christ in God. He points to Christ who can make pure the heart, from which are the issues of life, and, in His name and as His servant, he refuses all the outward inoperative nostrums which are offered as specifics for the deep disease of humanity; because they have no help or profit in them. He refuses the bad medicine only in favour of the good.

And now let us pass on to observe that the

Apostle adduces motives for this heavenly walk. And the motives he presents are three, drawn from the past, the present and the future.

There is a motive drawn from the past. "If then ye were raised with Christ." The motive presented is our gratitude to our Lord for the great work He has done for and in us. That we have been made partakers of so great benefits is reason enough for striving to walk worthily of Him. This motive is the same as, "The love of Christ constraineth us."

There is a motive drawn from the present. "For your life is hid with Christ in God." Notice here that Christ is described as, not the humiliated Christ, but the exalted Christ—"He is seated on the right hand of God." The motive presented is that as we all are one with Him, who is exalted to the right hand of God, we are to walk worthily of our high dignity. *Noblesse oblige.* If we are co-regnant with Christ, how should a king in this world walk? As grovelling in its dust and dirt? As subject to man's petty precepts? No! As superior to all the prescriptions of men and as above all the temptations to evil, because one with Christ and possessing a life hid with Him in God.

There is a motive drawn from the future. "When Christ, who is our life, shall be manifested, then shall we also with him be manifested in glory." The vindication, even before men, will come. We shall not always be misunderstood; we shall have the reward. And what a reward! Co-manifestation with Christ in glory! Do not our hearts spring within us with hope and joy!

ENTIRE SANCTIFICATION

1 Thess. 5:23–24:—"And the God of peace himself sanctify you wholly; and may your spirit and soul and body be preserved entire without blame at the coming of our Lord Jesus Christ. Faithful is he that calleth you, who will also do it."

THERE is no feature of Christianity more strongly emphasized by those to whom its establishment in the world was committed, than the breadth and depth of its ethical demands. The "salvation" which was promised in the "Gospel" or "Glad Tidings" which constituted its proclamation, was just salvation from sin and unto holiness. In other words, it was a moral revolution of the most thoroughgoing and radical kind. "Sanctification" is the Biblical word for this moral revolution, and in "sanctification" the very essence of salvation is made to consist. "This is the will of God" for you, says the Apostle to his readers in this very epistle, "even your sanctification." A great part of the epistle is given, accordingly, to commending the new converts for the progress they had already made in this sanctification, and to urging them onward in the same pathway.

No moral attainment is too great to be pressed on them as their duty, no moral duty is too minute to be demanded of them as essential to their

Christian walk. The standard the Apostle nas before him, and consistently applies to his readers, falls in nothing short of absolute perfection, a perfection which embraces in its all-inclusive sweep the infinitely little and the infinitely great alike. In the verses immediately preceding our text the Apostle had been engaged, as is his wont in all his epistles, in enumerating a number of details of conduct which he wished, especially, to emphasize to his readers. They are not chosen at haphazard, but are just the items of conduct which the particular readers with whom he is at the moment engaged required most to have urged upon their attention. But the Apostle would not have his readers suppose that their whole duty was summed up in the items he enumerates. As he draws to the close of his exhortations he therefore breaks off in the enumeration and adjoins one great comprehensive prayer for their entire perfection: "But may the God of peace Himself sanctify you wholly: and may your spirit and soul and body be preserved perfect without failure, at the coming of our Lord Jesus Christ. Faithful is He that calleth you who also will do it."

Here we have obviously a classical passage—possibly the classical passage—for "entire sanctification"; and it may repay us in the perennial interest which attends the discussion of the theme of "entire sanctification" to look at it somewhat closely, as such.

First of all, let us settle it clearly in mind that it is of "entire sanctification" that the passage treats. There can certainly be no doubt of it, if we will only give the language of the passage a fair hearing. It is so emphasized, indeed, and with such an accumulation of phraseology that it becomes almost embarrassing. The entirety, the completeness, the perfection of the sanctification, of which it speaks is, in fact, the great burden of the passage. In contrast with the details with which the Apostle had just been dealing, and which—just because they were details—could touch the periphery only of a perfect life, and that only at this or that point of the circumference, he here adverts to the complete sanctification that not merely touches but fills not the periphery only but the entire circle of the Christian—nay, of the human—life. It is a sanctification that is absolutely complete and that embraces the perfection of every member of the human constitution, that the Apostle here deals with.

Observe the emphatic repetition of the idea of completeness. May the "God of Peace"—and this very designation of God, doubtless, has its reference to the completeness of the sanctification, peace being the opposite of all division, distraction, hesitation and dubitation,—may the "God of Peace," the Apostle prays, "sanctify you completely"—so as that ye may be perfect and wanting nothing that enters into the perfection of your correspondence to the ends for which you were created. And not content with this, he adds explanatorily, "And may your spirit and your soul and your body be preserved entire, perfect," and not that merely, but "blamelessly entire, perfect"; "blamelessly"—that is, in a manner which is incapable of being accused of not coming up to its idea.

Observe further the distribution of the personality which is to be perfected into its component parts, of each of which, in turn, perfection is desiderated. Not only are we to be sanctified wholly, but every part of us—our spirit, our soul, our body itself—is to be kept blamelessly perfect. The Apostle is not content, in other words, with the general, but descends into the specific elements of our being. And for each of these elements in turn he seeks a "blameless perfection," that the sum of them all—the "we" at large—may be, indeed, complete and entire, wanting nothing.

Now, no doubt, this enumeration of parts is in a sense rhetorical and not scientific. The Apostle is accumulating terms to convey the great idea of completeness more pungently to us—something as our Lord did when He told us we must love the Lord our God with all our heart and soul and mind and strength. But even so he makes a certain distinction between the three elements he enumerates, by the accumulation of which he expresses completeness most emphatically. His meaning is that there is no department of our being into which he would not have this perfection penetrate, where he would not have it reign, and through which he would not have it operate to the perfecting of the whole.

By this double mode of accumulation, we perceive, the Apostle throws an astonishing emphasis on the perfection which he desires for his readers. Here we may say is "Perfectionism" raised to its highest power, a blameless perfection, a perfection admitting of no failure to attain its end, in every department of our being alike, uniting to form a perfection of the whole, a complete attainment of our idea in the whole man. There is certainly no doctrine of "entire sanctification" that has been invented in these later days which can compare with Paul's doctrine in height or depth or length or breadth. His "perfectionism" is assuredly the very apotheosis of perfectionism. The perfection proposed is a real perfection (which is not always true of recent teachings on this subject) and the man who attains it is a perfect man—every part of his being receiving its appropriate perfection (and this is seldom or never true of recent teachings). A perfect perfection for a perfect man—an entire sanctification for the entire man—surely here is a perfection worth longing for.

Let us observe next that Paul does not speak

of this perfecting of the entire man as if it were a mere ideal, unattainable, and to be looked up to only as the for ever beckoning standard hanging hopelessly above us. He treats it as distinctly attainable. He seriously prays God to grant it to his readers; and that as the end of his exhortation to them to study moral perfection as the aim of their endeavours.

He does not, indeed, represent it as attainable by and through human effort alone, as if man in his own strength could reach and touch this his true ultimate goal of endeavour. Rather he emphatically represents it as the gift of God alone. After exhorting men to their best endeavours, he turns suddenly from man to God and besieges Him with prayer. Strive, he says, strive always, do this thing and do that—and so work out this, your ethical salvation. "*But* may God *Himself*—the God of peace Himself"—the stress is on the "Himself." It is in God, in God alone, the God of peace alone, that hope can be placed for such high attainments.

But cannot hope be placed in God for this attainment? The whole gist of Paul's prayer—nay, the whole drift of his discourse—would be stultified, were it not so. Paul's prayer, and the way in which he introduces his prayer, all combine to make it certain that he is not mocking us here with an illusory hope but is placing soberly before us an attainable goal. This perfect perfection is then, necessarily, according to Paul, attainable for man. God can and will give it to His children.

Even more must be said. Paul not only prays seriously for it for his readers, and this implies that it may, nay, will be given them; he definitely promises it to them, and bases this, his definite promise, on no less firm a foundation than the faithfulness of God. May God sanctify you wholly, he says, and the rest of it. But he does not stop there. He follows the prayer with the promise: "Faithful is He that calleth you," and he adds, "who also will do it." Thus Paul pledges the faithfulness of God to the completion of his readers' perfection. And we must not lose the force and pointedness with which he does this by failing to pay attention to the sharp, proverbial character of this pledging clause. It has all the quality of a maxim; and the gist of the maxim is that God, this God of whom Paul was praying our perfection, is not a caller only, but also a performer. He has called us into the Christian life. This Christian life into which He has called us is in principle a life of moral perfection. And this God that calls is not a God that calls merely—He is a God that also accomplishes. His very calling of us into this life of new morality is a pledge, then, that He will perfect the good work in us which He has begun. "Faithful is He that calleth you: who also is one that shall do."

The accomplishment of this our perfection then does not hang on our weak endeavours. It does not hang even on Paul's strong prayer. It hangs only on God's almighty and unfailing faithfulness. If God is faithful, He who not only calls but does—then, we cannot fail of perfection. Here you see is not only perfection carried to its highest power, but the certainty of attaining this perfection carried also to its highest power. Not only may a Christian man be perfect—absolutely perfect in all departments of his being—but he certainly and unfailingly shall be perfect. So certain as it is that God has called him "not for uncleanness but in sanctification" as the very sphere in which his life as a Christian must be passed, so certain is it that the God who is not merely a caller but a doer will perfect him in this sanctification. Such is the teaching of the text. And assuredly it goes in this, far, far beyond all modern teaching as to entire sanctification that ever has been heard of among men.

And now, let us observe, thirdly, the period to which the Apostle assigns the accomplishment of this great hope. It is at once evident that he is not dealing with this perfection as a thing already in the possession of his readers. It is not a matter of congratulation to them—as some Christian graces were, for the presence of which in their hearts he thanks God,—but a matter of prayer to God for them. It is a thing not yet in possession but in petition. It is yet to come to them. He does not permit us to suppose, then, that the Thessalonians had already attained—or should already have attained—it. He thanks God, indeed, for their rescue from the state in which they were by nature. He thanks God for their great attainments in Christian living. But he does not suggest they had already reached the goal. On the contrary, a great part of the letter is taken up with exhortation to Christian duties not yet overtaken, graces of Christian living still to be cultivated. His readers are treated distinctly and emphatically as *viatores*, not yet as *comprehensores*. Not in and of them, but in and of God, is the perfection which he prays for. What we see is not hoped for, what we pray for is not already attained. Moreover the very pledge he gives of the attainment of this perfection bears in it an implication that it is yet a matter of hope, not of possession. He pledges the faithfulness of God, the Caller. Accordingly, the perfection longed for and promised is not given in the call itself; it is not the invariable possession of the Christian soul. He that is called looks yet for it; it is sought still; and at the hands of the Caller whose faithfulness assures the performance. The performance, therefore, still lags.

It is clear, therefore, that Paul, though promising this perfection as the certain heritage of every Christian man, presents it as a matter of hope, not yet seen; not as a matter of experience, already enjoyed. That it belongs to us as Christians we can be assured only by the faithfulness of God, the Performer as well as the Caller. Can we learn from Paul *when* we can hope for it? Assuredly, he has not left us in ignorance here. He openly declares, indeed, the term of our imperfection—the point of entrance into our perfection. "May the God of peace," he prays, "sanctify you wholly and may there be preserved blamelessly perfect your spirit and soul and body, *at the coming of our Lord Jesus Christ.*" You see it is on the second advent of Christ—and that is the end of the world, and the judgment day—that the Apostle has his eyes set. There is the point of time to which he refers the completeness of our perfecting.

And if you will stop and consider a moment, you will perceive that it must be so, for the entire perfecting, at least, of which the Apostle speaks. For you will bear in mind that the perfecting includes the perfecting of the body also. It is the perfecting of the whole man that he prays for, and this expressly includes the body as well as the soul and spirit. Now the perfected body is given to man only at the resurrection, at the last day, which is the day of the second coming of Christ. Until then the body is mouldering in the grave. Whether spiritual perfection may be attained before then, he does not in this passage say. But the analogy of the body will apparently go so far as this, at all events—it raises a suspicion that the perfecting of the soul and spirit also will be gradual, the result of a process, and will be completed only in a crisis, a cataclysmic moment, when the Spirit of God produces in them the fitness to live with God. This suspicion is entirely borne out by Paul's dealing with the whole matter of sanctification in this context, and in this whole epistle: as a matter of effort, long-continued and strenuous, building up slowly the structure to the end. There is no promise of its completion in this life; there is no hint that it may be completed in this life. There is only everywhere strong exhortations to ceaseless effort; and strong encouragements by promises of its completion in the end—against "that day." "That day" of judgment, that is, when God shall take account of all men and of all that is in man.

What is thus fairly implied here is openly taught elsewhere. Men here are not *comprehensores* but *viatores;* we are fighting the good fight; we are running the race. The prize is yonder. And not until the body of this death is laid aside shall the soul be fitted to enter naked into the presence of its Lord, there expecting until the body shall be restored to it—no longer a body of death but of glory. Meanwhile the gradual process of sanctification goes on in soul and body —until the crisis comes when the "Spiritus Creator" shall powerfully intervene with the final acts of renewal.

Certainly the gradualness of this process ought not to disturb us. It may be inexplicable to us that the Almighty God acts by way of process. But that is revealed to us as His chosen mode of operation in every sphere of His work, and should not surprise us here. He could, no doubt, make the soul perfect in a moment, in the twinkling of an eye; just as He could give us each a perfect body at the very instant of our believing. He does not. The removal of the stains and effects of sin—in an evil heart and in a sick and dying body—is accomplished in a slow process. We all grow sick and die—though Jesus has taken on His broad shoulders (among the other penalties of sin) all our sicknesses and death itself. And we still struggle with the remainders of indwelling sin; though Jesus has bought for us the sanctifying operations of the Spirit. To us it is a weary process. But it is God's way. And He does all things well. And the weariness of the struggle is illuminated by hope. After a while!—we may say; after a while! Or as Paul puts it: Faithful is He that calls us—who also will do it. He will do it! And so, after a while, our spirit, and soul and body shall be made blamelessly perfect, all to be so presented before our Lord, at that Day. Let us praise the Lord for the glorious prospect!

THE MYSTERY OF GODLINESS

I Tim. 3:16:—"And without controversy great is the mystery of godliness."

"CONFESSEDLY great," says Paul, "is the mystery of piety." This does not mean that piety is exceedingly "mysterious." There is no "mystery" in piety as such. As Paul means it here it rests simply, objectively on the great fact, subjectively on the hearty conviction that God was in Christ reconciling the world with Himself. The word "mystery," in the usage of Paul, does not imply inherent incomprehensibility, but only actual inaccessibility to the natural inquisition of men. Whatever is known by revelation rather than by unaided reason, is, in his usage, a "mystery"; and the employment of the word by no means implies that the revelation has not already taken place and the hidden truth been made fully known, but rather just the contrary. The "mystery of piety" is thus just "the opened secret of piety." And what Paul affirms of it is that this "opened secret of piety" is confessedly of the highest importance. "Confessedly great" he says, and he throws these words forward with sharp emphasis, "of admittedly the highest importance," "is the mystery of piety."

What Paul is doing in this clause, then, is simply impressing on Timothy's mind as deeply as possible a sense of the supreme value of the Gospel, which he calls a "mystery" only because it is a matter of revelation, but without the faintest implication that it is difficult to grasp when once made known, or that it includes in it any elements of the inscrutable or incomprehensible. Christianity, like other religions, had its mysteries, its sacred truths, made known to its initiates; and these mysteries, as they constituted its very essence, were to every Christian of the most supreme importance—to be carefully guarded, preserved intact, and kept whole and entire, pure and unadulterated, at every hazard. Confessedly great, says the Apostle here with marked emphasis, admittedly of supreme importance, is the mystery, the opened secret of Christian piety, the Gospel.

It is especially worth our while to observe two things here. First, preliminarily, why the Apostle is so strenuous in insisting here on the importance of the opened secret of piety, the value and significance of the Gospel. And, secondly, and more at large, because it is this that constitutes the burden of the text, what the Apostle conceived to be this "opened secret of piety," that is to say, what he conceived to be the contents of the Gospel which he pronounces here to have such confessed importance.

We need not delay long on the preliminary

point. A glance at the context is enough to inform us that the Apostle insists on the greatness of the Gospel here in order to impress Timothy with the importance of attending to the directions he had been giving him as to the proper ordering of the Church. Somewhat minute prescriptions had been laid down especially as to the conduct of public worship and as to the organization of the Church. In particular the officers of the Church had been enumerated, and the qualifications for their offices carefully described. At the close of these directions, now, the Apostle adds these pointed words: "I am writing these things to you, though I hope to come to you very soon: but if I am delayed that you may know what sort of behaviour is incumbent in God's house—seeing that it is the Church of the Living God, the pillar and buttress of the truth; and confessedly great is the mystery of piety. . . ." You see, his appeal to the confessed greatness of the truth, for the support and propagation of which in the world the Church exists, is intended to impress Timothy with a sense of the importance of the proper ordering and right equipment of the Church for this, its high function.

It is of the more importance that we should note this, that there is a disposition abroad to treat all matters of the ordering of public worship and even of the organization of the Church as of little importance. We even hear it said about us with wearisome iteration that the New Testament has no rules to give, no specific laws to lay down, in such matters. Matters of church government and modes of worship, we are told, are merely external things, of no sort of significance; and the Church has been left free to find its own best modes of organization and worship, varying, doubtless, in the passage of time and in the Church's own passage from people to people of diverse characters and predilections. No countenance is lent to such sentiments by the passage before us; or, indeed, by these Pastoral Epistles, the very place of which in the Canon is a standing rebuke to them; or, in fine, by anything in the New Testament.

On the contrary, you will observe, Paul's point of view is precisely the opposite one. He takes his start from the inestimable importance of the Gospel. Thence he argues to the importance of the Church which has been established in the world, so to speak, as the organ of the Gospel—the pillar and buttress on which its purity and its completeness rest. Thence again he argues to the proper organization and ordering of the Church that it may properly perform its high functions. And, accordingly, he gives minute prescriptions for the proper organization and ordering of the Church—prescribing the offices that it should have and the proper men for these offices, and descending even into the details of the public services. His position, compressed into a nutshell, is simply this: the function of the Church as guardian of the truth, that glorious truth which is the Gospel, is so high and important that it cannot be left to accident or to human caprice how this Church should be organized and its work ordered. Accordingly, he, the inspired Apostle—"an Apostle of Christ Jesus according to the commandment of God our Saviour and Christ, our Hope"—has prescribed in great detail, touching both organization and order, how it is necessary that men should conduct themselves in the household of God—which is nothing other than the Church of the Living God, the pillar and ground of the truth. In other words, it is God's Church, not man's, and God has created and now sustains it for a function; and He has not neglected to order it for the best performance of this function.

To imagine that it is of little importance how the Church shall be organized and ordered, then, is manifestly to contradict the Apostle. To contend that no organization is prescribed for it is to deny the total validity of the minute directions laid down in these epistles. Nay, this whole point of view is as irrational as it is unbiblical. One might as well say that it makes no difference how a machine is put together—how, for example, a typewriter is disposed in its several parts,—because, forsooth, the typewriter does not exist for itself, but for the manuscript which is produced by or rather through it. Of course the Church does not exist for itself—that is, for the beauty of its organization, the symmetry of its parts, the majesty of its services; it exists for its "product" and for the "truth" which has been committed to it and of which it is the support and stay in the world. But just on that account, not less but more, is it necessary that it be properly organized and equipped and administered—that it may function properly. Beware how you tamper with any machine, lest you mar or destroy its product; beware how you tamper with or are indifferent to the Divine organization and ordering of the Church, lest you thereby mar its efficiency or destroy its power, as the pillar and ground of the truth. Surely you can trust God to know how it is best to organize His Church so that it may perform its functions in the world. And surely you must assert that His ordering of the Church, which is His, is necessary if not for the "esse," certainly for the "bene esse" of the Church.

But our main attention to-day must be given to the Apostle's elaboration of the contents of this "truth," or this "mystery of piety," to support and buttress which he tells us the Church has been established in the world. He moves Timothy to zeal in properly ordering the church under his care, by the declaration that "the opened secret of piety," to support and buttress which the Church exists, is confessedly of the utmost importance. And then he deepens and vitalizes the impression which this declaration is calculated to make by abruptly enumerating the chief items which enter into this "mystery of piety"—this "truth" for which the Church exists.

This enumeration thus embodies Paul's conception of the essence of the Gospel, and takes its place among the numerous brief summaries of the essence of the Gospel which stud the pages of his epistles. It differs from most of them, however, in this circumstance—that it is not couched in language of his own, but the Apostle has availed himself here, as so often in the Pastoral Epistles, of a form of statement current in the churches, which would appeal to Timothy's eye and heart, therefore, with all the force of customary and well-loved words, in which he and the congregation had been wont to express their apprehension of the truth most precious to their hearts. Whether the words thus adduced are derived from some current liturgical form, or from a hymn, or merely from some formulary of accustomed speech, we have no means of knowing. We can only be sure that the whole document is not quoted here and, from the balanced, almost mechanical form of its structure, that the original document possessed an elevated and festal character.

The choice of the Apostle to adduce the essence of the Gospel from such a current formulary, rather than to frame it out of his own heart, naturally produces a certain abruptness in the words in which it is introduced. A fragment of current speech, torn out of its own context, is here simply juxtaposed by way of apposition to his own declaration, that the Gospel is a supremely important thing, and left to exhibit that importance by its contents. "Great," he says, "confessedly great, is the opened secret of piety," this to wit: "Who was manifested in the flesh, vindicated by the Spirit, observed by angels, proclaimed among peoples, believed in by the world, received into glory." There is not a word to tell us who was the subject of all these transactions; that was a part of the original context of the fragment, and here goes without saying; no one of his readers—least of all his primary reader Timothy, who knew as well as Paul the whole document from which the fragment was derived,—would hesitate to supply the subject, Jesus Christ. What Paul does is simply to avail himself of this fervent fragment and set out the contents of the "mystery of piety" by means of its rapid enumeration of the principal transactions which concerned the redemptive work of Christ—beginning with the incarnation and ending with the ascension.

Now, of course, this means that to Paul, Christ is the essence of the Gospel. As everywhere else, so here, he sums up the Gospel in Christ; not Christ, of course, merely as a person, but the active Christ—or in other words, in the great redemptive work of Christ. And it will repay us to observe in some detail how the redemptive work of Christ is presented to us in this somewhat artificially because artistically ordered fragment of old Christian confessional expression.

We observe, at once, that the fragment consists of a series of six passive verbs, rapidly succeeding one another, with the common subject "Jesus Christ," each further defined by a brief predicative qualification; the verb being put emphatically forward in each case: He was "manifested" in the flesh, "vindicated" by the Spirit, "seen" by angels. . . . We observe next that the clauses are so arranged as to fall necessarily into three contrasting pairs; and yet these three pairs are bound together by the contrast in each case being made to turn upon the contrariety of earth and heaven, or of the flesh and the spirit. Thus we have the successive triads on the one hand of the flesh, the peoples, the world; on the other of the Spirit, the angels, glory. There is no strict chronological order of occurrence followed in the enumeration, but the pairs so succeed one another as yet to suggest a beginning, a middle and an end; the inception, the prosecution, the consummation of Christ's work. On the one hand, he was manifested in the flesh and vindicated by the Spirit. Here clearly His earthly life is in mind, with the stress laid perhaps on its inception in the incarnation and its culmination in the resurrection. Then we have the declaration that He was seen of angels and proclaimed among the nations. Here the process of the saving work is referred to,—chiasmically adduced. Finally, we read, He was believed on in the world and received into glory. Here the stress is laid obviously on the result of His work. The whole constitutes an exceedingly comprehensive description of the process of redemption, antithetically set forth in balanced clauses, which advert, one by one, to a characteristic transaction of which Christ was the object.

Let us now briefly observe the several items of the description, *seriatim*.

He "was manifested in the flesh, vindicated by the Spirit." Here we have the redemptive work itself adduced. First, the incarnated life in the flesh—He "was manifested in the flesh"; next, the successful issue of that work,—He "was vindicated by the Spirit." The two clauses together constitute a singularly vivid though compressed picture of the incarnated work of redemption. Note the clear implication of the pre-existence—the deity—of the worker: He "was manifested,"—He existed then, hidden from human eyes, before; "in the flesh,"—in his pre-existence, then, he was something other than flesh. It is as clear a declaration of pre-existence and incarnation as the Johannean, "The Word became flesh," itself. There is a change of state implied, a change by virtue of which what was hidden is now brought to light, and it is brought to light because brought into flesh. Note next the perfection of His work established: He was "justified by the Spirit"; that is to say, though appearing in the flesh, yet by virtue of the Spirit that dwelt in Him, His work of salvation was vindicated; He rose from the dead, and could not be holden of death, and so manifested the completeness of His work.

He was "observed by angels, proclaimed among peoples." Here the progress of the saving work is outlined. It was not done in or for a corner. The object of the wondering contemplation of the hosts of heaven, it is made known also to the inhabitants of earth. Performed in Judea, in a life of confined and limited relations, to all appearance, yet it was all the time the focus of the observation of the angels of God, who anxiously desired to look into it; and when brought to its glorious completion, it was made the subject of a world-wide proclamation. Obviously it is the glory of the Christ—of the redemptive work of Christ—that is the theme of the whole fragment, and in this couplet we begin to see it come to light; and, indeed, the chiasmic arrangement might well have advised us of it before, what is most glorious in it being thrust forward to attract our first attention.

He was "believed on in the world, received into glory." Here we have the issue of the work adverted to; the earthly and the heavenly issue. So little chronological is the ordering that the conquest of the world by Christ is actually adduced first, while His ascension is adduced last. The order is climactic, not chronological; He has His earthly reward and also His heavenly. In these two items the whole comes to the appropriate end.

And now I think we are prepared to see clearly that the whole fragment is a hymn of praise to Christ. He was before all worlds; He was only "manifested" in the flesh and vindicated by the Spirit. He was the object of the contemplation of the angels of heaven and proclaimed in all the earth. He was believed on in the world and received into glory. It is the Glory of Christ that, according to Paul constitutes the essence of the Gospel. "O, Jesus, Thou art our head, we are thy body!"—so one of God's saints teaches us to pray. "How can the body but participate in the glory of the Head? As for Thyself, therefore, so also for us art Thou possessed of that heavenly glory: as Thou sufferedst for us, so for us Thou also reignest. . . . O then, my soul, seeing thy Saviour is received up into this infinite glory, . . . how canst thou abide to grovel any longer on this base earth? . . . With what longings and holy ambition shouldst thou desire to aspire to that place of eternal rest and beatitude into which thy Saviour has ascended, and with him be partaker of that glory and happiness which he hath provided for all that love him."

THE INVIOLATE DEPOSIT

I Tim. 6:20, 21:—"O Timothy, guard that which is committed unto thee, turning away from the profane babblings and oppositions of the knowledge which is falsely so called; which some professing have erred concerning the faith."

THIS short paragraph looks very much like a concluding summary, added, possibly, by the Apostle's own hand, in which the whole gist of the First Epistle to Timothy is summed up. It is almost as if the Apostle—after all the explanations and exhortations in which he had instructed and encouraged his own son in faith to perform the great duties laid on him in errant Ephesus—had paused suddenly and said in effect, "Hear the sum of the whole matter, Be faithful to the Gospel committed to you and shun all the pretentious show of superior learning which is proving a snare to many." Such an exhortation, it is manifest, has its universal and perennial value; and is peculiarly applicable to those in our situation. As we begin another year of our intellectual preparation for the ministry of the Gospel of grace, it is especially becoming that we should have in mind that it will be our wisdom too, as it is manifestly our duty, "to keep the deposit inviolate" and to shun the worldly inanities and contradictions of falsely so-called knowledge, by making profession of which so many in every age, and in our age too, have gone astray with respect to faith.

These latest epistles of Paul are commonly called Pastoral because of their direct address to the shepherds of the flock, and every word in such an exhortation as this, in such an Epistle as this, has a quasi-technical value. The key word among these words is the one which I have ventured to render after the Vulgate, "the deposit," and which the Authorized Version deals with by means of a paraphrase: "that which is committed to thy trust." It does not occur very often, but it does occur frequently enough to show that it and its cognate verb are employed by the Apostle as a well-known designation of the Gospel, considered as a body of Divine truth entrusted to those whom God has chosen as its ministers. As such, it stands in very clear relations with another technical term employed by the New Testament writers to describe the function of the ministers of the Gospel,—the term "witness." The Gospel is a "deposit"; the function of the minister is, therefore, "witnessing." The two ideas, you see, go necessarily together. The witness is in his essential nature not a producer but a reproducer; he is not the author of his message but its transmitter; his message is, therefore, not of his own devising but something committed to his trust,—a deposit. I do not know where the fundamental significance of the word "deposit" and its implications as to the duty of the minister is more richly developed than in a Fifth Century exposition of this passage, by Vincent of Lerins. His comment is so instructive that I cannot forbear quoting a part of it to you. "What," he asks, "is a deposit?" "It is something," he answers, "that is accredited to thee, not invented by thee; something that thou hast received, not that thou hast thought out; a result not of genius but of instruction; not of personal ownership but of public tradition; a matter brought to thee not produced by thee, with respect to which thou art bound to be not an author but a custodian, not an originator but a bearer, not a leader but a follower."

It is this that Paul means to emphasize when he calls the Gospel a "deposit." I rightly say he means to emphasize this. For he not only calls the Gospel a "deposit," but he sets it as such in contrast with its opposite, and that opposite proves to be just irresponsible speculation. O Timothy, he says, keep the deposit inviolate! And how is he to keep the deposit inviolate? "By shunning the profane inanities and contradictions of falsely so-called knowledge." You see the contrast is precisely between the Divine deposit and worldly knowledge. And he describes this worldly knowledge by epithets which are sufficiently discrediting to it. It consists of a mass of inanities and self-contradictions; it is, therefore, not real knowledge but only knowledge falsely so called. No doubt he had his eye on a specific instance,—the nascent Gnosticism, let us call it, which was disturbing the church at Ephesus, and to rebuke and correct which Timothy was in Ephesus. But I think that it would be wrong to suppose that the Apostle had this exclusively in mind. Rather he seems to be viewing it as a type of a whole class. Or, let us at once put it as broadly as we think it lay in his own mind; there is no reason to doubt that the Apostle would speak in exactly these terms of any worldly knowledge whatever, any form of earthly philosophy or science, that infringed upon or sought to substitute itself more or less for the "deposit" of the Gospel of Christ. Any speculation, any philosophizing, any form of learning, any scientific theorizing which sought to intrude itself, in the way of modifying it in the least respect, upon the Gospel of Christ,—which is a sacred deposit committed to its ministers not to dilute or to alter or to modify, but to learn, hold, guard and preach,—would be characterized by Paul without hesitation as among the profane inanities and contradictions of knowledge falsely so called.

Our memory reverts at once to the splendid passage in the opening chapter of the First Epistle to the Corinthians, in which Paul magnificently contrasts the wisdom of the world with the simplicity of the message of the cross, and passionately declares that God has made the wisdom of the world mere foolishness. Yes, there is passion, a holy passion, but real passion, in Paul's renunciation of all human wisdom and declaration that God will destroy the wisdom of the wise and reject the prudence of the prudent. And some of that same passion is throbbing in the vigorous language of our present passage. Not indeed knowledge as such, but all human knowledge as a substitute for, or a modifying force in, the Gospel of Christ, is to Paul a mass of mere profane inanities and self-contradictions, to give oneself to which is to miss the mark with respect to faith. Dirt has been illuminatingly defined as matter out of place. Any substance, no matter how precious in itself, if out of place is nothing more or less than just dirt. Gold-dust in your eye is just dirt; wash it out; it is an offence there. Diamonds scattered in your porridge are dirt; cast them out. To the starving man seeking nourishment and life, they are not only an offensive evil but a destructive evil. You all know how King Midas found that gold in the wrong place could become the worst of ills. So it is with knowledge. What, in its proper place, is knowledge,—to be sought, loved and cherished as such, to be valued and utilized for its own good ends,—becomes knowledge falsely so called whenever it intrudes into a place not its own; a mass of mere inanities and self-contradictions. And it is just this that Paul means here.

He is not condemning knowledge as such. He, too, would say with the poet—

> "Who loves not knowledge? Who shall rail
> Against her beauty? May she mix
> With men and prosper! . . .
> . . . Let her work prevail."

But just so soon as it presses beyond its mark and presumes to substitute itself for the Gospel of Christ, or to demand an alteration in that Gospel, or a modification of it, however slight, his righteous passion rises. Dirt! he cries,—matter out of place! the profane inanities and self-contradictions of falsely so-called knowledge!

"Falsely so-called knowledge"—that phrase is his tribute to the value of real knowledge. When thus debauched knowledge ceases to be knowledge and becomes mere "falsely so-called knowledge." "Profane inanities and self-contradictions," that is Paul's description of what knowledge out of place is; pressing beyond its mark to become procuress to the lords of hell. For, says he, those that make so much profession of such knowledge are too often observed to miss the mark with respect to faith. The passion that burns in these words rises to sight everywhere in these epistles, when the intrusion of human speculation into matters of faith falls to be mentioned, and quite a choice vocabulary of reprobation might be extracted from Paul's expression of it. On the other side, what a fervour of love is manifested for that "deposit" which is the Gospel of God's saving grace! He calls it in the present passage, to be sure, simply "the deposit," but I am not sure that the very simplicity of the designation is not surcharged with passionate devotion. "The Deposit," "*The* Deposit," "*The Deposit*," "Guard the Deposit," "Keep *The Deposit* inviolate." It is as if there were but one deposit conceivable to him and to those to whom he wrote. And see how he claims it as his own, in 2 Tim. 1:12, calling it "my deposit." "I know whom I have believed and I am persuaded—though I fall by the way—yet He is able to keep my deposit against that day." To Paul his deposit was more than life itself. Paul may go—but what then? "The deposit," "his deposit" is safe in the hands of Him who committed it to him. And then, again, two verses lower (2 Tim. 1:14), "Keep, O Timothy, keep inviolate, the beautiful deposit through the Holy Ghost that dwelleth in us." Ah, it is the devotion of Paul for "the deposit" that makes him speak such passionate words against that which would supplement or adulterate it. It is its surpassing glory which makes dull the glory of that which away from it would itself be glorious. The glory of the world of intellect itself fades like that of the face of Moses, like that of the old covenant in the presence of the new,—by reason only of the glory that surpasses all—the glory of that glorious Gospel of the grace of God. It is, in a word, the inherent preciousness of the Gospel, not the inherent valuelessness of knowledge, that makes all knowledge in contrast with it, but foolishness—but a mass of profane inanities and self-contradictions which should not be permitted to intrude into these sacred precincts.

A practical lesson imposes itself upon us. Preach a full-orbed, a complete Gospel. The deposit is not yours to deal with as you will; it is another's entrusted to your care. The deposit is not your product to be treated as you will; it is the creation of another placed in your keeping. You are but its witnesses. Bear your witness truly and bear it fully. Keep the deposit inviolate.

THE WAY OF LIFE

Titus 3:4–7:—"But when the kindness of God, our Saviour, and his love towards man, appeared, not by works done in righteousness, which we did ourselves, but according to his mercy he saved us, through the washing of regeneration and renewing of the Holy Ghost, which he poured out upon us richly, through Jesus Christ our Saviour; that being justified by his grace, we might be made heirs according to the hope of eternal life."

THE short epistle to Titus contains, amid its practical and ecclesiastical directions for the giving of which it was written, two doctrinal statements of quite wonderful richness and compression both of which have been easily brought into the compass of the passage read in your hearing this afternoon. They differ from each other in intent and content, as you will doubtless have observed. But they are alike in gathering into the narrow space of a few words the essence of the Gospel, and expressing it in words of a singularly festal and jubilant character, words which strike the reader as at once precise and comprehensive, as at once theologically exact and peculiarly fitted for public credal use.

Statements of this kind are characteristic of these latest epistles of the Apostle Paul, which we class together under the common title of the Pastoral Epistles, and which share not only the late date but also a character appropriate to their origin at the end of Paul's life when he was busied with consolidating and extending the churches he had founded rather than with the first planting of Christianity in the fresh soil of an unbelieving world. They present the doctrines of Paul, after they had been used, and worn round by use. They represent the sifting down of his doctrinal expositions into compact form; their compression into something like pebbles from the brook ready to be flung with sure aim and to sink into the foreheads of the Goliaths of unbelief. They represent the form which his doctrinal expositions had taken as current coin in the churches, no longer merely Paul's teaching, though all of that, but the precious possessions of the people themselves, in which they were able to give back to him a response from their listening hearts. They are no longer mere dialectical elaboration of the truth; but have become forms of sound words. As such, such passages are sometimes accompanied by a phrase peculiar to these Pastoral Epistles, which advertises these statements as something other than a teacher's novel presentations of truth to as yet untaught hearers: "This is a faithful saying." "This is a faithful saying"—a "trustworthy saying"—in other words, this is a saying well-known among you, that has been long repeated in your ears, that has been tested and found not wanting. This is good coin; and "worthy," it is sometimes added, "of all acceptation."

Our present passage is one of these "faithful

sayings." "Faithful is the saying," the Apostle adds on completing it, "and concerning these things I will that thou shouldst affirm confidently." Thus he tells us how important, how well-considered, how final and trustworthy this statement of truth is. Let us approach its study in a spirit suitable to so solemn an injunction.

The first thing that we observe in the passage is the melody that rises from it of praise to God. It is the "kindness of God our Saviour and his love towards men" which sets its key-note. The special terms in which God's goodness is here praised, His "benignity" and "philanthropy," are due, indeed, to the context. The Apostle had just been thinking and speaking about men; and he could not think or speak of them as either "benignant" or "philanthropic." He would have them exhorted to be subject to those over them, obedient, prone to good works, and averse to evil speaking and contentiousness, gentle and meek. But such they were not showing themselves. Christians themselves could remember how aforetime they lived in malice and envy, hateful and hating one another. What could be expected from man? What a contrast when one lifted his eyes from this scene of lust and malice and envy and hatred—men striving with one another to surpass each other in doing injury to their fellows—and set them on God, to see His benignity and philanthropy! The whole passage is pervaded by the suggestion of God's kindness and humanity; thrown out into sharp relief by its contrast with man's malice and hatred. Nothing can be expected of or from man; but God has manifested His benignity and philanthropy to us and by them saved us. Man would destroy, God saves.

But there is much more than this to be said. The passage is not only pervaded by the suggestion of God's general goodness; it is a psalm of praise to God for His saving love. It sings not only "Gloria Deo" but "Soli Deo Gloria." Our salvation is its subject. It not only ascribes salvation in its root to God's love; it ascribes it in every one of its details to God's loving activities and to them alone; it ascribes its beginning and middle and end to Him and to Him only. The various activities that enter into our salvation are enumerated; and every one of them is declared to be a loving activity of God and of Him alone. This passage is even remarkable in this respect. Even in that classical passage in Ephesians, which is designed to ascribe salvation wholly to God, and to empty man of all ground of boasting, we have faith, at least, mentioned: "We are saved by grace, through faith"; though it is immediately added: "And that not of yourselves, it is the gift of God." But this passage leaves faith itself to one side as not requiring mention. There are no subjective conditions to salvation, in the sense of conditions which we must perform in order to obtain or retain salvation. It is God alone who saves, "not by means of any works in righteousness which we have done ourselves but in consequence of his mercy" and of that alone. Not even faith itself, that instrument of reception to which salvation comes, can be conceived of as entering causally into God's saving work. It is He and He alone who saves; and the roots of His saving operations are set deep in His mercy only. If we are saved at all, it is because—not that we have worked, not that we have believed,—but that God has manifested His benignity and philanthropy in saving us out of His mere mercy. He has, through Jesus Christ, shed down His Holy Spirit to regenerate and renovate us that we might be justified "by His grace,"—in other words, gratuitously, not on the ground of our faith,—and so be made heirs of eternal life.

Our passage empties man of all glory in the matter of salvation and reserves all the glory to God. But this is not because it does not know how to distribute honour to whom honour is due. Man has no part in the procuring or in the applying of salvation, but there are Three Persons who have; and our passage recognizes the praise due to each, and distributes to each Person of the Holy Trinity the saving operations which belong to Him. "*God* . . . according to His mercy, . . . saved us, through the washing of regeneration and renewal of the *Holy Ghost*, which He poured out on us richly through *Jesus Christ* our Saviour." The source of our salvation is to be sought in the loving mercy of God the Father. The ground of the saving activities exerted on us is to be sought in the work of Jesus Christ our Saviour. The agent in the actual saving work is to be sought in the Holy Ghost. Here are brought before us God our Lover, Christ our Redeemer, the Spirit our Sanctifier, as all operative in the one composite work of salvation. To God the Father is ascribed the whole scheme of salvation and the entire direction of the saving work; it is His benignity and philanthropy that is manifested in it; it is according to His own mercy that He has saved us; it is He that saved us; He saved us through the Holy Spirit; He poured out the Holy Spirit through Jesus Christ; it is His salvation and it is He that has given it to us. To Jesus Christ is ascribed the work of "Saviour" by which the outpouring of the Holy Spirit was rendered possible to God. The nature of His work is not precisely outlined in our passage; but in the preceding passage we are told that "He gave Himself for us, that He might redeem us from all iniquity." This it is that the Son does for us. To the Holy Spirit is ascribed the actual application of the redemption wrought out by Christ. The items of this application are very richly developed, and the development of them constitutes the strength of the passage.

If we will scrutinize the items in which the applying work of the Holy Spirit is developed, we shall perceive that they supply us with a complete "order of salvation." We are told that God saves us in His mere mercy, by a renovating work of the Holy Spirit, founded on the redeeming work of Christ; and we are told that this renovating work of the Holy Spirit was in order that we might be justified and so become heirs. Here the purchase by the death of Christ is made the condition precedent of the regeneration of the Holy Spirit; but the action of the Holy Spirit is made the condition precedent to justification and adoption. We are bought unto God by Christ in order that we may be brought to God by the Holy Spirit. And in bringing us to God, the Holy Spirit proceeds by regenerating us in order that we may be justified so as to be made heirs. In theological language, this is expressed by saying that the impetration of salvation precedes its application: the whole of the impetration, the whole of the application. And in the application, the Spirit works by first regenerating the soul, next justifying it, next adopting it into the family of God, and next sanctifying it. In the more vital and less analytical language of our present passage, this is asserted by founding the gift of the Holy Ghost upon the work of Christ: "which He poured out upon us richly through Jesus Christ our Saviour"; by including in the work of the Holy Ghost, regeneration, justification, adoption, and a few verses lower down, sanctification; and by declaring that the regeneration of the Holy Spirit is "in order that being justified we might be made heirs."

Now what are the practical fruits of this teaching? The Apostle says it is faithful teaching, which he wishes to have confidently affirmed, to the end that they which have believed God may be careful to maintain good works. It is encouraging teaching to believers to tell them that they are not their own saviours but God is their Saviour; that their salvation is not suspended on their own works or the strength of their own faith, but on the strength of God's love and His mercy alone; that all Three Persons of the Trinity are engaged in and pledged to their salvation; that Christ's work for them is finished and they are redeemed to God by His precious blood and are, henceforth, God's purchased possession; that it is not dependent on their own weakness but on the Spirit's strength whether they will be brought into the enjoyment of their salvation; that the Spirit has been poured richly out upon them; that He has begun His work of renovation within them; that this is but the pledge of the end and as they have been regenerated and justified, so have they been brought into the family of God and made heirs of eternal life. This is encouraging teaching for believers! Shall they, then, because they are saved out of God's mercy and not out of works in righteousness which they have done themselves, be careless to maintain good works? I trow not; and the Apostle troweth not. Because of this, they will now be careful "to maintain good works." Let us see to it then that by so doing we approve ourselves as true believers, saved by God's grace, not out of works but unto good works, which He hath afore prepared that we should walk in them! This is what the Apostle would have us do.

THE ETERNAL GOSPEL

2 Tim. 1:9, 10:—"Who saved us and called us with a holy calling, not according to our works, but according to his own purpose and grace, which was given us in Christ Jesus before times eternal, but hath now been manifested by the appearing of our Saviour Christ Jesus, who abolished death, and brought life and incorruption to light through the Gospel."

SECOND Timothy is the last letter written by Paul. More than that, it was written during the last days of his life. He had fought his fight and finished his course. What had the Gospel he had preached done for him? What was his attitude towards the salvation in Christ Jesus which he had so long proclaimed, now that life was over and he could look back in a detached sort of a way over its whole course? Did it seem to him in those sad disillusioning days as—scarcely worth while?

It certainly is interesting to catch Paul's last thoughts about the Gospel; to learn what that Gospel was and what it was to him as the sands of his life ran out; to compare it with the Gospel he had grasped with such enthusiasm at the outset and propagated with such zeal during the days of his strength and freedom. Well, it is reassuring to find that the Gospel Paul preached at the end was just the same old Gospel he had embraced at the beginning. And more than that, that it was the same to him.

There is even an odd echo in the very language he uses here to describe the Gospel of that which he had employed in the earlier, lustier days. To the Romans he had written that he was not ashamed of the Gospel, because it was the power of God unto salvation. To Timothy he gives the exhortation not to be ashamed of the Gospel but to endure manfully in its behalf, with an endurance measured only by the power of God manifested in the salvation it had brought.

The echo in the language, I say, is oddly close, because there is no direct connection between the two passages; and when closely scrutinized they are perceived to speak of two very different things. In Romans we have an objective statement; in Second Timothy an intensely subjective one. In the one case the contrast is with the scorn of the world. Paul will not be deterred by that; he cannot be ashamed to preach a Gospel in which is enshrined the power of God to save. In the other case, the contrast is with the persecution of the world. Timothy is not to shrink back before the dangers that now hang over the proclamation of the Gospel, but to witness straight on, emboldened by the saving power of this Gospel in his own heart.

One passage is then in no sense a repetition of the other; both are rather embodiments of the same fundamental idea for completely different ends. This fundamental idea is that the Gospel is the power of God to salvation and therefore a thing of which no man with a mind to see can possibly be ashamed, and which no man with a heart to feel can possibly be frightened away from proclaiming. Because it has the dynamics of life in it, it stands immeasurably above all the so-called Gospels that men can proclaim. Nay, because it has the dynamics of life in it, he who has it hidden in his heart cannot fear death.

One sees the enheartening power there is in this perception of the Gospel as the power of God to salvation. We cannot wonder that Paul uses this conception, whether to enhearten himself in preaching it despite the scorn of men, or in enheartening Timothy in preaching it despite the persecutions of men. It is natural then that it should crop out here again, where the Apostle would fain put new courage into Timothy in the sad time that had come upon the Gospel proclamation. The propagation of the Gospel through the Roman world had hung largely on the arm of Paul. But that arm was now stricken down, and Paul was lying in the Roman prison with nothing to anticipate except an inglorious death. Something like a panic seems to have fallen upon the little circle of helpers on whom he was accustomed to depend as on hands and feet in the prosecution of his great missionary task. Though in prison and nearing the fatal issue, the burden of the churches still rested on his stricken arm. He enumerates the disposition of the forces he had made and was making.

For the work at Rome, however, he was short-handed and felt helpless. One of those whom he had depended on for the dangerous work there had fled. Only Luke remained with him; he needed two additional helpers. He turns to Timothy and Mark; and it is striking to see him turn to these two in his hour of need, and with obvious trust and confidence in them. On a former occasion Mark had forsaken him at a juncture of importance. And many commentators have thought that his general tone to Timothy implies that Paul thought him little endowed with the quality of daring. This appears to rest on a mistake; the effort which the Apostle makes to enhearten Timothy for his work does not seem to imply special timidity suspected in him so much as the need of special courage for what he asks of him. At all events, his choice of Timothy for aid in this hour of need and the express encomium which he passes on Mark as one fitted to be his companion in the arduous service asked of him would seem to be a diploma of trustworthiness given to these helpers. We may be sure that he wishes for Timothy and Mark in this sad time to be standing by his side, because he had special confidence in just Timothy and Mark.

Nevertheless Paul recognizes that there is very special need of courage and boldness for the service he is asking. And in asking the service he points Timothy to the source of strength. That source of strength to which he points Timothy is, briefly, the Gospel, conceived as embodying the power of God to salvation. He reminds Timothy first of his hereditary faith; next of his endowment with grace by the laying on of the Apostle's hands; but finally and chiefly of the power of God he had himself experienced in the Gospel which he was called on to preach and for which he was to be ready also to suffer. It was not his human strength that was to be called on for this great endurance; haply that might soon be exhausted. His endurance was to be limited only by the power of God, of that God who had saved him and called him with a holy calling, not according to any works of his own, but according to only to God's own purpose and the grace that was given him in Christ Jesus before times eternal, and has now been manifested by the epiphany of our Saviour Jesus Christ, in His making naught of death, and bringing to light of life and incorruption through the Gospel.

Surely there is gathered together in this great exhortation everything that could be needed to fill with deathless courage in the behalf of the Gospel even the most timid hearts. Let us try to point out one or two of the things that Paul does here, calculated to enhearten his companion.

First, we shall certainly take notice that he places beneath Timothy the eternal arms of God Almighty. He lifts the eyes of Timothy from himself to God, and says to him in effect, There, there is your strength. And observe the pains Paul is at to impress on Timothy that the relation in which he stands to this God, by virtue of which God becomes his strength, is not, in any sense,—not in the remotest degree, not in the smallest particular,—dependent on Timothy himself, or anything that he has done, is doing, or can do. He would withdraw Timothy utterly from the least infusion of dependence on self and cast him wholly on dependence on God, that he may realize that his weakness is not in question, but the whole strength of God is behind him to uphold him and bear him safely through.

Therefore Paul describes this God on whose power he would throw Timothy back as one "who saved us and called us with a holy calling; not according to works of ours but according to His own purpose"—where the words "His own" are thrown out with a tremendous energy,—"and a grace that was given to us in Christ Jesus before times eternal,"—where the words "was given," not "was promised" or even "was destined for," but actually and finally and unequivocally "was given" us before times eternal, are used with equally tremendous emphasis, to declare that what has appeared in time has been only a manifestation of what was already done, concluded, accomplished in eternity. How could this power of God fail us now because of aught we can do, or fail to do, when its gift to us is so thoroughly independent of everything or anything that we can do? Obviously, what Paul is doing is so completely to take away Timothy's consideration of himself in this whole matter of the Gospel that he will trust exclusively in God and feel that, therefore, there can be no failure—just because it is God alone and not he himself on whom the performance rests.

An appeal to the well-recognized fact that it was thus and thus only that Timothy received his call from God, is nothing other, then, than to cast him back on the Almighty arms and to make him poignantly realize that it is God and not he who is conceived as carrying through the work so begun. "O Timothy," says Paul, in effect, "Faint not! It is not your own strength—or rather weakness—that is here in question; it is the power of Almighty God. Do not you remember how you were brought into relations with this God? Was it of yourself that you were called with this holy calling? Nay, no works of your own entered in. It was of His own purpose that He called you; the grace that has come to you was given you from all eternity. What has come to you in time is only the manifestation of what was eternally done. It is this Almighty God who is using you as His instrument and organ. Nothing depends on your weakness; all hangs on His strength. Take courage and go onward." Thus Paul strengthens Timothy for the conflict before him.

But there is another element in Paul's enheartening exhortation which we must not fail to take notice of if we would feel all the subtlety and force of its appeal. Paul not only throws Timothy back on the eternal arms of Almighty God; he fixes his eyes firmly also on an eternal Christ. For not less clearly than in the prologue to John's Gospel itself is the pre-incarnate Son of God brought before us in this great passage. So vivid, indeed, is the Apostle's realization of the great transaction in eternity; so pointed is his representation of all that has been wrought out in time as but the manifestation of what was already prepared in eternity; that it would be easier to read him as throwing an air of unreality over the temporal acts than as treating the eternal ones as merely ideal.

The use of the word "given," the "grace given" to us before times eternal, is already a mark of his intense perception of the reality of the eternal transaction. But this is carried much further by the other terms emphasized. This grace given in eternity is only "manifested" in time; made visible—the conception being that it was already in existence and is only now brought to sight. And in like manner the Christ Jesus in whom the grace was given us before times eternal, can by no possibility be conceived as existing only ideally in this eternity, as if the notion were only that in foresight of Him and His work, the gift of grace was determined upon and so His historical life on earth was the logical prius and this eternal transaction rested on it in prevision and provision. On the contrary, it is His eternal existence that is the actual reality and His historical manifestation is described as an "epiphany"—a term which distinctly describes a glorious apparition of what already exists and now only breaks forth to the illumination of the world. As such it is elsewhere confined in the New Testament to the second coming of Christ, and when here applied to His first coming as fully implies as in the parallel case that He who is thus manifested exists and has existed beforehand gloriously, and now only bursts on Man's astonished sight like the breaking forth of the sun from thick clouds. The grace that was given us before all eternity, was given us in that eternity in Christ Jesus, as the then present mediator of grace; and as the grace then given has only been "manifested" in time, so the Christ Jesus in whom it was then given has only "appeared" in time. So clear and vital is Paul's realization of the eternal transaction in a word, that the danger would be not that we should read him as speaking of only an ideal eternal pre-existence of His and our Lord, but rather, as giving too little significance to the outworking of the eternal plan in the actual historical realization.

It is interesting to observe this very complete doctrine of the eternal pre-existence of Jesus

Christ in this epistle, for theological reasons, and more particularly, for biblical-theological reasons. Our interest in it now, however, turns on the use which Paul makes of it for the enheartening of Timothy. By fixing his eyes thus on the eternal Jesus and subtly suggesting that the events of time are (in a sense) but the shadows of the eternal realities; that the salvation wrought out on Calvary was but a corollary (so to speak) of the determining transaction in heaven; the Apostle leads his pupil to attach less importance to the course of affairs on earth in comparison with the eternal things thus vividly pictured before his eyes. The fashion of the earth passes away; the heavenly alone abides. This eternal Jesus—may He not be relied on quite independently of the temporary appearances of the things of earth? For how many ages did He abide above—before He was manifested as Saviour! He may have removed again into the glory He had with the Father before the world was. But is He, therefore, non-existent—unable to help? We have seen his epiphany once, when He burst from the skies bringing salvation. Shall we not see it again? Sufferings meanwhile may come—persecutions, trials—above what flesh is capable of enduring. But as the grace of God has appeared already bringing salvation, shall we not be sure that, in due season, there shall be another epiphany of our great God and Saviour Jesus Christ?

Perhaps it is too much to say that the exhortation of Paul bids Timothy to look forward to this second epiphany. But perhaps it is not too much to say that the use of the word here, consecrated elsewhere to our Lord's second coming, and the whole cast of the passage, can scarcely have failed to suggest by analogy this second coming to Timothy. And if so, the remembrance of it would add to the force of the exhortation to endurance. In any case, this vision of the eternal Christ forms a substantial element in Paul's great exhortation.

There is, however, a third element in it that we must be sure that we perceive before we can say that we have appreciated its whole force; it fills Timothy's heart with the sense of an eternal salvation. We have seen that it points him back into eternity for the inception of this salvation. There, we will not say merely it was prepared for, provided for; it was rather, prepared, provided. Before times eternal there was a purpose of God—His own sovereign purpose, independent of all works of man—in accordance with which we have in time been called. But there was also more—even a grace that had been given to us already in Christ Jesus, our eternal Lord. And it is in accordance with this grace also that we have been called with a holy calling and saved; in accordance with this grace, existent eternally, and only manifested in time, when Jesus burst on the astonished view of man and abolished death and brought to light life and immortality. This salvation, thus manifested, therefore, is an eternal salvation. There was no time when it was not. Can there be any time when it shall cease to be?

What we must, above all, however, see to it that we do is to focus our eyes on what this eternal salvation thus manifested in time consists in. It consists in just the abolishment of death and the bringing to light of life and immortality. Ah, this death that Timothy may have been in danger of fearing—that is the real shadow. This salvation—so long hidden in the heavens—that is the reality. It may again seem to be hidden in the heavens; death—does it not loom before him as a hideous threat of the immediate future? Nay, the eternal salvation, revealed in Christ Jesus, is revealed in this very act—that He has abolished death and brought life and immortality to light through the Gospel. Surely if Paul can quicken and give life and force to this conception in Timothy's mind and heart, his encouragement of him to face persecution and death with him for the Gospel's sake is complete. Then, this threatened death is naught; the Saviour has abolished death and brought life and immortality to light.

In essence, shall we not say, then, that this appeal finds its deepest root in the assurance of a blessed immortality? That it unveils the life beyond the tomb? And puts the heart into us that was in Paul when he declared that he viewed with unconcern the wearing away of this earthly house because he knew he had a building of God, a house not made with hands, eternal in the heavens? It is because the salvation brought thus to Timothy is not only eternal in its inception but eternal in its endurance, that the appeal has such force. Paul is seeking to fill the heart and mind of his follower with the realization of an eternal salvation, and so to lead him to courage in facing temporal trials. Is it not our wisdom to apply his words to ourselves? Shall we, too, not endure as seeing the invisible?

COMMUNION WITH CHRIST

2 Tim. 2:11–13:—"Faithful is the saying: For if we died with Him, we shall also live with him: if we endure we shall also reign with him: if we shall deny him, he also will deny us; if we are faithless, he abideth faithful; for he cannot deny himself."

THE words which are before us this afternoon form one of those "faithful sayings" taken up by Paul from the mouth of the Christian community and given fresh significance and force by his employment of them to wing his own appeals and point his own arguments to his fellow Christians. It is exceedingly interesting to observe the Apostle thus acting as a member of a settled community with its own standards of belief and maxims of conduct already to a certain degree established; and none the less so that he was himself the founder of the community, who had impressed on it the faith to which it was now giving expression. The special "faithful saying" he now adduces bears in it traits which point back to his teaching as the germ from which it had grown, but also to the teaching of our Lord Himself, a witness to the wide diffusion of which in the churches it thus supplies. If the phrase, "If we died with him we shall also live with him" is Pauline to the core and takes the mind of the reader irresistibly back to such a passage as Romans 6:8; and the next succeeding phrase, "If we endure we shall also reign with him," reminds us more remotely of such passages as Rom. 5:17; 8:17; the clause which follows that, "If we deny him, he, too, will deny us," cannot fail to remind us of Matt. 10:33, or rather, of the saying of Jesus there formally recorded.

How this "faithful saying" had been formed in the church, whether merely as a detached gnome, or maxim, which Christians were wont to repeat to one another for their enheartening and encouragement; or, as a portion of some liturgical form often used in the church service, until its language had become fixed; or as a passage from a hymn that had grown popular, as its rhythmic form may perhaps suggest, it may be difficult or impossible to decide. The way in which the Apostle adduces it appears in any event to bear witness that the words were a current formula in the church, to which he could appeal as such, and which would, from their familiarity and devout, if not sacred, association, appeal powerfully to Timothy's heart. Perhaps we may venture to say that the Apostle himself felt the appeal of these devout associations, and employs the "saying" precisely because it had become by use the natural expression of his own strong feelings, at the moment aroused to a particular fervour. He, the great Apostle, yet leans with comfort on the church's own expression of its faith. What a testimony we have here to the solidarity of the church of God; or, as we prefer to put it, to the communion of the saints. And what an enforcement of the great commands that we bear one another's burdens, that we neglect not the assembling of ourselves together, that we do not indulge the vanity of living each one to himself. The Church is ever to Paul, the inspired teacher of the Church, in a deep and true sense, the pillar and ground of the truth, on the testimony of which he gladly rests.

The purpose for which he adduces this particular "faithful saying" is to clinch his appeal to Timothy to steadfast adherence to his high duty and privilege of teaching the Gospel, despite every difficulty and danger besetting the pathway. He appears in this context to be urging three motives upon Timothy to induce him to face bravely the hardships of the service he is pressing upon him. He points him first to the source of his strength: "Remember Jesus Christ as risen from the dead, of the seed of David"; keep your eyes set on the heavenly majesty of the exalted Christ, our King. Surely he who keeps vivid in his consciousness that He with whom he has to do is the Lord of heaven and earth, who, though He had died, yet lived again, and is set on the throne of universal dominion, should have no fear in boldly obeying his behests. Paul points Timothy next to the important function performed by the preacher of the Gospel, faithfulness in proclaiming which he is urging upon him as so prime a duty that no danger must be allowed to intermit it. It is by it that the elect of God attain the salvation destined for them in Christ Jesus. Who will draw back when he realizes that he is a fellow-worker with God in bringing to their salvation God's own elect—those elect whom God has loved from the foundation of the world, for whom He has given His Son to shame and death, and sent His Spirit into the foulness of men's hearts? Surely he who apprehends that it is laid on him to carry this salvation to those whose own it is will never weary in conveying it to them. Let us learn how a brute beast may respond to an appeal to share in such a service of good by reading Browning's "How they brought the good news to Ghent." Shall we be less responsive to such appeals than even the brutes? Lastly Paul plies Timothy with this "faithful saying," the force of whose appeal lies in its subtle blending of encouragement and warning: encouragement because it tells us what a glorious prospect lies before him who gives himself to Christ unreservedly here; warning because it discloses to us the dreadfulness of the award that lies before him who is unfaithful here to the service he owes his Lord.

"If we died with him, we shall also live with him; if we steadfastly endure we shall also reign with him," but also, "if we shall perchance deny him, he will also deny us"; though of one thing we may be firmly assured, "though we prove faithless, He abideth ever faithful, for He cannot deny Himself." Was ever warning and encouragement so subtly blended in a single composite appeal? So subtly indeed that one remains in doubt whether the appeal comes to its close on a note of hope or on one of despair. Is it that God will remain faithful to His gracious purposes of love despite our weakness; that, though we prove untrustworthy, yet He abides ever trusty—is it on this note of high hope and encouragement that the Apostle's great song sinks down to rest? Or is it rather, that the God who has threatened to deny those that deny Him, will abide ever faithful to this dreadful threat, so that he who disowns Him here need cherish no hope that he shall escape the announced disavowal there—is it on this note of profoundest warning that the Apostle pauses? The language is flexible to either sense; the context leaves the way open to either; the appeal would be alike strong under either interpretation; but it is strongest of all, doubtless, under the subtle blending of the two, to which the phrasing of the whole "faithful saying" seems to invite us.

For this "faithful saying" has the characteristic pregnancy and subtlety of all its fellows, which is the hall-mark of all true popular sayings that have passed from mouth to mouth until they have been compacted into the thought of a whole community. For its interpretation we should confine ourselves primarily to its own narrow compass and remember that the context in which it comes to us is not its own original context, and can help us to its interpretation only so far as the propriety of its adduction here is concerned. So looking at it, it is clear that much of the current exposition of its clauses falls away of itself. For example, it seems obvious that the "dying with Christ" here adduced is not physical dying with Christ, martyrdom, but forensic dying with Christ, justification. It is clear that our fragment is a fragment of a piece in which the main theme is Christ's work of redemption. It is especially clear that we have no right to supply "with Christ" with the second clause. It is not endurance "with Christ," but "steadfast endurance to the end" alone that is intended, and the conjunctive preposition is left off of this verb just to advise us of that. Nor may we omit to note and give effect to the changes of tense: first the aorist, then the present, then the future, then the present again; all of which changes are significant. Lastly, a careful observation of the consecution of the clauses will certainly bid us pause before we fall in with their division into two pairs, the first encouraging, the last warning; a division far too simple to do justice to the subtlety of the whole thought, or even the surface considerations derived from the sequence of the tenses and verbs.

Let us look at the saying then a moment in its

own light and then ask how it lends itself to Paul's purpose in adducing it here.

We perceive at once that the passage consists of four conditional sentences which stand, therefore, in a certain formal parallelism with one another. The first of these sentences declares that sharing in Christ's death entails sharing in Christ's life. The idea is a frequent one in the New Testament and must, indeed, in all Pauline churches at any rate, have become long ere this a Christian commonplace. The language in which it is expressed is the same as that which meets us in Rom. 6:8, and stands in express relation with that of, say, 2 Cor. 5:14f. It would be most unnatural violently to separate the statement here from the ordinary connotation of the language. This is reinforced by the fact that the aorist tense is employed, and thus a dying with Christ already accomplished by every Christian who took this language on his lips, most naturally suggested. It is most unnatural, therefore, to understand here a dying with Christ not yet accomplished, perhaps never to be accomplished; the language implies rather a dying which has been the invariable experience of every Christian heart. Are we to say that the passage teaches that only if we share in Christ's death in the sense that we like Him die for the Gospel, are we to share in his life? Or, are we to say that the meaning is rather that every faithful Christian that dies shall live again? The latter is too flat a sense to be attributed to our passage; the former, obviously too narrow. The reference is neither to martyrdom, not yet merely to a Christian death. The death here is obviously ethical or rather, spiritual, and yet not quite in the exact sense of Rom. 6:8, but more in that of 2 Cor. 5:14. The simple meaning obviously is that he who is united with Christ in His death shall share with Him His life also; that all those "in Christ Jesus" as they died with Him on Calvary, as that death which He there died, since it was for them, was their death in Him, so shall share with Him in His resurrection life, shall live in and through Him.

The appeal is clearly to the Christian's union with Christ and its abiding effects. He is a new creation; with a new life in him; and should live in the power of this new and deathless life. For there is a stress laid also on the persistence of this life and a pointing of the reader to the deathlessness of the life in Christ. Know ye not, says the Apostle in effect, that if ye died with Christ ye shall also live with Him, and that the life ye are living in the flesh ye live by the power of the Son of God, and it shall last for ever? The pregnancy of the implication is extreme, but it is all involved in the one fact that if we died with Christ, if we are His and share His death on Calvary, we shall live with Him; live with Him in a redeemed life here, cast in another mould from the old life of the flesh, and live with Him hereafter for ever. This great appeal to their union and communion with Christ lays the basis for all that follows. It puts the reader on the plane—sets him at the point of view—of "in Christ Jesus."

Now, the second and third clauses present the contrasting possibilities, emerging from the situation presented in the first clause, and belong as such together, as positive and negative statements. He who is in Christ may by patient continuance in well-doing abide in union with his Lord, and he shall not fail of his reward. The metaphysical possibility remains open, however, that he may deny his Lord, in which case, he shall, himself, in accordance with our Lord's own express threat, be denied by Him. Observe the precise justice of the contrasting expressions employed in these alternatives. The tense changes first from the aorist to the present, because not the act of incorporation in Christ, but the process of steadfast endurance, is in question. The verbs in the apodosis are also varied to meet the exact case; we begin as sharers in Christ's life; if we continue steadfastly in that life we shall share in its glories. The thought is precisely that of Rom. 8:16, 17; if we are God's children, we are heirs, joint heirs with Christ, "if so be that we suffer with Him, that we may be glorified with Him also." Only in our present passage the matter is not conceived so distinctly as suffering or as suffering with Christ; in preparation for the companion clause yet to come the idea of "with Christ" falls away here. The two cases rest with us—abiding steadfastly or disowning. The "reigning with Christ" is an advance on "living with Christ"; it throws the emphasis on the reward: if we have died with Him we are sharers of His life; if we abide in this life we shall inherit with Him the Kingdom.

The companion clause presents the other possibility. The "deny" corresponds to "the steadfast endurance" and Christ's disowning us corresponds to the "reigning with Him"; both as opposite contrasts. The tense is changed in accordance with the new nature of the case. It is not a matter of continually disowning Him; it is a matter of breaking the continuance of our steadfast endurance. This is done by an act. Hence the future, expressing the possibility of the act: "should we disown Him,"—if we shall disown Him, why then, *He* (emphatic), also will disown us! This is the dreadful contingency; all the more dreadful on account of three things: (1) the simple brevity of its statement as a dire possibility to be kept in mind and steadfastly guarded against; (2) the express reminiscence of our Lord's own words in Matt. 10:33 carrying the mind back to the most solemn of associations possible to connect with the words; (3) the emphatic "He," thrusting the personality of Christ for the first time upon the consciousness of the reader; as before, He is only gently kept in mind by the implications of the "with." This emphatic "He" is partly due, of course, to the change of construction, by which a new subject is needed for the succeeding verb; though it would be, perhaps, better to say the desire for emphasis is the cause of the change of construction. We might have had a passive verb, "If we deny we shall be denied," with or without the "by Him." But the personality of Christ is too strongly felt here for mere suggestion or even for relegation to the predicate. The change to the active construction and the expression of the subject and its expression by the demonstrative "He," all pile emphasis on emphasis; "If we disown, HE, too (not merely He, but HE, too), will disown us!" This is the climax of the sentence and a fitting pause is reached. "If we died with Him we shall also live with him; if we steadfastly endure we shall also reign with him; but if we shall ever, by any possibility, deny Him, He, too, will deny—us!" The thought is complete with this. Both alternatives are developed. And the effect of the whole is a powerful incentive to abide in Christ. Patient endurance—nay, bold, steadfast, brave endurance—has its reward—reigning with Christ. But if we fall from this and disown Christ, do we not remember His dreadful threat: "He, too, can and will disown—even us!"

Surely there is nothing required to enhance the terror of this situation. The poignancy of the appeal to steadfast endurance seems scarcely to need heightening. But on the other hand there would seem need for a closing word of encouragement to weak and faltering Christians. And there would seem a way open for it. For the very sharpness of the assertion that if there is disowning on one side there will be disowning on the other, too, seems to hint something else. The contrast between the present tense of the second clause expressing continuance and the tense of the third clause expressing an act, calls for consideration: "If we continue to—," "If we shall perchance ever—." Nothing is said of the continuance of the disowning on either side. Disowning begets disowning. True; but is that all? Shall one act of even such dreadful sin divide us from all that we had hoped for, in a long life of endurance? What shall poor weak, faltering Christians do in that case? It does not seem impossible, to say the least, that the last clause comes in to comfort and strengthen. There is hope even for the lapsed Christian! For "though we prove faithless, He (emphatic), HE, at least, abides faithful: for deny Himself He cannot!" Deny us He may and will; every denial entails a denial. But deny Himself, He cannot. Our unbelief shall not render the faith of God of none effect.

If this be the construction, the whole closes on a

note of hope. The note of warning throbs through even the note of hope, it is true, for He who cannot deny Himself must remember His threats also; and no Christian holding this wonderful "faithful saying" in his heart will fail to note this. But the note of hope is the dominant one, and I take it this last clause is designed to call back the soul from the contemplation of the dreadfulness of denying Christ and throw it in trust and hope back upon Jesus Christ, the faithful One, who despite our unfaithfulness, will never deny Himself—will never disown Himself,—but will ever look on His own cross and righteousness and all the bitter dole He has suffered, and will not let anything snatch what He has purchased to Himself out of His hands.

In this view of the matter, then, the arrangement of the clauses is not in a straightforward quartet—two by two—but rather this:

If we died with Him we shall also live with Him;
  If we endure we shall also reign with Him;
  If we shall deny, He too will deny us.
If we are faithless, He abideth faithful, for Himself He cannot deny.

PRAYER AS A PRACTICE

James 5:16b:—"The supplication of a righteous man availeth much."

I WANT to speak to you this afternoon about prayer, and I have chosen a text which, if we cannot quite say of it that it brings prayer before us at the height of its idea, yet, certainly, presents its value to us in the most emphatic way.

Men ask, What is the use of praying? Above all, What is the use of bringing specific petitions to the throne of the Almighty? "To crave boons you know little of, from a God of whom you know nothing at all, save that you have made him in your own image—of what profit can that be?" That is the language of unbelief.

Much, however, which passes for belief asks practically the same thing in somewhat more chastened forms of speech. This half belief also asks, What is the use of praying? We must have a very low conception of God, it suggests, to suppose that He does not know how to govern His universe without our telling Him. Do we really think He will subordinate His wisdom to the demands of our folly? Cannot we leave the direction of affairs to Him? If He be, indeed, a good and wise God, must we not leave it to Him? Why rush hysterically into His presence and demand that the universe be ruled according to our notions? Are we competent to give Him advice? Do we fancy that we know what is best even for ourselves, as He does not? He cannot hear us unless He be God; He certainly ought not to hearken to us if He be God. If He is "mighty enough to make laws," why should we think Him "weak enough to break them" at our request? Prayer is in effect an attempt to undeify the Deity and substitute our will for His will. It is not only foolish and immoral, therefore, but supremely self-contradictory. We cannot attempt it save on the supposition that it is God whom we are addressing; we would not attempt it if we really believed that He whom we are addressing is God. Of one thing, at least, we may be assured, that it is of no use to pray.

Well, you see, it is precisely to this point that our text speaks. It speaks not of prayer in general, but of the specific act of petition. "Supplication," our Revised Version calls it. It is that precise act of prayer which is the making of a request, the urging of a desire, the preferring of a petition. And what it says about it is that so far from its being of no use, it is of very great use. "The prayer,"—or more specifically, the "petition," the "request," the "supplication"—"of a righteous man availeth much," "is of great value," "exerts great power." There is another word in the sentence, but as it is of somewhat doubtful interpretation and in no way qualifies the sense of the declaration for our present purpose, we may pass it by here. It is variously rendered as qualifying the prayer of the righteous man that availeth further as "earnest"; or as indicating the source from which such a prayer alone can come, by affirming that it is "inwrought" in him, that is, by the Holy Ghost; or as further describing the value of it as availing "in its working." It is obvious that whether we say "the fervent prayer of the righteous man availeth much," or "the prayer of a righteous man availeth much, seeing that it is inwrought," or "the prayer of a righteous man availeth much in its working," the one main thing asserted in every case is that a righteous man's prayer is of high value; that it is strong to obtain its end; that it is fully worth offering up.

And this emphatic assertion is buttressed immensely by its context. The assertion is made in order to encourage the readers to pray for one another, and for themselves. To pray for one another when they are sick; to pray for one another when they are soul-sick. If any is sick among you, exhorts James, send for the elders of the Church and have them pray over such an one; and the prayer of faith shall heal the sick; yes, and if he have any sin on his conscience, it will heal that sin. And all of you—why, confess your sins to one another—and pray for one another, and the prayer will bring healing. Take everything to God. If you are suffering go in prayer; if you are in joy go in praise. But in any and every case, go. It is strong and reiterated advice, you see. Go continually, go always, to God. Go, go, because prayer is not of no profit; but, on the contrary, the "prayer of a righteous man profiteth much!" And then James supports this central declaration with a most telling example. It is taken from the life of Elijah. Elijah prayed. He was a man just like us. And he got what he prayed for. And it was no little thing he asked for. He asked for drought and he asked for rain. And he got the drought and the rain he asked for. See, says James in effect, see, how much the prayer of a righteous man is good for!

It looks as if we could not easily find a stronger assertion of the value of prayer; and of prayer at the very apex of its difficulty as I have said; prayer, specifically as petition. But I do not wish this afternoon to confine our thoughts to this one point the value of petition, but to take encouragement from this emphatic assertion of the value of prayer, and direct our minds to a general consideration of prayer in the large.

First, then, the idea of prayer. In its most general connotation, prayer is the Godward expression of subjective religion. Subjective religion is the state of mind consequent on the apprehension of God. Prayer is, therefore, in its most general sense the Godward expression of that state of mind which is consequent on the apprehension of God. In short, all conscious communion with God is prayer. A great many elements, therefore, enter into prayer. It is not to be confined to petition. Every form of expression of the soul Godward is a form of prayer. Many terms, therefore, are employed in the Scriptures, Hebrew and Greek alike, to give expression to the various forms and modes of praying. In some passages several of these are accumulated and that with full consciousness of the variety of mental state and action expressed by them. One of the most formal of these summations occurs at the opening of the second chapter of First Timothy. Here four terms are gathered together to give more adequate expression to what Paul would have us do when we pray; four terms which emphasize the mental movements we call respectively adoration, petition, urgency, thanksgiving. These four elements, at least, ought, therefore, to intertwine in all our acts of prayer. When we come before God, we should come with adoration in our hearts and on our lips, with thanksgiving suffusing all our being for His goodness to us, and making known our desires with that earnestness which alone can justify our bringing them to Him.

Next, the presuppositions of prayer. Obviously they are the presuppositions of subjective religion. And these may be summed up in the existence, the personality, the accessibility and the continued activity of God in the world. The Scriptures themselves tell us that to come to God implies that we believe that He is, and that He is the rewarder of those who diligently seek Him. We must really believe in the existence of God and in His care for the works of His hands, or we cannot pray to Him. Not only then cannot the atheist, or the agnostic, or the pantheist, pray; nor yet the deist or the fatalist. But neither can adherents of many a variety of our modern thought which baptizes itself with the Christian name, pray as men ought to pray. I have particularly in mind in saying this, on the one hand, those extreme advocates of the reign of law in external nature who love to call themselves either speculative theists or non-miraculous Christians; and on the other those extreme advocates of the autocracy of the human will, who fancy that the whole cause of liberty is bound up with the self-sufficiency of the human soul.

The one of these would forbid us to pray for any external want; the other for any internal effect on the soul. So, between the two, they would take away the whole sphere of prayer. Unless we should prefer wisely to look at it from the opposite angle, and to say that each refutes the other, and between the two they allow us the whole sphere of prayer. Certainly, that is what the Scriptures do. They authorize, or rather require, us to pray both for external and internal blessings; for rain and drought like Elijah; for the healing of sickness like the elders of the Church; for the healing of sin-sick souls like Christians at large. There is, no doubt, a problem of how God answers prayers for external effects; and we may be chary of supposing that miracles will be wrought when special providences will serve the end; and there is a problem of how God answers prayer for internal changes and we may be chary of supposing that violence is done to our nature, when confluent action along psychologically indicated lines will suffice. But one thing we must hold firmly to: God answers prayer. And that equally, and equally readily and equally easily, for internal and for external things.

Now, the conditions of acceptable prayer. Let us study here the simplicity of Scripture. We need not multiply conditions where the Scriptures do not multiply them. And, speaking strictly, Scripture knows of but one condition. It conduces to the peace and comfort of our souls to remember that there is but one condition to acceptable prayer. It is easiest and best, however, to state this one condition in a twofold manner: objectively and subjectively. There is an objective condition of acceptable prayer and there is a subjective condition of acceptable prayer. The objective condition is that we should have access to God. The subjective condition is that we should have faith. The objective and subjective conditions are one, because it is only in Jesus Christ that we have access to God and only through faith that we are in Him.

Whatever may be said of men as men—the creatures of God—you and I have nothing to do with. You and I are not men as men; we are sinners. And sinners as such have no access to God. They may go through all the motions of prayer, no doubt. It is like bodily exercises that profit nothing; one might as will turn a prayer wheel like the Thibetans. It goes no higher than our own heads. For this is of the very essence of sin—that it breaks communion with God. God is deaf to the sinner's cry. He owes the sinner punishment, not favour. In Jesus Christ alone has the breach between God and sinful man been filled in. In the blood of His sacrifice only can we penetrate within the veil. In Him only, as Paul repeatedly tells us, do we have our introduction into the Divine presence. All prayer that is acceptable and reaches the ears of God, therefore, is prayer that is conveyed to Him through Jesus Christ. For sinners the atonement of Christ lays the only basis for real prayer.

The subjective condition is faith; and faith is the sole subjective condition. No other condition is ever announced in Scripture. And the promises to faith are repeated, emphatic and unlimited. He that prays in faith shall surely receive. For faith can no more fail in prayer than in salvation; and if faith and faith alone is not the only but all-sufficient instrument of salvation, then we are yet in our sins and are of all men the most miserable. If any one is puzzled by so unlimited a promise, let him reflect what faith is and whence faith comes. If faith is the gift of God in this sphere, too—as assuredly it is—then faith can no more fail than the God who gives it can fail. Or think you that God will deceive you by working faith in you by His Holy Spirit when He has no intention of correspondingly blessing you? Man-made faith—that might fail; for that is no faith at all. But God-inspired faith, as it is God within you working, so is it sure to find God without you hearkening. That is what Paul says in that great passage in the eighth of Romans about the Holy Spirit groaning within us unutterably, and God knowing the mind of His Spirit. It is possibly also what James says in our present passage, when he says that it is an "energized prayer" which is effective. But the gist of the whole matter is that there is no condition of successful prayer but faith.

No condition, but not therefore no characterizing qualities, which are always present where faithful prayer is; and the presence and absence of which you and I can observe as marks of acacceptable or unacceptable prayer. These are customarily enumerated as sincerity, reverence, humility, importunity, submission. Many more similar characteristic features of acceptable prayer could be added. We need not dwell on these in detail.

Lastly, the effects of prayer. These too are both objective and subjective. Which are the more important? That depends very much on the specific exercises of prayer which we have in mind; and on the specific things we pray for, if it is of the exercise of petition that we are thinking.

The main point to emphasize is that prayer has an objective effect. It terminates on God, and does not merely bound back like a boomerang upon our own persons. We do not throw it up towards the heavens to have it do nothing but circle back to smite our own heads. But though this is to be mainly insisted upon, it does not follow that prayer may not also have subjective effects; or that these subjective effects may not be of unspeakable importance to us; or even that in some exercises of prayer, they may not be almost the most important of its effects. If the specific exercise of prayer in which we are engaged is adoration or thanksgiving, may not what we call its subjective effects be the most important? No doubt, if we are engaging in petition, it may be different; may be even here, not must. If our petition be, Father, hallowed be Thy Name!—or, Thy Kingdom come, Thy will be done in earth as in heaven!—no subjective effects can compare with the objective value of the petition. But suppose the petition be, "Give us this day our daily bread!" Or for some lesser blessing "of this life"! Is not the enjoyment in prayer of communion with God of more value than any of these things? Let us bless God that man does not live by bread alone; nay, not even chiefly.

If we seek to enumerate the benefits obtained by prayer, then, I think we must say that they are, at least, threefold. There are the objective blessings obtained by means of the prayer in the answer to its petitions. There is the blessing that consists in the very act of prayer, that communion with God which is the highest act of the soul. There are the blessings that arise from the assumption in prayer of the proper attitude of the creature, especially of the sinful creature, towards God. Perhaps these last alone can be strictly called purely subjective. The first we may speak of as purely objective. It is the second in which the highest value of prayer is to be found.

We must not undervalue the purely subjective or reflex effects of prayer. They are of the highest benefit to us. Much less must we undervalue the objective effects of prayer. In them lies the specific meaning of that exercise of prayer which we call petition. But the heart of the matter lies in every case in the communion with God which the soul enjoys in prayer. This is prayer itself, and in it is summed up what is most blessed in prayer. If it be man's chief end to glorify God and enjoy Him for ever, then man has attained his end, the sole purpose for which he was made, the entire object for which he exists, when he enters into communion with God, abides in His presence, streaming out to Him in all the emotions, I do not say appropriate to a creature in the presence of his Maker and Lord, apprehended by him as the Good Lord and Righteous Ruler of the souls of men, but appropriate to the sinner who has been redeemed by the blood of God's own Son and is inhabited by His Spirit and apprehends his Maker as also his Saviour, his Governor as also his Lover, and knows the supreme joy of him that was lost and is found, was dead and is alive again,—and all, through the glory of God's seeking and saving love. He who attains to this experience has attained all that is to be attained. He is absorbed in the beatific vision. He that sees God shall be like Him.

GOD'S HOLINESS AND OURS

I Pet. 1:15:—"But like as He which called you is holy, be ye yourselves also holy in all manner of living."

The first chapter of the First Epistle of Peter ranks with the most precious in the Bible. It opens with a singularly rich and beautiful description of what God has done for us, and of the glory of that salvation which He has provided. He has given His Son to die and rise again that by His resurrection from the dead He might beget us anew unto a lively hope. Though we may have to suffer now and enter not yet into this hope, He Himself preserves for us the hoped-for inheritance, incorruptible and undefiled; and keeps us by His power for it, until the day comes when we shall enter into it. This glorious salvation He had prepared for us, indeed, before we were born, even from the beginnings of the ages, announcing it from time to time through the prophets who well knew that it was for us and not themselves that they ministered, but revealing it in its full glory not even to the angels as it has now been made known to us. Thus Peter makes known to his readers that it was not they who chose God but God who chose them; that their salvation is not dependent on their own effort but rests on God's almighty power; that the inheritance for which they hope in the end is not such an one as they could obtain with human weakness, but such an one as only God could prepare—more splendid than prophets could tell, more glorious than angels could imagine, prepared by God just for us from the foundation of the world. By this far-off glimpse of it, Peter would quicken our hope and awaken our love and gratitude to God.

"Wherefore," he adds,—turning suddenly from this glorious prospect to stir us up to make this precious inheritance surely our own—"wherefore" see to it that you enter into this hope and lay such hold upon it that it cannot slip away. As we approach the text for the day, thus, we pass from the contemplation of the glorious inheritance of the saints to the most earnest exhortations to make our calling sure. Peter admonishes us by the greatness of the hope that is set before us, in other words, to a mode of life conformable to it. We must gird up the loins of our minds, be sober and set our hope perfectly on this grace that is to be brought to us at the revelation of our Lord. It is ready for us; it is kept in store for us in heaven; when Christ comes it will come with Him. Would we be meet for its reception? How then shall we be made meet for it? We are told first negatively and then positively.

Christ is our King and to Him we owe our duty. Not with eye service only; not with grudging honour; but as the very children of obedience we must offer Him our willing service. And this service which He demands of us is summed up broadly in the negative rule that we must be separated wholly from our former evil desires which we followed in the days of our ignorance, before He recalled Himself to us and made known to us what a glorious inheritance He had for us. Children of the flesh, born in the flesh, we have lived according to the lusts of the flesh; for who is there that sins not? But now that the eyes of our hearts have been opened that we may see what it is that we have done, and that we may know the evil that we have wrought, we must turn away from evil. This is the negative rule of life. But mere negation brings us nowhere. To separate from sin is not enough; we must go on to positive holiness; "like as He which called you is holy, become ye also yourselves holy in all manner of living." Here is the positive rule of life.

Now let us look at this precept somewhat more closely. Doing so we will observe (1) what it is that we are exhorted to become—holy; (2) in what we are to become holy—in every manner of living; and (3) to what degree we are to become holy in all our life and all its activities,—as holy as God Himself is. In other words, we may observe here (1) that God draws back the veil and exhibits His own holiness to His children; (2) that He makes His holiness the incitement to them to become holy also; (3) that He holds His own holiness forth as the standard of the holiness which they must strive to attain; and (4) that He actually proposes to share this His highest attribute with us.

Observe, then, first, that God here proclaims His own holiness and so exhibits this His crown and glory to His children; "like as He which called you is holy"—"for I am holy." What, then, do we mean when we speak of the "holiness" of God? We need not trouble ourselves with the derivation of the Hebrew word, although, no doubt, its etymological sense of division, separation from, is conformable with its usage. The usage of the word, which is applied primarily to God, and only afterwards and secondarily to those that belong to Him,—especially if we will observe its contrasts—clearly indicates as its central idea that of separation; and specifically separation from the world conceived of as a sinful world. When we call God holy, then, the central idea in our minds concerns His absolute and complete separation from sin and uncleanness. Not that the idea has this negative form as it lies in our minds. There is no idea so positive as that of holiness; it is the very climax of positiveness. But it is hard to express this positiveness in a definite way, simply because this idea is above the ideas expressed by its synonyms. It is more than sinlessness, though it, of course, includes the idea of sinlessness. It is more than righteousness, although again it includes the idea of righteousness. It is more than wholeness, complete soundness and integrity and rightness, though, of course, again it includes these ideas. It is more than simpleness, high simplicity and guilelessness, though it includes this too. It is more than purity, though, of course, it includes this too. Holiness includes all these and more. It is God's whole, entire, absolute, inconceivable and, therefore, unexpressible completeness and perfection of separation from and opposition to and ineffable revulsion from all that is in any sense or degree, however small, evil. We fall back at last on this negative description of it just because language has no positive word which can reach up to the unscaleable heights of this one highest word, holiness. It is the crown of God as mercy is His treasure; as grace is His riches, this is His glory. Who is like unto God, glorious in holiness?

Such is the challenge of the Old Testament and safely might it be given. The holiness of God is a conception peculiar to the religion of the Bible. None of the gods of the nations was like unto our God in this, the crown and climax of His glory. But it is just this His ineffable perfection that He calls us to imitate. It is just the exhibition of this His glory that He trusts to quicken an unquenchable thirst in us to be like Him. For observe, secondly, that it is by this exhibition of His holiness that God incites us to holiness. "Like as He which called you is holy, become ye also yourselves holy." "Ye shall be holy for I am holy." God exhibits His glory to us for our imitation and expects the sight of the beauty of holiness in Him to beget in us an inextinguishable longing to be like Him. Holiness is a dread attribute. Reverence and awe attend its exhibition. Who can look upon the holy God and not tremble? To the sinful man, no words so quickly spring to the lips when he is brought in sight of holiness as "Depart from me, for I am a sinful man, O Lord!" It is pre-eminently the holiness of God which constitutes the terror of the Lord, and as often as He appears to men we read the record that they feared a great fear. Does its contemplation not silence our tongues and abase our hearts rather than rouse our endeavours and quicken our efforts? It is but too true that sin and holiness are antagonistic and that holiness hates sin no less truly than sin hates holiness. Sinful man cannot be incited to holy activity by the sight of holiness; it begets no longing in his heart except a longing to hide himself away from it. When Adam sinned, he no longer wished to meet God in the garden.

The very fact of the proposal of God to show us His holiness as an incitement to holiness in us means something, then, of infinite importance to our souls. It means that we are no longer averse to all that is good; no longer God's enemies but

His friends. Peter is addressing here not man as man but Christian men as Christian men. Those to whom he speaks have been bought with a price, have been begotten anew unto a lively hope by the resurrection of Christ from the dead. As God's sons they are already like God, and he only exhorts them to become more like Him. It is only as God's sons that they could be attracted by the exhibition of His holiness; it is only as God's sons that they could find in it an incitement; it is only as such that they can hope to attain it. And it is just because we are God's sons that the exhortation is necessary to us. If we are to call on Him as Father we must vindicate our right to use that ennobling name by living as His children. Thus the very proposal of God to incite us to holiness by the exhibition of His holiness to us, is itself an encouragement to and a pledge of our attainment of it. He expects us to see and to feel the beauty of holiness and that means that He has already recreated our hearts.

Thus we observe, thirdly, that God not only exhibits His holiness here as an incitement to us, but also reveals to us by that act His gracious and loving purpose with us. We see God here not calling us up to seek communion with Him in our own strength; but rather stooping down that He may raise us to that communion. For let us observe that it is, after all, communion with Him to which He has summoned us. There can be no communion between the holy and the sinful. He is here beseeching us to hold communion with Him, and He is providing the way by which it may be consummated. The Holy God has by the resurrection of Christ from the dead begotten us again into a living hope and here He holds out to this already formed hope the incitement of the sight of His holiness as the goal to which we must strive to attain.

It is not unadvisedly that we say that His holiness is here exhibited as the goal to which we must seek to attain. For not only is it in the text the incitement, but also the standard of the holiness for which we are to strive. We are to become holy as God is holy. Of course the finite cannot attain the infinite. But as the asymptote of the hyperbola ever approaches it but never attains, so we are eternally to approach this high and perfect standard. Ever above us, the holiness of God yet is ever more and more closely approached by us; and as the unending æons of eternity pass by we shall grow ever more and more towards that ever-beckoning standard. That is our high destiny and it is not unfitly described as partaking in the Divine Nature.

CHILDSHIP TO GOD

1 Jno. 2:28–3:3, especially 3:1:—"Behold what manner of love the Father hath bestowed upon us, that we should be called children of God: and such we are."

THE conception of the divine birth as the root of the Christian life is a specially Johannean one. Not that the other New Testament writers do not also teach all that is expressed by the term "regeneration." But that they teach it prevailingly under other figures, such as those of a repristination, a new creation, and the like. The Johannean expressions, "to be born again," "begotten of God," do not occur at all, for example, in Paul, whose use in a single passage of a similar term only serves to bring out the contrast. There is a corresponding difference in the use by Paul and John of the conception of childship or sonship to God. In accordance with his juridical point of view, Paul speaks of sonship as conferred by adoption, and thinks of our acquisition of the rights and the inheritance of sons. In accordance with his essential point of view, John speaks of childship as conveyed through birth and thinks of growing up into the likeness of God. Accordingly Paul prefers the term "sons." We are adults received by God's grace into the number of His sons. And John prefers the term "children" or even "little children." We are born into the family of God as the infants of His household.

This difference in the use of the conception of childship is not a difference of doctrine; it is only a difference in the illustrative use of the conception of childship in the setting forth of doctrine. It will not do to say on its ground that John teaches that our sonship to God is due to regeneration and Paul that it is due to justification. It will not be accurate even to say that John emphasizes regeneration and Paul justification. What is true is that Paul has adopted the conception of sonship to illustrate the title to life and holiness which we obtain through justification, and John to illustrate the communication of a new principle of holy life to us in regeneration. Paul uses it of an objective fact, John of a subjective one. Paul, to point us to what becomes ours through the work of Christ without us; John, to what is made ours by the working of Christ within us. It would lead to confusion to treat the several passages in John and Paul as if they were teaching us the same sonship to God. It would lead to even greater confusion to suppose that because they illustrate different portions of the doctrine of salvation by the same figure, they teach a different doctrine of salvation,—one by the Christ without us, the other by the Christ within us.

Perhaps no passage could be pitched upon which would more richly and completely than that before us outline to us John's presentation of his doctrine of childship to God, begun in regeneration and growing up in ever-increasing sanctification to its goal of likeness to God. It may repay us to run over the points of doctrine that emerge in the course of these five verses.

First then we are to observe that the childship of God of which John teaches us—as truly as the sonship to God of which Paul teaches us—is not a natural but a graciously conferred relation. Neither in John's sense nor in Paul's sense, nor in the sense of any New Testament writer, can we speak of a universal Fatherhood of God. The idea of the All-Father is rather a heathen than a Christian notion; that is to say it is a conception belonging to the sphere of natural religion, voicing the yearning of the human heart to find in its Creator and Ruler something more than a Master or a Sovereign Lord. It contains no more Biblical truth than arises from the fact that according to the Bible we are like God in so far as by our first creation we were made in His image; He is in this sense the Father of our spirits. For from the Biblical point of view, sonship presents primarily the idea of likeness. Therefore, the bad are the sons of Belial and the good are the sons of God; and the high name of the children of God is, from Genesis to Revelation, reserved for those whose likeness to Him extends beyond the mere natural fact that they have a spiritual nature similar to

God's, to the moral fact that they have a spiritual character like God's.

Holiness of heart, not immateriality of essence, is the ground in the Scriptural view of Divine sonship. And as men are by nature not holy but wicked, they are naturally the sons of the Devil, the sons of wrath. Sons of God they can become only by an act of Divine mercy. The idea of the universal Fatherhood of God represents therefore, from the Biblical point of view, what God would fain have been when He made man in His own image, creating him in righteousness and true holiness; what God still fain would be; not what God is. He is in the Biblical sense, the Father only of those who are renewed unto holiness. So John puts it; so Paul puts it. Paul exhorts his readers to "do all things without murmurings and disputings, that they may be blameless and harmless, children of God, without blemish": and John in our present passage represents only those who do righteousness as the children of God.

To John then, as we say, as to Paul and to the whole New Testament, childship to God is not a natural but a graciously constituted relation. It is so in our passage, "Behold what manner of love the Father hath *bestowed* upon us, that we should be called the children of God." It is a matter of bestowment; it is a gift. And it is an undeserved and unmerited gift. John cries out in wonder and surprised gratitude at the love—

not only the greatness, but the high quality of the love—which God bestowed on us, with the intent of having us called children of God: "Behold, what *manner* of love the Father hath bestowed upon us to the end that we should be called children of God." And then his feelings overcome him as he contemplates this great, this indescribable, kind of love, and he adds, not as part of the statement but as an unrestrainable comment on the statement, "and such we are." The words themselves point out the ineffable mercy and love of God in making us—such as we—children of God. But these two words of comment of the responding heart of the beloved disciple pierce even deeper into our souls. As he declares the Father's love in making us His children, he cannot help jubilating over the blessed fact. "It is true," he cries, "it is true!" "And we are." Assuredly, to him this is no natural relation. We are the children of God only by the ineffable love of God, constituting us sons. It is not a thing we have by nature but of grace; it is not a thing to which we are born as men, but to which we are born again as Christians; it is not a thing to which all are born, but only those who are born not of blood, nor of the will of the flesh, nor of the will of man, but of God.

It is as clear as day, then, that this childship to God, of which John teaches us, is not a product of our own endeavours; it is a gift, a free favour, from God; and it has its root in the ineffable and indescribable and sovereign love of God. "Behold what manner of love the Father has bestowed upon us that we should be called the sons of God." We have not earned it; the Father has given it; not paid it to us as our just due for effort made, labour performed, righteousness practised; but given it to us out of His free and inexplicable love; not out of His justice but out of His incomprehensible love. It is a sovereign gift. So the New Testament everywhere and under all its figures represents it; so John always represents it. And it is therefore that he sings pæans to God's love on account of it. "Behold!" "What manner of love is this!" "To seek us out and make us the sons of God!" Language could not convey more clearly, more powerfully, the conception of the absolute sovereignty of the gift of childship to God. Elsewhere it is conveyed more didactically, more analytically; here it is conveyed emotionally. Elsewhere we are told that it came not of blood, nor of the will of the flesh, nor of the will of man, but of God; here we have the answering thrill of gratitude of the human heart at this unexpected, undeserved gift. Elsewhere the sovereignty is asserted, explained; here it is acknowledged, honoured. Elsewhere it is claimed, here it is yielded, admired, glorified.

But the passage gives us not merely the origin and source of our childship to God in His love—

free, and freely giving us this great benefit; it points out to us the evidence of its reality. Though we cannot purchase it by our righteousness, it is freely bestowed, it yet evidences itself through righteousness. It is not by righteousness that we obtain it; but only the righteous have it. As it is sonship to the righteous God that is conferred; as sonship implies likeness; it follows that the test of such a sonship having been conferred is the presence of the likeness, the presence of the righteousness. Accordingly we read: "If ye know that He is righteous, ye know that every one also that doeth righteousness is born of Him." This is the test. None but the righteous are sons of God. The Apostle does not say, None but the righteous can become the sons of God. Then it would not be true that the sonship is a free gift of ineffable, sovereign love. But he does say that none but the righteous are the sons of God.

This is, indeed, essential to his point of view, that sonship hangs on an inward fact. Paul, too, teaches the same doctrine even though he is looking upon sonship as a juridical fact. For God leaves none of those whom He constitutes His sons by adoption without the Spirit of sonship in their hearts, crying Abba, Father; and only those who are led by the Spirit of God are sons of God. But much more will John, who is thinking of regeneration rather than justification, under the figure of sonship, teach the same. Only he who doeth righteousness can really be begotten of the Righteous One. That we do righteousness becomes thus the test and evidence of our sonship. Begetting is the implanting of a seed of life, and it is the very nature of life to live, that is, to manifest its essential nature in outward activities. But the seed implanted in this begetting is the seed of holy living; how can it be said to be there if it is not manifested in holy living? It is of the very nature of the thing that only those who do righteousness can have been begotten by the Righteous God unto newness of life.

But is not John then blending regeneration with sanctification? If none is born of God—regenerated—unless he doeth righteousness, is not this to say that by the mystical act of being begotten of God—regeneration—a man must be made holy, and unless he has been made holy, he is not born of God? Yes, and no. For John, while insisting that no one is born of God who does not do righteousness, does not represent him as having already in his new birth attained his goal. An infant is not a full-grown man. Nor is he who is born of God already perfected in likeness to God. John, too, represents this as a growth. He asserts that only those who do righteousness are the children of God; but he claims to be himself—he claims that his readers are—already children of God. "And such we are." "Are"—already. "Beloved, *now* we are children of God."

(4) The hope of the children of God, developed likeness to God.

(5) The duty of the children of God, to purify themselves as God is pure.

(6) The end of the children of God—the as yet unmanifested glory of perfect assimilation to their Father's character.